Pretext:
Anti-Communism in Latin America

Pretext:
Anti-Communism in Latin America

James Trapani

&

Drew Cottle

Vij Books India Pvt Ltd
New Delhi (India)

Published by

Vij Books India Pvt Ltd
(Publishers, Distributors & Importers)
2/19, Ansari Road
Delhi – 110 002
Phones: 91-11-43596460, 91-11-47340674
Mob: 98110 94883
e-mail: contact@vijpublishing.com
web : www.vijbooks.com

ISBN: 978-93-89620-74-0 (Paperback)

ISBN: 978-93-89620-37-5 (ebook)

Contents

Introduction

The Cold War struggle against the perceived enemy of communism dominated the politics of every Latin American republic for a generation. Between 1948 and 1990, the fear and hysteria surrounding communism, and the foreign policy of the USSR, impacted every election, revolution, military coup, and internal conflict in twenty individual Latin American republics.[1] This was based upon the premise that communism could, and potentially would, overtake the region and impose tyrannical authority to the detriment of the great majority. This book will demonstrate that this premise was in fact a pretext. The leaders of the United States created a prolonged era of paranoia based upon exaggerated and fabricated communist threats throughout the hemisphere, beginning in the 1920s and continuing throughout the era of the Cold War. In doing so, they characterized a generation of social democratic reformers as a part of the monolithic, and foreign, global movement for communism and Soviet global domination. As this pretext continued to grow, by the 1960s, all debate over whether 'communism' was the regional ideological enemy ceased. Rather, debate turned to how to contain the so-called insurgencies that threatened the status quo with violent revolution. In the absence of the substantial liberal and economic reform proposed by the social democratic, and other populist, politicians, the region became increasingly unstable and polarised between the status quo of social conservatism and neoliberal service to the American led global capitalist economy. Few thought to question what created these 'insurgencies'. This 'pretext' shaped Latin American politics for the duration of the global 'Cold War' despite its political, economic and geographic distance from the Soviet led world.

This ideological Cold War has obscured the analysis of democratic movements of the Americas. This book will trace those movements for 'social democracy' within the Mexican Party of the Institutionalized Revolution (PIR), the Peruvian American Popular Revolutionary Alliance (APRA), the Venezuelan Democratic Action Party (AD), the Colombian Nationalist Leftist Revolutionary Union (UNIR) and leftist faction of the

1

Liberal Party, the Authentic Party of the Cuba Revolution (PRC-A), the Guatemala Revolutionary Action Party (PAR), the Costa Rican National Liberation Party (PLN), and the Dominican Revolutionary Party (PRD). These movements were forged in the struggles against their respective national dictators and their ideology sought to form a progressive democratic community in the vacuum that followed long-term autocratic governance. Commonly associated with post-war Western Europe, the policies of 'social democracy' prioritize the protection of labor from the worst ravages of the free market.[2] Meyer argues that a "self-sustaining society" required the protection of "labor from the vicissitudes of the market" to ensure the collective wellbeing of all members of society.[3] In Europe, this meant income redistribution to ensure the safety, education and wellbeing of all sectors of society regardless of their social class.[4] While each Latin American example is unique in its political, social and economic circumstances, there is a clear transnational ideology based upon the anti-dictatorial struggle and the establishment of "survival coalitions" in their aftermath.[5] The Mexican Lazaro Cardenas' political strategy was defined by "radical social policies," "economic nationalism" and sovereignty from foreign capital.[6] The Peruvian Victor Raúl Haya de la Torre's platform professed "nationalism," "anti-Imperialism" and "social security".[7] The Cuban Eduardo Chibás defined the original PRC-A movement through "nationalism, socialism and anti-Imperialism", which he continued in his, later formed, Ortodoxo Party.[8] In Venezuela, AD professed "nationalization," "social reform" and unity against "imperialist finance".[9] Meanwhile, Jorge Gaitán, the leader of Colombian left liberalism, diagnosed the "social problem" between capital and labor as unsustainable inequity.[10] It is evident that the Latin Americans were coming from a less developed base than Europe. The fundamental social problem of inequality was entrenched and causing agitation between the dictatorships, the oligarchs and the masses. There was no single theorist that determined this philosophy of 'social democracy'. Rather, it became a framework for anti-dictatorial struggle and the formation of populist coalitions to fill their post-revolutionary voids, which claimed to create more equitable and developed societies. This came at the expense of the ruling oligarchs and foreign capital, setting the stage for the Latin America's unique Cold War, which was distinct from the global conflict between communism and capitalism.

Anti-communism emerged in the North American psyche immediately after the 1917 Russian Revolution. President Woodrow Wilson declared that "Bolshevism represented the antithesis of everything" he believed in.[11]

Communism is antithetic to American foreign policy for far greater reasons than professed global commitments to democracy, individualism and human rights. Communist countries nationalize the trade, investment and production of the economy to the, perceived, benefit of the nation. By 1919, the US was committed to a policy of economic expansion that required the 'openness' of the world economy to allow for constant capitalist growth in markets and access to the requisite resources to fuel that growth.[12] While communism posed a direct threat to American capitalism and it global ambitions, the threat of 'communism' was not unique to 'communism'. The policies of economic nationalism were not communist, in and of itself, but the threat to US capitalism was the same. Nationalists also prohibited the growth of US trade and investment in specific nations. Stephen Niblo has referred to this version of anti-communism as the "Communist Line".[13] In reference to the nationalism of 1940s Mexico, Niblo reasoned that the US labelled as communist, any economic policy that opposed US interests, both private and public.[14] The social democrats were, in most cases, anti-imperialists and economic nationalists which confronted foreign investment to support their populist coalitions. By the 1940s, the US were the greatest imperialists in their region. The redistribution of both income and capital goods was central to the social democratic coalitions for power. The redistribution of income was performed through increased taxation on the domestic oligarchs and foreign corporations. That income returned to the people in the form of social security, increased wages, and programs for health and education. The redistribution of capital goods was also undertaken by several of the social democratic leaders. Most common were the measure of nationalization of subsoil rights and the redistribution of land which was seized from peasants and sold to foreign corporations during the first decades of the twentieth century. These actions hindered the capitalist expansion of the US from the 1920s onwards, as it made small Latin American nations increasingly self-sufficient. It also negatively impacted those US citizens that owned the land and subsoil rights. This gave the US a motive to oppose economic nationalism from the early twentieth century.

The anti-communist pretext began within the US during 1919. Leffler argues that American politicians "would brand their enemies as communists" despite no detailed knowledge of the doctrine, or of events in Russia.[15] Boyle asserts that "the deep fears and anxieties of America in the Cold War created the irrationality of the Red Scare".[16] Moreover, communism was labelled as an evil doctrine without any general thought about it. People were coerced to express their loyalty to the US or risk being alienated by civil society, first during the red scare and much more explicitly during the McCarthy era of the 1950s.[17] This opinion was also expressed in their foreign policy. In 1927, US Secretary of State Frank Kellogg warned of the Bolshevist threat in Mexico and its influence upon Augusto Sandino's guerrilla campaign in Nicaragua.[18] The US Ambassador to Peru, Fred Dearing, described APRA as "the reddest of the red" and "under the influence of Moscow" during the 1931 presidential election.[19] In 1933-34 the US Ambassador to Cuba, Sumner Welles, accused the short-lived Grau administration of supporting communist land seizures in rural areas, leading to the overthrow of his government.[20] As the international Cold War descended, in 1948, US Secretary of State George Marshall accused rioters responding to the assassination of Jorge Eliécer Gaitán in Bogotá of having communist motivations.[21] By 1948, the anti-communist paranoia was so ingrained that few members of the US State Department were willing to question it. To do so would attract accusations of treason under the crusade of McCarthyism. To determine the origins of this paradoxical pretext, one must look back to the development of contemporary Latin America in its relations to the US. In doing so, the stories of the region's social democrats will be reclaimed. This book will demonstrate that the social democrats were not loyal to communism or the Soviet Union. Rather, they were middle-class reformers who sought to realign their national roles within the international capitalist economy through their social and economic programs to empower a greater majority at the expense of the oligarchy, foreign investment, and regional militarism. As Rómulo Betancourt indicated during the 1930s, their inspiration was much closer to the American 'New Deal' of Franklin Roosevelt, than to a violent revolution modelled after Russia.[22]

A New World in the service of the Old

The political origins of the Latin American republics are based upon their colonization and the conflicts for their independence. In Spanish America, a European elite of conquistadors ruled over a predominate Indigenous and mestizo population. Their role was to exploit the natural wealth of the hemisphere by commodifying agricultural, mineral and light manufactured products. In a land of plenty Eduardo Galeano states that, Latin America "continues to exist at the service of other's needs".[23] That is, Latin America was colonized as a source of raw materials for Europeans, and eventually North Americans, who sought to control and profit from the sale of those goods. Liberation in the early nineteenth century did not change their condition. The descendants of the conquistadors formed 'creole' oligarchies that replaced Spanish domination with their own. The demise of the Spanish Empire during the Napoleonic period brought independence but little substantive change. No democratic inclusion was offered to the Indigenous masses. Those masses continued to labor for the oligarchs without the promise of political or economic change. Meanwhile, the Creoles became increasingly dependent upon the British Empire to purchase their export commodities.[24] This made political power and economic wealth intrinsically linked. They continued to exploit labor to serve their private economic needs. In El Salvador, for example, a dozen families ruled the nation for over a century.[25] That level of control was required to produce the goods demanded in the North Atlantic, and to monopolize wealth.

The creole oligarchs diverged into two great camps following their independence from Spanish rule. The intellectual and political traditions of Latin America have often been defined through the polarization of Liberal and Conservative Parties. While their coalition against progressive ideologies is more significant than their opposition, it is relevant to define the two positions. Woodward defines Latin American "conservatism" as a reaction to radical philosophies that emerged in nineteenth century Europe.[26] Conservatism was ideologically very close to the Catholic Church, which "upheld the existing order" in the predominately Catholic countries of the Americas.[27] Hence, the emergence of conservatism in Latin America was a response to the arrival of liberal thought during the national independence revolutions inspired by France and the US. Henderson asserts that the emergence of Latin American conservatism "illustrate[s] both the unity of Western history and the element of lag in the spread and acceptance of new ideas".[28] This lag was both geographic and programmatic. Conservative parties are a continuing part of the political landscape in Latin America.[29]

Latin American liberalism originated from within European thought. Fawcett defines "liberalism" as the belief, "that societies were constantly evolving" with a specific emphasis "on people's rights, toleration, constitutional government, the rule of law, and liberty".[30] All Liberalism seeks to harness the power of people, who may be unequal and even immoral.[31] This analysis is based on classical liberal works including Hobhouse, Wallerstein and Weber.[32] It is, however, important to make a distinction between economic and social components of liberalism. Grampp defines "economic liberalism" as a "laissez-faire" approach to the economy that utilizes human energy.[33] Hence, economic liberals have sought to unleash the powers of the free market to rapidly expand economic output in their respective nations. Alternatively, the social liberal, or 'progressive', agenda requires several reforms including the improvement of the working conditions. Progressivism began as an isolated strand of liberalism that sought to regenerate society by utilizing the potential of the working class. However, according to Peeler "most Latin American liberals were less deeply committed to the political side of liberalism, with its emphasis on constitutionalism, limited government and freedom of expression" as they were preoccupied by 'economic liberalism', which advantaged the entrepreneurial oligarchic class.[34] Hence, when it is said that the principle conflict in Latin American politics was between liberalism and conservatism, the statement concerns economic theories rather than progressive notions of egalitarianism. That would not materialize until the twentieth century.

Despite this ideological divide between members of the oligarchy, nineteenth century politics was mostly undemocratic. The landowning oligarchic class, both conservative and liberal, influenced government policy for personal economic and political gain.[35] International trade rapidly expanded in the second half of the nineteenth century due to the industrial revolution, global population expansion and improved naval technology.[36] This created intense competition between these factions, which led to many civil wars. But of greater significance was the control of the disgruntled masses. The increase of trade and technology brought formerly isolated peasant communities into the national economy. The advent of rail transportation rapidly increased the amount of arable land in Latin America available for agricultural exploitation. These land seizures cemented the power of oligarchic rule over the lives of peasants. But to maintain that power against an increasingly agitated peasant and working class, they turned to the military. The late nineteenth and early twentieth century saw the oligarchic democracies give way to military caudilloism.[37] The 'caudillo' military presidents maintained the stability that was demanded by international trade and investment. By the dawn of the twentieth century the only Caribbean nations that could make any reasonable claim to constitutional rule were Costa Rica and Nicaragua.[38] Every other nation in the region went through a continual cycle of militarism, elitist elections and coup d'états.[39]

A Rising Star in the North

The British established a settler society along the Eastern coast of North America during the seventeenth century that was fundamentally different to the majority of the 'Latin' American colonies. Europeans replaced the Indigenous population of British North America with each class of their society to form a new Europe in the New World. The American Declaration of Independence expressed the notions of nationalism and individualism, which created a large democratic community. While a moneyed oligarchy remained dominant over the political system, the European citizens of the US supported the general maneuvers of the Federal Government that they had elected, believing in the concept of 'America'. Peripheral members of this new society, such as Native Americans and African slaves, were excluded through forced unpaid labor, persecution and genocide; however, the majority of the European citizens were free to undertake independent economic and social activities. The United States began its path towards regional economic leadership through its implementation of a rapidly expanding capitalist economy that created internal markets, industrialization, innovation and rapid geographic expansion. The thirteen colonies began to expand at the conclusion of the Revolutionary War in 1788. The continuing threat of British aggression to the North directed the US both southward and westward; into conflict with the newly independent Latin American republics. Following the politically peaceful acquisitions of the regions of French Louisiana, in 1803, and Spanish Florida in 1819, the US engaged in the eradication of Indigenous peoples throughout their westward expansion. Foreseeing this great expansion into 'Latin' America, US President James Monroe declared that European colonization of the Americas would amount to a declaration of war against the US.[40] While the US lacked the military capacity to prevent European colonization, an informal agreement was forged with the dominant regional economic power, Britain.[41] Both nations sought to prevent further economic competition in the Americas as they continued to control resources and markets without formal colonization. Meanwhile, the US continued its continental expansion. North American settlers pushed into the sparsely populated region of Tejas and seceded from the Mexican Empire in 1836.[42] Tension over 'Texas' and America's newfound doctrine of "manifest destiny" sparked the Mexican-American War of 1846-1848.[43] The war gained the US 2.5 million square kilometers, over half of Mexican territory, and provided the US with access to the Pacific Ocean and the impetus to become a global power.[44] By 1848, the US had announced itself to the region.

America's first engagements in Latin American politics were conducted by private citizens outside of Washington's control. US citizens were competing with the British and other European powers for control of commodities, markets and infrastructure investment throughout the region. In doing so, they were impacting regional politics without the official oversight of the US government. For example, the renegade trader William Walker declared himself the President of Nicaragua in 1856 following a dispute between his employers and the local government.[45] Of more significance though, was the US rail magnate James Stillman's support of the 1876 coup conducted by Porfirio Díaz in Mexico.[46] Díaz remained in power until the 1910 Mexican Revolution, granting generous concessions to US transport, mining and agricultural consortiums.[47] Meanwhile, the federal government was unsure of the necessity of this expansion. The American economy remained dependent on goods and capital from Europe until World War I. However, the severe depression of the 1890s demonstrated to US policy makers that the US required markets beyond Europe for its export commodities. The "open-door notes", outlined by WA Williams, initiated an expansionist trade policy in both East Asia and Latin America.[48] From this moment, the US adopted a policy of trade liberalism and military expansionism. During the 1890s, the US transformed its economic position from raw material exporter for Europe, to industrial exporter to Asia and the Americas. Hence, the US became dependent on foreign sources of raw materials to fuel their growth. The aggressive foreign policy in the Caribbean between was motivated by their shifting place in the global economy. Therefore, their attitude towards Latin American sovereignty, politics, and economics was self-interested.

The US turned the Caribbean into an American lake between 1898 and 1910. The US had only US$600 million of direct foreign investment in 1897.[49] The US$200 million invested in Mexico was the only foreign country where the US were the major investor.[50] This was due to their support for the authoritarian Díaz regime who, in turn, favored American over European businesses. The establishment of similar relationships in the Caribbean was the major motivation for the era of 'gunboat diplomacy'. The Americans also monopolized shipping routes and the prospective Panama Canal, under this policy. As such, the actions of William McKinley, Theodore Roosevelt and Howard Taft were a secured trade and strategic dominance with the assistance of local oligarchies, militaries and American soldiers of fortune. This physical expansion began with the demolition of the defunct Spanish Empire in 1898 leading to the annexation of Puerto Rico and the 'protection' of Cuba under the 1903 Platt Amendment.[51] It then provided military support for the secession of the Panama region from Colombia in order to create the inter-Oceanic canal within a dependent client state.

To support this new wave of interventionism, the US congress approved US$115 million to create Roosevelt's "Great White Fleet" in 1900.[52] The combination of military expansion, the transoceanic canal and increasing US trade and investment shaped the Caribbean as an 'American Lake'. However, continuing European trade, investment and naval presence temporarily obstructed Washington's advance. In the 1904 State of the Union Address, Theodore Roosevelt offered a far-reaching corollary to the 1823 Monroe Doctrine. Roosevelt advocated for expansion of US political and economic control in "every country washed by the Caribbean Sea".[53] He described the interests of the regions as "identical" as they possessed "great natural riches" that would bring "prosperity" to the region.[54] However, those nations that continued to defy the Monroe Doctrine by maintaining their relationships through European trade and investment, through their "impotence" would be subject to "international police powers".[55] The interventions in Venezuela 1903, the Dominican Republic 1903, Nicaragua 1911 and Honduras 1911 created pro-US governments and treasury departments.[56] These nations, and their military leaders, became increasingly dependent upon US trade. Their governments gave favorable deals to US businesses, as Díaz had done in Mexico. The process for expansion became clear; intervene in foreign nations to ensure that American economic interests were directly served.

Forces for Change

Political power was monopolized throughout most of Latin America at the end of the nineteenth century. While Central America and the Caribbean struggled with the forceful expansion of US capital in the first decades of the twentieth century, their contemporaries in the 'Southern Cone' were for the first time experimenting with representative democracy. The mass immigration of Europeans to the Americas in the last decade of the nineteenth century brought new political ideals that translated to reform in Argentina, Uruguay, and, to a lesser extent, Chile. In most cases, political change comes from below through radical coalitions of workers, small business owners and university students. However, the region's first experiment with large scale representative democracy came from above. José Battle y Ordonez was the son of a former Uruguayan President and a lifelong politician.[57] During his second interlude as President between 1911 and 1915 he expanded the philosophy of the Liberal 'Colorado' Party to become the people's party. Uruguay possessed very different demographics to other Latin American countries. It had a large European population, of primarily Spanish and Italian descent, that arrived and urbanized the nation between the 1890s and the 1920s.[58] Pendle suggests that

> "Ordonez maintained that the employer should always set the public welfare above private gain; that the employer should pass on a greater share of profit than formerly to his employees; and that the employer and the state should aid the poor, the sick, the old, and the young".[59]

Above all, the renewed constitution of 1918 allowed for universal male suffrage. And although several years behind Ecuador and Chile in granting women the vote, the universal measure meant that Uruguay was the most democratic nation in the region. It was also the most socially progressive with federally mandated 48-hour working week and a more generous minimum wage.[60] While Ordonez is unique, both regionally and globally, in his efforts to reform Uruguayan society, it did prove that democracy was not monopolized by 'Northern' countries and that the model could be implemented in 'Southern' nations with significant social benefit for the population.

Along with the concept of a more "liberal" Liberalism, as exemplified Ordonez in Uruguay, came a plethora of new beliefs on how to run a society. These ideas were disseminated by European immigrants to Argentina, and Southern Brazil. They brought the ideas of the worker's internationals, including anarcho-syndicalism, socialism and eventually communism. They also brought progressive versions of liberalism that emphasized individual rights and mass participation. However, ideas that did not directly apply to the Latin American, and specific national, condition had no mass appeal. While these European ideas had some influence upon events and movements for mass democracy, they all become 'Latin-Americanized' before they become successful. One such example is the efforts for Argentine 'Radicalism'. Upon seeking election in 1910, the Radical leader Saenz Peña proposed universal education, universal male military service and, above all, compulsory voting for all segments of society.[61] Peña attempted to forge an Argentine nationalism that emphasized the collective good, an experiment that had only previously been trialed in the remote British dominion of Australia. Nevertheless, Argentine Radicals came to power in 1916 under the leadership of Hipolito Yrigoyen.[62] While not proposing a 'radical' social revolution, Yrigoyen brought all sectors of society into the political community, effectively ending the era of oligarchic control of Argentina. Democracy was the first requisite change along the road towards social and economic modernization for all Latin American countries. Argentina had achieved this, only decades after most

European nations. At this moment, all Latin American revolutionaries saw that attracting the oppressed masses to their movements was necessary to fulfill their social revolution.

The Presence of the United States was also deeply unpopular throughout the Latin America. This was exemplified in the works of José Marti. As a Cuban Revolutionary living in exile, Marti saw the handicaps that Latin America faced when dealing with the US. He blamed US business for the Caudillo style regimes of Antonio Guzmán Blanco in Venezuela, Porfirio Díaz in Mexico and Juan Ruffino Barrios in Guatemala.[63] He reasoned that those regimes served US capitalists at the expense of their nations by stating, "they have made money the chief good so as to create prosperity. Cursed be prosperity at such a cost".[64] He continued to state, "Let us imitate the - No! Let us copy them - No!".[65] Marti's attacks on US capitalism predated the era of expansion that followed the Spanish American War. Following those aggressive acts, he was joined, posthumously, by further critics such as Santiago Iglesias and Diego Vincente Tejara among other radical authors.[66] Their main critique was that the US sought to lead Latin America. Indeed, Monroe's 1823 doctrine professed as much. The US attempted to control the economies of the region and provide Latin Americans with specific roles serving their industrial economy. Marti, among others, sought independence from all foreign powers as the central tenet of any revolution. The US were confirming Marti's hypothesis in Cuba and expanding it to many other countries. By the 1920s, many of the larger Latin American nations were opposed to US aggression, especially the direct military intervention against Mexico in 1914 and 1917. US expansionism was opposed by the residents of the hemisphere. Moreover, the seeds of a continent-wide democratic revolution had been planted prior to the Russian Revolution. This book will document how many of these necessary political, social and economic revolutions throughout Latin America have been misinterpreted as part of an international Cold War, and the belligerents incorrectly labelled as 'communist'.

Chapter One

'Our People Have Never Had Justice'

Emilano Zapata symbolized the injustices of the economic expansion that struck much of Latin America in the late nineteenth century. The increased market for exportable agricultural products led to the annexation of traditional lands that had been used for subsistence agriculture for generations, in turn, making those peasants dependent upon plantation farming for survival. With no political options provided to the peasantry, they took up arms against their government, and their perceived oppressors. Zapata's followers in Morales, Southern Mexico, were committed to a social revolution that would redistribute land from the 'haciendos' to the peasants.[67] Zapata stated that, "our people have never had justice. Nor given freedom. The rich have got all the major landholding, while the poor wear rags and work from dawn til' dusk. I believe things must be different in the future".[68] Zapata's army became a major part of the Mexican Revolution. This struggle for 'justice', land and freedom from the political and economic elite continued to define the multiclass transnational revolution for social democracy and revolutionary nationalism that emerged in the 1920s. These movements in Mexico, Peru, Venezuela, Cuba and Colombia required the destruction of the military dictatorship and those who profited from it. From that base, an alliance between peasants, industrial workers and the liberal bourgeoisie became necessary. This chapter will examine the first attempts for social democratic revolution in Latin America. It will also explain the counter-forces of US economic expansion that continued to work against these revolutionary movements during the first decades of the twentieth century.

The Mexican Revolution

Porfirio Díaz ruled Mexico, directly and indirectly, between 1876 and 1910.[69] During that time, Mexico underwent substantial economic development during that time, however, the vast majority of that development served foreign trade and investment and a small segment of 'technocratic oligarchs'.[70] Foreign investment had monopolized lands that had been worked by Indians for generations.[71] Meanwhile, the expansion of mining in Northern Mexico, and manufacturing in the cities, created a sizable industrial working class, organized through mass unionization.[72] Many Mexicans were opposed to Díaz continuing as President in 1910. There was also growing opposition to the amount of foreign American investment and the rising inequality in Mexico. Therefore, when Díaz cancelled the 1910 general election against the Liberal candidate Francisco Madero, several groups began clamoring for revolution.[73] Madero forged alliances with disparate revolutionary movements, including: the Zapatista peasant armies of Morales to the South; the northern ranchero armies of Pancho Villa; the constitutionalist armies of Victoriano Carranza and Alvaro Obregon; and the anarchist-syndicalist unions of Mexico City.[74] These movements represented the disaffected masses of Mexican society, from peasant, to worker, to petty bourgeoisie, to soldier of fortune. They also represented a wide array of intellectual traditions that were both Indigenous to Mexico and adopted from the Atlantic region. Moreover, this was a complex multiclass, anti-Díaz, alliance that collapsed soon after it achieved its primary objective.

Madero's inability, and unwillingness, to fulfill the revolutionary ambitions of his supporting factions led to the dissolution of the alliance soon after his ascension to presidency. With chaos ensuing, the Porfirian general Victoriano Huerta overthrew Madero in February 1913.[75] Huerta and his military sought to stabilize rural Mexico by eliminating the resistance of Zapata and Villa. However, the peasant armies drove the military back to Mexico City during 1914.[76] Villa, Zapata and thousands of rebel peasants-controlled Mexico City during the winter of 1914-1915.[77] Madero's failure to govern Mexico demonstrated the necessity of mass political consent within the multiclass revolutionary movement. The alliance had removed Díaz, but the destruction of the alliance had allowed the conservative military to return. Thus, Mexico required an institutionalized revolutionary alliance that could manage diverse class segments and deliver on its promises. In 1915, Villa and Zapata held the capital while the more moderate constitutionalists occupied much of Northern Mexico.[78] These constitutionalists required a coalition large enough to monopolize power and eventually return peace and stability to Mexico. Their victories in 1915 gave them the legitimacy to organize the constitutional convention of Aguascalientes in 1916, selling their vision for post-revolutionary Mexico.[79] Gonzalez states, "despite his patrician manners and thinly veiled elitism, Carranza expanded his political base by promising peasants and workers land, higher wages, and political voice by unifying Mexicans through revolutionary nationalism that focused on the condemnation of US imperialism".[80] Those measures to ensure independence and liberty from the Americans are explicit in the Mexican constitution of 1917.

The Mexican constitution was a radical document but was not fully implemented in the aftermath of the Revolution.[81] It is a reflection of the multiclass alliance that eventually supported the revolution. Indigenous rights are represented through: anti-discrimination measures; explicit recognition of Indigenous cultures; and land redistribution for communal ownership under article 27.[82] This brought in many of Zapata's rural peasant supporters who fought for land and equality for Indigenous peoples.[83] Classical liberalism is represented through: freedom of ideas; freedom of speech; rights to petition and protest; freedom of movement; and, freedom of personal affairs.[84] This brought in members of the old liberal oligarchy and constitutional movements. Social Democracy is represented through: mandated government support for free primary, middle and higher education; exclusion of titles of nobility; planned economic growth to favor the masses; nationalization of some economic ventures; capped commodity prices; commitment to nationalism and democracy.[85] This was a token gesture of nationalism in providing support for their collective future. Worker's rights are represented through article 123 which commits to: the 8-hour day; prohibition of child labor under 15; the 6-day working week; minimum wage; provisions for reduced duties during maternity and a formal 12-week maternity leave; equal wages for equal work; profit sharing mechanisms; housing for rural labor; health and safety mandates; and the right to strike.[86] This rewarded the 'red-battalions' who fought for the constitutionalists during the revolution.[87] Women's rights are represented through: legal equality for women including health services and the protection of children; full citizenship rights including voting rights.[88] Equality is also ensured through maternity provisions and equal pay within article 123. This brought in increased support from women who were now, rhetorically, liberated from the paternalistic society. Anti-Imperialism is represented through article 27 which prohibits foreign ownership of natural resources, and land of vital national interest, such as that near borders and coastlines.[89] While these measures were not directed at a single country, the US who had intervened in Mexico during 1914 and

1916, in addition to condoning the Huerta coup of 1913, were the implicit target.

This radical constitution created the framework for a multiclass coalition to collectively govern Mexico following the violent revolution. Significantly, it also claimed to make Mexico independent from the US led Caribbean sphere through 'nationalist' measures. This was a serious challenge to the American expansionist agenda, inasmuch, the US had sought to stop the revolution throughout the 1910s. The US Ambassador to Mexico, Henry Lane Wilson, gave US support to the Huerta coup of 1913.[90] Upon learning of this, the newly inaugurated President, Woodrow Wilson, dismissed the ambassador and became antagonistic towards Huerta, invading the Northern territory of Veracruz in 1914.[91] Wilson again invaded Mexico in 1916 to catch and kill Pancho Villa who was responsible for the deaths of 17 US citizens during a train heist.[92] American action briefly united the Mexican Revolutionary factions. The constitutionalists and Villa combined to drive the American forces out of Mexico in early 1917.[93] This revolution was misunderstood by the Americans. Mexicans sought a quality of life comparable to the North Americans. This was a threat to US businesses that sought to exploit the low Mexican wages and the nation's resources. More significantly, it was also a threat due to precedence. American foreign policy towards Mexico in the 1920s demonstrates these two clear positions. When Obregón and Warren Harding assumed their respective presidencies, in 1920 and 1921, the bilateral relationship was at an impasse. For Secretary of State, Charles Evan Hughes, America's objective was "the safeguarding of property rights against confiscation".[94] The US argued that the 'retroactivity clause', which led to the nationalization of land and subsoil rights in the 1917 constitution, was illegal.[95] While it still had revolutionary ambitions, the Mexican Civil War left the government indebted, fatigued, and in need of revenue. To appease Washington, Obregón imposed a 25 per cent tax on the export profits of US companies in the place of the full and immediate expropriation of oil rights.[96] Hughes accepted this agreement and the tensions were temporarily eased. The Americans contained and limited the effects of the Mexican Revolution during the 1920s. For Mexico, however, their revolution was merely delayed.

The Expansion of American Power

World War I altered the American position within the global economy. By financing the militaries of the allies, the US became a major creditor to the Europeans. However, much of that investment was made privately by US financiers outside of the control of the federal government, which professed neutrality in the early years of the war. Public enquiries into American involvement in WWI, found that the financial institutions' desire to protect their investment was a major cause for America's military involvement in 1917. As of the 1910s, the US public did not want its government to be the international arbiter or policeman. The US had long been 'isolationist', and many resented the 'robber baron' class for sending them to war. This sentiment was at odds with Woodrow Wilson's proposed ideology of internationalism. Wilson created a new post-war regulatory body to prevent future European wars. The League of Nations (LoN) was the forerunner to United Nations (UN), which attempted to balance power in a world that was rapidly changing.[97] WWI shattered the international order of the 'long nineteenth century'. Despite their eventual victories, the British and French Empires were weakened by economic obligations and the overextension of their colonial subjects. Following WWI, both Empires faced major calls for decolonization in their large colonial empires, especially in Asia. Meanwhile, much of the large Tsarist Russian Empire was now under the control of the USSR and the order of the Austro-Hungarian Empire and German Republic in continental Europe was shattered.

American public opposition to internationalism handed the Republicans the presidency in 1921. The republicans saw internationalism in different terms to Wilson and focused on rapid capitalist development without explicit control of international markets. Under pro-business Republican leadership, from 1919 to 1929 the US experienced a 70 per cent increase in industrial output.[98] The rapid industrialization of export commodity industries, such as automobiles, electronics and light consumer goods, was fueled by global demand. However, the US were not the only industrial nation. Inasmuch, the foreign policy of the US required the procurement of markets for finished American goods and the monopolization of the resources required to produce those industrial consumer goods. The US possessed significant capital investment in Central America and the Caribbean by 1920. Foreign policy under the Republican administrations of Harding, Coolidge and Hoover focused on returning the US to "normalcy".[99] In Latin America, this meant a return to the interventionism of gunboat diplomacy and the support of US capitalist enterprise. They also committed to the "protect American life and property" abroad.[100] Simply put, the Republicans would protect and promote US trade and investment abroad. Washington's economic relationship with Latin America was required for this industrial expansion. However, much of this influence was turned over to private corporations.

US businesses thrived with official government support for their actions. The United Fruit Company (UFCo) of Boston became the largest landowner in the Caribbean.[101] It was an agricultural enterprise that sought to mass produce bananas. Their operations expanded to such a point that they became a dominant political force in Guatemala, Honduras, Costa Rica and Panama.[102] Their large land purchases were integrated with infrastructure development to service their enterprise. Their leader, Sam Zemmurray, often became involved in politics. He was personally responsible for the Honduran coup in 1911 and was heavily involved in choosing Nicaraguan leaders after the US intervention in 1911.[103] Pliable governments aided their enterprise by providing cheap land and paying for infrastructure that was exclusively used by the UFCo. Standard Oil of New Jersey (SONJ) was the largest oil producer in Mexico prior to the Revolution.[104] Foreseeing the setbacks of Mexican nationalization, SONJ moved further South to find more pliable governments. They monopolized oil extraction in Colombia, and Bolivia while taking a major share of Venezuela's vast reserves.[105] SONJ was amongst the biggest oil exporters in the world due to its large Latin reserves. The Guggenheim American Smelting and Refining Company (ASARCo) were the largest mining company in Chile by the end of the 1910s. They ensured that the US accounted for 87 per cent of Chilean copper exports by 1918.[106] They also initiated largescale mineral extraction and refinement in Bolivia, Colombia and Peru. There are countless other examples. International Telegraph and Telephone Company (ITT) monopolized the communication infrastructure of western South America and the Caribbean.[107] Ford motors established a rubber plantation deep in the Amazon to ensure constant supplies to its American factories.[108] Pan American airlines began monopolizing regional air travel and mail services from the 1920s.[109] The Associated Press (AP) bought newspapers across the continent to advertise American goods.[110] While Washington did not directly control this rapid capitalist expansion, it did provide them with support under the assumption that this would serve American interests in the long term. Many Latin Americans did not differentiate between the corporations and direct American foreign policy as they were inseparable during the 1920s.

Despite their advances, the US only accounted for 40 per cent of Latin American trade in the 1920s.[111] The continuing presence of European trade, investment and infrastructure prohibited the creation of an American sphere of influence. Britain was the major investor in Eastern South America with projects in communication and transport since the nineteenth century.[112] Germany was the major ammunitions supplier to Argentina and Chile who viewed their military technology and training as superior to that of the British and Americans.[113] The Royal Dutch Shell Company monopolized the oil supplies of Paraguay and held a large proportion of Venezuela's reserves.[114] British and French banks were preferred to the US, and even had branches throughout the Americas.[115] However, the larger obstacle was the perception of 'Yankee Imperialism'. The Latin Americans opposed US invasions in the Caribbean. Writing in the 1920s, the future Secretary of State, Cordell Hull, stated, "the United States has pursued policies towards some of the Latin American nations" which has led to "prejudice and feeling throughout Central and South America against our country".[116] The Latin Americans did not want to come under the imperial influence of the US because they had seen the consequence for nations like Cuba. They also opposed American businesses for the way that they treated Latin Americans. In the example Magdalena Massacre in Colombia, the UFCo refused to yield and pushed the conservative government of Miguel Méndez to resolve protests over pay and conditions with force. Estimates of casualties vary from 47 to several hundreds.[117] It was clear to many in the region that the UFCo valued profits over human life. While these types of incidents were out of Washington's control, they were in their name and they did nothing to reprimand UFCo's owners or regional managers.

Communism and Anti-Communism in the Americas

The Russian Revolution of 1917 reverberated around the world. Beyond the European theatre, Vladimir Lenin professed global revolution against Imperialism through the "third international of workers" in 1919.[118] The Cold War between American capitalism and Soviet communism began in the aftermath of the Revolution. The US actively prevented the expansion of Soviet Communism by promoting the independence of former Russian territories from the Soviet sphere.[119] They also worked against the short-lived Hungarian Revolution. For their part, the Soviets promoted global revolution through the "Comintern". Lenin promoted the Comintern as a means to the "dictatorship of the proletariat and the Soviet Power".[120] This differentiates their purpose from the first international anarchist parties and the second international socialist parties. The Comintern prioritized the expansion of the Soviet sphere of influence and the potential for global revolution. The Communist International declared, "to fight by all available means, including armed struggle, for the overthrow of the international bourgeoisie and for the creation of an international Soviet republic as a transition stage to the complete abolition of the state".[121] Hence, the participants of the third international in 1919, and subsequent meetings of international communism, followed a direct line from the Soviets. However, the limited place of the Latin Americans must be kept in context.

Latin American Communist Parties were established in the first two years after the Communist International. By 1921, Communist Parties were formed in Argentina, Brazil, Uruguay, Mexico and Chile.[122] These parties were composed of the educated, middle-class segments of their societies.[123] Most had defected from socialist, anarchist and radical parties in their respective nations and sought to follow the radical path to violent revolution in the Americas, having exhausted other means to mass participation. The Communist Parties, struggled for membership due to their inability to translate the Marxist ideas for revolution to the Latin American economic position.[124] Communism, as professed by Karl Marx, was an economic stage that would come after capitalism and socialism.[125] In many parts of Latin America, the transition from feudalism to bourgeoisie capitalism was only recently initiated, while in some regions it was yet to occur. The developed parts of the 'southern cone' resembled Europe enough for communism to grasp relevance, hence the limited success of parties in those regions. The most successful regional communist leader was Carlos Luis Prestes of Brazil who had emulated the Chinese 'long march' in order to preach revolution to the peasants.[126] In other nations, the communists infiltrated the union movement. The Confederacion Sindical Latino Americano (CSLA) preached Latin American revolution to their membership in several Latin American nations.[127] However, party membership remained low. In Mexico, for example, they did not have enough members to register for elections.[128] Their limited place in international communism was reflected by their isolation within the "Latin Bureau" with French and Iberian parties.[129] The that Latin American communists did not earn their own section until late 1920s.[130] But as the Comintern preached strict adherence to Soviet policy, the Latin American communists remained irrelevant through the 1920s.

Communism became a focal point for global capitalism, despite its limited role in Latin America. The 'Red-Scare' of 1919 was a major challenge within the United States. The doctrinaire expressions made by communists against their government caused significant concern among business and government elite.[131] However, civil discontent in the US was not solely caused by communists. Many of the mass strikes were staged by anarchist unions and anarchists were also responsible for acts of domestic terrorism during 1919.[132] However, the term communism was an effective measure to label unions as pro-Soviet and anti-American. Conservative

American politicians began using this term 'communist' indiscriminately, during the red scare, to target pro-union politicians and union leadership as un-American.[133] This was effective both domestically and internationally. The Mexican Revolution was not a 'communist revolution' and did not serve the interests of international communism. In fact, it significantly predates the outbreak of revolution in Russia. However, broadly speaking, it was anti-American and opposed foreign investment. Hence, the label of Communism was directed towards Mexico by US Secretary of State Frank Kellogg in 1923, while still a Minnesota Senator.[134] After his 1925 promotion he adopted a hostile stance towards the Elias Calles Mexican government. He furthered this claim in 1927 to state, "the bolshevist leaders [have] set up as one of their fundamental tasks, the destruction of what they term as American imperialism" in the memorandum – 'Bolshevist aims in Mexico'.[135] He continued his assault on Mexico to claim that it had inspired the domestic insurgency of the liberal defector Augusto Sandino in Nicaragua.[136] The claim that either Calles or Sandino were communists was not scrutinized by the American press, but they justified a decade of harassment of both nations by the Republican Coolidge and Hoover administrations – exacerbating Latin American accusations of American Imperialism. Anti-communism had become a pretext of convenience during the 1920s. It was hugely popular within the US and it served the interests of the American business community in their Latin American operations.

The Origins of Social Democracy

The social democratic revolution in the Americas does not have a precise moment of origin. Rather, it was the product of four individual movements against the tyrannical rulers of Peru, Venezuela, Cuba and Colombia. Haya de la Torre, Betancourt, Grau and Gaitán were all university educated and led their movements from that discontented middle revolutionary class. They were all deep thinkers about the social problems in their nations, offering revolutionary ideas about democracy, nationalism and socialism They had all spent time abroad, where they learnt lessons on democracy and social progress. They were all charismatic leaders that were able to construct broad coalitions of peasants, workers and middle-class people against elite military control. They all experienced victories, and suffered defeats, which inspired them to continue their struggles until old age, or ultimately death. But above all, they were revolutionaries. They saw the problem of tyranny as something to be defeated. They also realized the challenge of creating a coalition to protect their movement.[137] This is represented in their philosophies, party names and actions throughout their lives. These four movements would define the struggles in their own nations and also inspire their neighbors in Guatemala, Costa Rica, the Dominican Republic in addition to less successful movements for democracy in Honduras and Nicaragua. They have a significant regional legacy to be examined.

Victor Raúl Haya De La Torre was born on February 22, 1895 to a wealthy family in Trujillo, Peru.[138] Despite the luxuries of wealth, the Haya de la Torre family had lost prestige and opportunities due to familial opposition to his parent's marriage. Because of perceived injustices against him, Haya began to identify with the poor. At a very young age, Haya denounced "the treatment of labor and lament[ed] that much of the wealth of the coast has fallen into foreign hands".[139] Haya actively opposed this hypothesis of 'status insecurity' put forward by the historian Peter Klaren during his life. Nevertheless, Haya's thoughts and actions diverged from those of his social class. Prior to his departure from Trujillo, Haya wrote and produced a play that demonstrated "resentment against the plutocrats", which explained his coming exile from that community.[140] In 1917, at age 22, he arrived at San Marcos University in Lima to continue his studies. While Haya's concept of an ideal society was being developed in Lima, the dictator Augusto Leguia seized power expressing a view for Peru that was the exact opposite.[141] Leguia advocated for a pluralist society of elites with relative freedom, while the masses received few civil liberties. While those at the top would thrive under Leguia, the great masses would continue to be impoverished. The challenge to the dictator came from two places, José Carlos Mariategui's socialists, and from San Marcos University.[142] By 1920, Haya had been elected to lead the university movement. More significantly, he fostered ties with organized labor and began establishing "popular universities" to educate workers in political theory and gain their support against the government.[143]

While expanding the political movement of San Marcos, Haya took a job as a teacher. There he learnt from John A. Mackay that the task of an educator is "to attack everything in society that seems responsible for the suffering and backwardness of men".[144] Haya forged new ideas for a utopian Peru that would be built upon Christianity, nationalism, democracy and equality. Haya was a well-known figured in Peru by 1923. He preached revolution to receptive the masses. This revolutionary fervor caught the attention of Leguia. In November 1923, he was expelled from Peru by the regime. Haya retorted "I have been exiled…by the government of Leguia, which is an agency of Yankee imperialism, to which it is selling all the riches of Peru".[145] Abroad in Mexico, Haya continued his message of student revolution. In doing so he declared a new movement for the Americas – the Alianza Popular Revolucionaria Americana (APRA).[146] APRA sought to internationalize the Peruvian struggle against Leguia. While in Mexico, Haya worked as a secretary for the Mexican Education Minister José Vasconceles.[147] By the end of the 1920s, Haya was ready for his return to Peru. He had also initiated a regional anti-dictatorial movement in the Americas. The political and economic policies of the APRA, however, would not be made clear until the 1930 presidential campaign. At this moment in time, it was merely an alliance, of students, workers and the other 'have-nots' against the dictator, the US and the oligarchs who profited from inequality.

Rómulo Betancourt was born in 1908, the same year that Vincente Gómez seized power in Venezuela. He was a mixed-race Venezuelan with a Spanish father and a Native American mother. His father, Luis Betancourt, was of modest means but was remembered as "an educated man, of outstanding intelligence and an expert accountant".[148] During the 1918 global influenza epidemic, Luis and Rómulo Betancourt assisted his community by distributing medicine. It was at this time, that a young Betancourt "began to know the misery of the peasants".[149] His father died in this epidemic and a 10-year-old Rómulo commented,

> "he died poor, leaving me an invaluable legacy: that of his permanent teaching of dignity…if I have known how to remain loyal to profound moral convictions, in public acts and private life, it is because in my home I learned from an exemplary Venezuelan that lesson which will bind me all my life".[150]

After this, Betancourt continued his education in his native Gautier demonstrating an interest in literature and political philosophy. His dissertation focused on the life and works of the Venezuelan philosopher Cecilio Acosta. Betancourt concluded that

> The fatality of history has been the separation of Venezuelan generations from the noble preoccupation with things of the spirit; and for that of reason…I imagine that there is reserved to my generation…all the pride of being one which incorporates that eminent life and work, as efficient factors of evolution, into the currents of national life.[151]

The young Rómulo Betancourt saw the need for a spiritual revolution that incorporated his life experience of expressed suffering.

Betancourt studied constitutional law at the Central University of Venezuela. However, this was a theoretical topic of enquiry given Gómez's continuing military reign. Despite the problems of broader Venezuela, Betancourt favored literature over politics during his first 18 months of studies. His life was turned upside down during the violence of 'student week', February 6-12, 1928. The Federation of Venezuelan Students (FEV) staged, what was intended to be a peaceful march in the center of Caracas. However, the speeches quickly turned political. Chants of "Down with the Yankees" and "Viva Nicaragua" were heard at the strikes.[152] This attitude of revolution was unexpected but began to gain momentum. On February 9, Betancourt gave an impassioned speech alluding to "the poor people, forgotten by god and crucified by Republican anguish".[153] This revolutionary rhetoric was not ignored by Gómez, who on February 11 had Betancourt and three other leaders of the FEV arrested. Their brutal treatment by police inspired street demonstrations, which eventually led to their release. Once free, Betancourt began planning the April Rebellion with the FEV leaders and some disgruntled military members. According to the historian Robert Alexander, "The April 1928 plot was a failure. However, it contributed to the political education of the students who participated in it. It helped convince them that the overthrow of Gómez and the caudillo system would be the result of long and patient effort".[154] Betancourt escaped this revolutionary 'failure' and his new commitment to overthrowing the Gómez regime was galvanized while exiled in Costa Rica.

Ramón Grau San Martin was born into to a wealthy Cuban family in 1887.[155] Grau was afforded a high-quality education and graduated from the University of Havana in 1908. Like many wealthy Latin Americans, Grau continued his studies throughout Europe and North America over the next decade.[156] This period seems to have been formative for Grau. Having lived through the first Cuban Revolution of 1898, he also got a close look at university politics during the height of the Great War in Europe.[157] Unlike Haya, Betancourt and Gaitán, Grau was not the architect of his political movement. Rather, he was thrust into political power on the wave of anti-Machado sentiment that rocked Cuba in the late 1920s, primarily amongst his students. Grau was a professor at the University of Havana, from 1921, and became increasingly involved in the politics of the university throughout the 1920s. Cuba had been a protectorate of the US under the Platt Amendment of 1903.[158] This made representative democracy virtually unattainable in the Caribbean Republic. However, the election of Garrardo Machado in 1924 began to raise the expectations of the masses. Machado's populism was pure rhetoric as the President was extremely corrupt, loyal to the US and demonstrated a violent streak. In 1925, Machado had Armond Andre killed over a series of distasteful cartoons.[159] In 1926, a series of labor leaders were also killed by the regime.[160] Amidst this violence, Machado sought to change the constitution to allow his continuation for at least a decade.[161]

Grau was just one of many Cubans who opposed the repressive regime of Machado in the late 1920s. The activist Wilfredo Fernandez stated that, "the proper thing to do for anyone who accuses a government of being tyrannical or murderous is to try to overthrow it by revolutionary methods".[162] Much of the opposition originated in the University of Havana, which drew Grau closer to the struggle. After years of anti-Machado activism, the University Student Directorate (USD) expanded their resistance. At one such protest a police officer fatally wounded Rafael Trejo.[163] Jaime Suchlicki stated, "Trejo's death was the turning point in the struggle against Machado", with the students in this protest movement labelled, "the generation of 1930".[164] Among this movement was Grau's long-term ally and future President Carlos Prio, and ideological leader of the "Autentico" movement Eduardo Chibás.[165] Prío and Chibás began to see themselves as the protectors of the national will and the opponents of tyranny and US imperialism. After the fall of Machado, the USD placed Grau in charge of their movement as a compromise between the supposed 'radical' students, the military, led by Fulgencio Batista, and the US delegation, led by Sumner Welles.[166] Grau became the leader of the USD and evolved that ideology into the Party of the Cuban Revolution – Autentico (PRC-A). Chibás stated that this movement's ideology was "Nationalism, Socialism and anti-Imperialism".[167] Unlike, Venezuela, Peru and Colombia, Cuba lacked one central ideological leader of their social democratic movement. Rather, Grau became the figurehead of the USD and PRC-A's social mission in Cuba.

Jorge Eliécer Gaitán was born on January 23, 1898. At that time, Colombia was at the onset of the "War of the Thousand Days" which began the thirty years of uncontested conservative rule.[168] His father, Eliécer Gatian, was an informal scholar, journalist, teacher and distributor of secondhand books. His father was eccentric and struggled to provide for the family, but he served as a formative influence through his passions for Colombian history and politics in an era of chaos. His mother, Manuela Ayala de Gaitán also influenced Gaitan's development. She worked as a teacher and was an advocate for progressive and feminist views, often at professional and personal sacrifice. Gaitán described her as "an extraordinary woman…of forceful spirit, who cared lovingly for my destiny. The sanctity of her life was illuminated always by a studious intelligence and an indomitable will".[169] Gaitán's upbringing was made difficult by his family's economic struggles, and his need to support his six younger siblings. Gaitán was a fiery youth who clashed his teachers. Despite this, his obvious skills were recognized and the Colegio Araujo provided him a scholarship at the age of 15.[170] Its founder, Simon Arauja was a liberal scholar who influenced Gaitán's thoughts on politics. However, persecution from church and government made life at Araujo difficult and Gaitán transferred to the Colegio of Martin Resprepo Mejia in 1919. His biographer, Richard Sharpless, attributed much of Gaitán's drive for personal success and political change to his own class status and physical appearance.[171] His dark complexion demonstrated obvious Indian heritage which was a common obstacle to political and economic success in conservative Colombia. Hence, this deep drive to prove his place in society molded Gaitán in his early years.

In 1920, Gaitán was admitted to the National University of Colombia. While enrolled in law, Gaitán spent much of his time continuing his father's work on Colombian history and politics. The four years at university were the most formative of Gaitán's life. In writing 'Las Ideas socialistas en Colombia' in 1924, he laid out his political philosophy that he would commit to throughout his career.[172] Braun argues that "in positivism Gaitán found a conception of society as a coherent entity".[173] For Gaitán, the social problem in Colombia was that of capitalism, which had shattered the equilibrium of society. He disagreed with the communists who described capitalism as the process towards socialism. Rather, Gaitán saw socialism as the return of the social equilibrium between the classes which had been eroded over time. He proposed that both ends of society, the poor workers and the wealthy capitalists, needed to be bound by the same social order that they originated within. Gaitán "argued for a return to a social organization that preceded the unrestricted, individual accumulation of property, the centralization of wealth and power, and the monopolization of the means of production".[174] That is, if the equilibrium could be reestablished by government and both groups brought back within the social order, then there would be no need for revolution. But Gaitán must have realized that achieving this, in 1920s Colombia, would amount to a revolution, in and of itself. Gaitán's desire to study abroad in Europe led his mother, Manuela to ask the Conservative President Marco Fidel Suarez to grant her son a small diplomatic posting in the Rome embassy that would allow Gaitain to study political positivism under Enrico Ferri from 1925.[175] His ideas on

Colombian society were so impressive that he delivered them directly to the Italian King, Fascist President Benito Mussolini and his entire cabinet.[176] Ferri then turned Gaitán's conception of society into a unit for study at the University of Rome in 1929. Gaitán returned to Colombia with a desire to see his ideas turn to action.

These four future political leaders formed movements that professed a vision for a fundamental change in Latin America. No single theorist is responsible for the philosophies of Latin American social democracy, and that their implementation would be unique to each nation. Their inspirations range from classical liberalism, to legal positivism, to socialism, to democratic action, to nationalism, and to populism. During the 1920s, most Latin American societies were at an impasse. The increased trade integration with the United States created unprecedented wealth for the economic and social elites. Meanwhile, these new ideas of democracy and socialism were being distributed to the increasingly literate, yet, impoverished masses. The status-quo was no longer an option. Change was both necessary and inevitable. These four leaders were thrust into a position to mold that change. Through their disgruntled experiences of class inequity, they began forging a platform for contemporary Latin America that would be based upon nationalism, socialism and anti-imperialism. These leaders were influenced by variations of socialism throughout their personal and political development. However, unlike those Latin Americans who chose to join the doctrinaire Communist and Socialist Parties, they acknowledged that there was no simple road forward to revolution in Latin America. Each nation possessed unique challenges that required localized solutions. They were not loyal to the foreign power of the USSR. Rather, they took inspiration from lessons from Europe, the United States and of course other Latin American nations. Hence, the anti-communist pretext was both inaccurate, and calculated to ensure their demise. The social democrats attempted to realign their societies and begin to redistribute income, through social security, education and healthcare, and even wealth, through expropriations of land and subsoil rights. However, their loyalty was to the people of Latin America – not to an alien power. This line would continue to blur throughout the Cold War and make this social democratic revolution largely impossible due to the anti-communist paranoia that would undermine them.

Chapter Two

'I Fell Because Washington Willed It'

The Great Depression of the 1930s provided a unique opportunity for independent economic, social and political development in the Americas. US foreign policy was both broadly unpopular and 'protectionist' under the Hoover administration. The newly elected President, Franklin Roosevelt, was forced to admit US regional wrong doings to rebuild those fractured regional relations. This brief interim period of economic and political independence provided the opportunity for several social democratic organizations to reemerge into the national conscience. During 1931, APRA contested national elections, coming very close to success. Colombian liberalism came to power granting Gaitán a national populist platform. Even Venezuela's seemingly endless autocratic rule subsided allowing for the brief re-emergence of AD before it was, again, forced underground. However, the events in Cuba and Mexico demonstrate the two distinct sides to the so-call 'Good Neighbor Policy' (GNP). In Mexico, the former revolutionary general, Lazaro Cardenas, initiated a broad program of land and resource redistribution to fund ambitious social programs. He fulfilled the objectives of the Mexican Constitution of 1917 to solidify the populist gains of the Revolution. In Mexico, the US adopted a lenient stance under Roosevelt, allowing for the controversial oil expropriations. As Word War II approached, Roosevelt prepared a hemispheric alliance that required Mexican cooperation and regional good-will. The situation for Cuba was very different. Following the fall of the autocratic Machado regime, Grau emerged as President of Cuba. The US accused Grau of supporting pro-communist land seizures and gave its support to the head of the military, Fulgencio Batista. Upon leaving office in 1934, Grau claimed that "I fell because Washington willed it".[177] The US had a direct role in supporting a military regime in Cuba against the populist will of the people. This was also true in the Dominican Republic, Nicaragua and Guatemala. Despite their improved regional image, Washington began its Cold War against regional social democracy through targeted accusations and their direct support for militarism in the Caribbean and Central America.

The Good Neighbour

Franklin Roosevelt became during the Great Depression, which had devastated the international economy and left millions of Americans unemployed and impoverished. The collapse of the global economy decreased the real value of US exports by 78 per cent. In response, the Republican Hoover administration promoted isolationism through the protectionist "Smoot-Hawley Tariff Act".[178] Hoover, and his advisors, neglected to realize that US jobs were dependent on markets for exportable goods. This led to 5,000 US banks defaulting and 13 million American workers becoming unemployed.[179] The second consequence of Smoot-Hawley was to divide the world into economies 'spheres-of-influence'. Much of African and Asian trade was closed by their European colonial masters. Meanwhile, the trade race in the Americas escalated as the fascist powers of Germany and Italy expanded their influence. Roosevelt's proposed New Deal to the American population was, in effect, a socialist program of government spending to reinvigorate the domestic economy through government control. He sought to get the US back to work by providing government support for infrastructure, agriculture and industry. Roosevelt also required raw materials and markets for finished goods. Hence, his proposed GNP was the global arm of the domestic New Deal.

The GNP was not a philanthropic attempt to improve the lives of Latin Americans. It was a calculated policy to change the American image and to increase its American economic sphere of influence. In his inaugural address on March 4, 1933, Roosevelt alluded to the GNP by stating, "I would dedicate this nation to the policy of the good neighbor".[180] He committed to fulfil US global commitments while respecting "the rights" of other nations. He stated that "we now realize…our interdependence on each other", clearly indicating the economic ambitions of the new administration.[181] To gain support for GNP, Roosevelt swiftly renounced three decades of direct US interference in Latin American politics. Cordell Hull was tasked with winning allies when he renounced the American "right to intervene in the internal or external affairs of another nation" in Montevideo in December 1933.[182] In effect, he was abandoned 'gunboat diplomacy' as the principal mechanism of US foreign policy and beginning a new era of 'pan-Americanism'. Hull also made tangible gestures the region. In 1934, the US repealed the Platt Amendment of the Cuban constitution that gave the US jurisdiction to intervene and police Cuban politics.[183] They also committed to non-interference in the domestic affairs of Panama and increased the lease amount for the canal from US$250,000 to US$430,000 per annum.[184] Finally, in 1935, the US marines were withdrawn from Haiti. In 1935, the US had returned all sovereignty back to domestic governments and committed to never intervene in their domestic matters.

The US made these commitments in return for new economic alliances, as defined by the Reciprocal Trade and Tariffs Act of 1934 (RTTA).[185] The RTTA was a reversal in American foreign economic policy from protectionism to internationalism. Given the closure of most of Afro-Eurasia to international trade following the London Economic conference of 1932, the US looked to the Americas.[186] In 1930, prior to the major contraction, the US accounted for approximately 40 per cent of Latin American trade.[187] The majority of this was mandated by US foreign intervention in the Caribbean and capital investment in areas such as Mexico. Their penetration into the more significant markets of the Southern cone was hindered anti-Americanism and a preference for European technology. The anti-Americanism was fostered by US actions under successive regimes of 'gunboat diplomacy'. The GNP attempted to reverse their image. Meanwhile, German penetration into the economic and political systems of Colombia, Argentina and Chile posed a serious threat to US Pan-American ambitions prior to WWII. The RTTA sought to eliminate their German, Italian and British counterparts by allowing the President to reduce tariffs, establishing reciprocal trading relations. Roosevelt signed 1,000 decrees between 1934 and 1940 and returned the US to its status as regional economic power.[188] This was a country by country approach and not all Latin American nations entered Washington's sphere of influence under this policy. Indeed, many remained dependent upon British, German and Italian trade well into World War II.

This economic policy worked upon two false premises. The first was that these arrangements were reciprocal. Colombia actually experienced economic growth and diversification as a result of decreasing dependence on coffee exports during the early Great Depression. In 1933, Colombia exported US$47 million worth of goods, mostly coffee, to the US while importing only US$14 million.[189] The preference for German cars, planes and capital goods, as well as a program of Import-Substitution Industrialization (ISI) in Bogota improved the economy. However, like many governments who had defaulted on loans during the 1929 market collapse, Colombia owed US$130 million to American banks and citizens.[190] Hull forced the RTTAs onto Latin American nations in return for softer loan terms with creditors. Hull also threatened to impose tariffs on Colombian coffee to the advantage of competitors in the Caribbean should the Alfonso López government turn down the RTTA.[191] This economic leverage forced arrangements that advantaged the US economy in several Latin American countries. From an American perspective, this was seen as good business. However, the immediate effects in Colombia were devastating. The depression worsened as cheap imports of textiles and processed foods from the US cost thousands of Colombian jobs.

The second false premise of the RTTA was that the US was not interfering with the domestic politics of sovereign Latin American countries. The US had made the rhetorical commitment to regional self-determination during the 1923 Washington Conference, and committed to non-interference in 1933.[192] However, democratic and constitutional governments were less likely to cooperate with RTTAs that were against the national interest. Rather, the progressive Roosevelt administration developed close ties to regional despots. In the example of Guatemala, the authoritarian Jorge Ubico was granted US recognition in return for his signing of the RTTA. Ubico sought to convert his elite conservative constitutional regime to a permanent dictatorship in 1936 against popular calls for democratic elections.[193] At that time Germany purchased 40 per cent of Guatemalan exports.[194] By achieving the RTTA, the US managed to decrease that number to 11 per cent by 1939, and by 1944 the US was directly purchasing 92 per cent of all Guatemalan exports.[195] By endorsing the Ubico dictatorship, the US created an economic protectorate in Guatemala. This was also true of their tacit alliances and RTTAs with Maximiliano Martínez in El Salvador, Anastasio Somoza in Nicaragua, Rafael Trujillo in the Dominican Republic, Fulgencio Batista in Cuba, and Carias Andino in Honduras.[196] That is, the US were simultaneously renouncing their power to interfere in regional affairs at the same time that they were deciding who should lead each country based on who would best serve their economic interests. Roosevelt's version of regional imperialism reaped instant results and didn't cause the same negative publicity as 'gunboat diplomacy'. While he was absurdly decried as a socialist by his Republican advesaries, Hull's "philosophy of the RTTA became the bipartisan cornerstone of American foreign economic policy during and after WWII".[197] Greg Grandin asserts, "this economic expansion into Latin America [became] the keystone of the New Deal state for the next three decades: liberalism at home and internationalism abroad".[198] Latin America's military dictators aided the

US in escaping the Great Depression of the 1930s and becoming the global power of the 1940s and beyond.

Lazaro Cardenas and the Mexican Revolution

Lazaro Cardenas was born on May 21, 1895 in the city of Jiquilpan, Mexico. His father, Damaso Cardenas, was a philanthropic physician who gave his services to the local people in return for what little they could afford.[199] Cardenas was impressed by his father's medical practice and influenced by his sympathy for the poor. He studied at the only boy's school in Jiquilpan, demonstrating commitment to academics while also exhibiting a rebellious side.[200] Following the orders of Díaz, local schoolchildren were organized into citizen militias and Lazaro began weekly military drills at age 11.[201] He left school at the age of 12 and worked as a revenue collector for Donaciano Carreon. Carreon was a liberal who favored Madero's movement and demonstrated the injustices of tax collection to a young Cardenas. He was also exposed to liberal works on the French and American Revolutions. The convergence of his father's death and the turn of the Revolution in early 1913 shook Cardenas from his isolated existence in rural Mexico at the age of 17.[202] The assassination of the liberal leader Madero turned more Mexicans against Huerta. After some small-scale guerilla activities in Jiquilpan during 1913, Cardenas joined the passing constitutional army of General Zuninga.[203] In 1915, Cardenas took refuge in Agua Prieta, administered by General, and future revolutionary ally, Elias Calles, and asked "give me a chance to show my loyalty in battle".[204] Once entrenched as a commander in the Constitutionalist Army, Cardenas continued his rapid advance through the political ranks.

Lazaro Cardenas was just 25 years old at the end of the revolution in 1920. He was given enormous responsibility in battle and emerged as one of the few trusted men during the Carranza-Obregon feud of 1920. While military governor of Michoacan, he decreased crime and returned stability. But by 1925, few of the goals of the revolution were achieved and constant infighting meant that revolutionary instability continued indefinitely. Cardenas, at this point, stated his intention to leave the army by declaring, "it's time the promises of the Revolution be converted into tangible deeds. All of us who believe in the ideal of the Revolution should put into constructive and energetic action".[205] He was elected as governor of Michoacan in 1928 and committed to installing the promises of the Mexican Revolution. As governor, Cardenas experimented with largescale land reform and the social policies of the Mexican constitution. His popularity quickly brought him into the national political sphere. In May 1929, Calles formed the Party of the National Revolution (PNR) to permanently instill the constitutional ideals of 1917.[206] Cardenas became the 'theoretical' head of the party, but still worked under Calles. His primary function was to prevent the fracturing of the revolutionary movement. Mexico needed unity over more conflict, in order to fulfil the goals of the revolution. Hence, Cardenas began expanding government services and programs, while also defending those already in place such as Obregon's education policies. His success in unifying the party earned Calles' endorsement in the 1934 Presidential election.

Lazaro Cardenas enacted a program of "agrarian reform, socialistic education and economic nationalism" between 1934 and 1940.[207] These programs were both political and pragmatic. Cardenas looked to the constitution of 1917 for a program to govern Mexico. He targeted the Catholic Church's monopolization of education by funding state primary and secondary education. He claimed a preference for 'socialist education' which would be secular from religious teaching and free of charge. This received backlash from the church but was widely popular elsewhere. The depression exacerbated the poverty of Mexico and the nation required substantial development. Cardenas turned to land and resource nationalization and programs of education and healthcare during his presidency. In doing so, enough good-will was earned to keep the PNR together. The promises of land reform had not been delivered by 1934, hence, Cardenas engaged in a program of rapid expropriation, buying back US$102 million worth of agricultural land from wealthy Mexicans and foreign corporations.[208] Cardenas made this newly redistributed land immediately productive by organizing communal "ejido" farms.[209] Cardenas additionally established the National Bank of Ejido Credit to lend money to these communal farms.[210] This was an instant success both politically and economically, which gave Cardenas freedom to tackle bigger opponents.

Cardenas also relied upon the support of organized labor. In 1938, the large oil companies were engaged in dispute with unions over layoffs in Northern Mexico. Cardenas used the threat of Article 27 expropriations to bring a favorable resolution for the workers.[211] When the oil companies continued to act in defiance of the government, Cardenas nationalized the properties of SONJ and Royal Dutch Shell in 1938, commenting that "the petroleum expropriations marks the beginning of our independence".[212] Cardenas was fortunate that the US ambassador Joséphus Daniels was favorable to policies, which resembled Roosevelt's New Deal. The American and British oil companies demanded invasion and heavy embargos. The British attempted to incite anti-communism by demanding that Roosevelt "deal with those communists down there".[213] However, the US required Mexico as a WWII ally and to be seen as a good neighbor to prevent Argentina, among others, from abstaining the Pan-American alliance. The nationalist fervor for this move pushed Cardenas to nationalize other segments of the economy. The implementation of ISI under Cardenas decreased Mexico's import of consumer goods from 35.2 per cent in 1929 to only 6.9 per cent in 1950.[214] This meant more jobs for Mexicans. Those businesses were also tightly regulated and were decreed to be majority owned by Mexicans. Moreover, Cardenas gave the people what they asked for, he: opened schools, gave peasants land and access to loans, protected workers against foreign corporations, created more jobs, nationalized core parts of the economy, limited foreign ownership and investment, and ended the infighting of the revolutionary factions. Cardenas made a social democratic revolution in Mexico which temporarily led to peace and prosperity. He also set an example for his neighbors by fulfilling the promises of the 1917 constitution. However, the freedom that the US gave to Mexico would not be offered to all of Latin America.

A Cold War Emerges

Mexico was unique in its dealings with the Roosevelt administration. Both Daniels and Roosevelt were sympathetic to Cardenas' position. They were also very sensitive towards accusations of interference in Mexico's domestic politics while attempting to establish their Pan-American alliance. But while all eyes were on Mexico, their neighbors embarked on the first phases of their Cold War against the US and their creation of the anti-communist pretext. This Cold War was about competing visions for each nation's future within the international capitalist economy. The US attempted to establish a 'sphere of influence'. In order to achieve this, they favored pliable and conservative politicians who allowed and supported the economic integration of the two unequal regions. The social democrats sought to limit foreign control by emulating Mexico. Through their pragmatic version of nationalism, socialism, and anti-imperialism, they formed alliances with the disaffected classes of their nations. This required formal expressions of policy that favored peasants, workers and the liberal bourgeoisie against the rhetorical enemy of US imperialism. These movements expanded the anti-dictatorial struggles in an attempt to form post-revolutionary coalitions. In many cases the US had readily identified its mission as an obstacle to their national interest of economic expansion.

These competing visions were best exemplified in American handling of the Cuban democratic revolution of 1933. The fall of Machado had placed Cuba in the hands of the largely unknown Dr Ramón Grau San Martin. At the end of 1932, the Cordell Hull clarified that the US would not intervene on behalf of either group, which emboldened both the military and the USD to act against Machado and seize power. However, Grau's insistence on implementing a social democratic revolution under the PRC-A posed a challenge for the US. The US did not want Grau and the students in charge of Cuba. Simultaneously, they could not be seen to intervene in Cuban politics. Sumner Welles was the lifelong diplomat who given the task of resolving the conflict between Machado and the opposition groups. Welles mediated the creation of a junta to replace Machado after he was deposed in July 1933. The junta was formed in the USA by exiles of the major resistance groups. The communists labelled the junta as "enemies of Cuba and lackeys of Yankee imperialism".[215] However, they believed they were in the process of creating Cuba's first independent and democratic government and removing the tyrannical Machado and replacing him with the interim president, Cespedes. Unfortunately, as Welles' chosen leader Cespedes was not approved of by any of the revolutionary members and eventually replaced by the Junta on September 5. The revolutionary chief of the armed forces of the Republic, Fulgencio Batista, approved the appointment of Dr. Ramón Grau San Martin on September 10. Once President, Grau ruled by decree to fulfil the promises of the 'authentic revolution'. The decrees included: the abrogation of the Platt Amendment, the creation of a department of labor; ensuring university autonomy, outlawing the importation of foreign seasonal workers in all industries, gave women the right to vote, decreased the cost of utilities, and declared "Cuba for the Cubans".[216] These decrees made Grau extremely popular amongst the masses. But because of these increased freedoms some members of the Communist Party and the student left wing declared it as a social revolution, which drew criticism from Welles.

Welles had condemned Grau's government to defeat almost immediately. By January 1934, Welles had formed a bond with the future dictator, Batista.[217] Welles decided the fate of the Grau government just days into his rule through his memoranda to the State Department and orchestrated the downfall of Grau's short-lived government. Another representative of the US government, Jefferson Cafferey, described supporters of the Grau government as the "ignorant masses" and reported that the "better classes" would support his removal by the army.[218] Faced with the threat of a coup, Ramón Grau resigned on January 15, 1934 after just months as president. Communism was successfully trailed as a pretext for explicit US support of a military coup. This became common place in the Cold War. The actual threat posed by Grau was economic nationalism. Those 'ignorant masses', as Cafferey had deemed them, would continue to demand economic nationalism during the coming decades and ultimately led to Castro's Revolution of 1959. Elite attitudes towards class and race in this era continued to foster dissatisfaction with American foreign policy in Cuba.

The Peruvian dictator Augusto Leguia's term as president ended in early 1930. The Great Depression brought increased pressure for democratic action amongst the unemployed urban masses. The 1931 Presidential election lured Haya de la Torre back to Peru. The brief respite from political repression allowed APRA to put their platform to the Peruvian people. Up until this point, APRA was a protest movement that opposed imperialism and the dictatorship. Hence, Haya needed to convince the masses that he could govern them. APRA developed both maximum minimum programs for Peruvian development. The maximum program emphasized: anti-Imperialism; unity with region's social democratic parties; nationalization key industries and land; the internationalization of the Panama Canal; and solidarity with oppressed people of the world.[219] While this was the core of APRA's philosophy, a minimum program was developed to appeal to the suffering masses who wanted work, security and social mobility.[220] This minimum program emphasized: ending corruption; strengthening bureaucracy; nationalization of mining and oil; separation of church and state; and social security policies.[221] The US Ambassador, Fred Dearing, feared the APRA revolution and declared that Haya was the "reddest of the red and a very dangerous man", and APRA as a "subversive in character and not entitled to the freedom of a normal and natural political party…it is almost certain they are still under the influence of Moscow".[222] Dearing advocated exclusion of APRA from the election. This harassment played a minimal role in APRA's eventual loss. They still received 36.4 per cent of the popular vote.[223] APRA claimed that fraud had cost them the election.[224] While there was little evidence for this claim, voting was limited to only the 300,000 most privileged citizens, around 5 per cent of the population, and completely excluded peasants who would have directly benefitted under the APRA revolution. Moreover, there was an appetite for this revolutionary even in the upper classes of Peruvian society. For their moderate success, the government spent the next decade persecuting APRA as a threat to the status-quo and echoing American accusations of communism.

Colombia elected its first Liberal government of the twentieth century in 1930. The successive governments of Enrique Olaya Herrera and Alfonso López Pumajero failed to initiate wide scale change due to the great depression.[225] Gaitán's ideas on the socialization of the public sector to decrease the vast gap between rich and poor was not initiated by the Liberal oligarchs. Gaitán accused the Liberals of in fact being conservatives. President Pumajero asserted "Gaitán defended the rights of the poor without first asking the permission of the rich".[226] Unfortunately for Gaitán, the Liberals were the rich. While Pumajero had fought the US state department over the RTTA that destroyed Colombian industry, he yielded to threats of coffee tariffs that would impact Liberal landowners.[227] Many of those landowners were directly involved in producing and exporting coffee. Hence, they put their own economic interests ahead of Colombia's. Gaitán found this unacceptable and seceded from the Liberals in protest in 1934. He used the Union Nacional Izquierdista Revolucionaria (UNIR) as his own social democratic party to run for offices and eventually the presidency.[228] After two years alone, Pumajero convinced Gaitán to return to the Liberal Party by offering him the position of Bogota Major.[229] From there, Gaitán formed a populist coalition of workers and peasants that took him towards the Presidency in the 1940s. The failure of UNIR demonstrated the hold that the Liberals held on the voting public. However, Gaitán's emerging populist identity signaled the fragility of that system. Gaitán appealed to the disaffected people of Colombia.

Venezuela remained under the control of Laureano Gómez until 1936. Betancourt had lived in exile through the 1930s, working briefly as an editor for a Costa Rican 'communist' newspaper. Betancourt continually sought to distance himself from this 'job', but there is some significance to be drawn by this association. Nevertheless, when Gómez died, Betancourt returned to Venezuela and established the AD political party. He stated that the movement,

> "aspire to the formation of a provincial united front with the exploited sectors of the city and the countryside, semi-proletariats, poor peasants, schoolteacher, commercial employees working for starvation wages…to oppose the reactionary front which will result from the collaboration between imperialist finance capital and the international bourgeois-caudillo bloc".[230]

At the onset of the new regime, the political left, including AD, were outlawed and persecuted pushing the movement underground.[231] The philosophy of the AD underground included: Political democracy including mass suffrage; higher taxation on oil companies as path to nationalization; anti-fascism; ISI industrialization; land reform; social services; new labor laws and conditions.[232] This form of government appealed to the disaffected sectors of Venezuelan society, however, they were not yet able to overthrow the dictatorship. Hence, they continued to appeal to allies in rural areas and in the union movement. Betancourt came to admire the US under Roosevelt due to his lenience in Mexico and advocated the New Deal as a platform for a new Venezuela.[233]

This era provided a brief window into the Cold War between Latin America's social democrats and the American anti-communist pretext utilized against them. The US demonstrated their preference for conservative and military rule in the Caribbean. This wasn't necessarily motivated by malice, rather it was a pragmatic strategy to increase the share of US trade and investment in the region. This preference became clear when dealing with the region's social democrats. Lazaro Cardenas was in the fortunate position of spotlight. The US had spent decades harassing the Mexican Revolution. Hence, Mexico became a public testing ground for the GNP. Cardenas was allowed to expropriate land and subsoil rights to demonstrate American good-will and benevolence towards the region. Significantly, the US required Mexico and the larger South American countries to commit to political and economic collaboration to combat the approaching threats of Nazism and Japanese militarism. The smaller social democratic movements were less fortunate as the US controlled the message. The US labelled APRA in Peru and the PRC-A in Cuba as communist in order to demonize their political platform and ultimately persecute their movements. While events were mostly domestic in Peru, Grau's Cuban government would not have fallen during 1934 without US intervention. Persecution based on false communist accusations was extended to the Venezuelan AD movement also. Meanwhile Gaitán continued to struggle within the Colombian Liberal Party to bring forward his social revolution. Herein lies the roots of the Latin American Cold War. American intervention in Latin American politics and economics motivated greater anti-Imperialist ideas and made the social democrats more relevant, drawing greater appeal. Meanwhile, the further that they went to tackle the injustices of imperialism, the easier it was to label them as communist, demonize their actions, and inevitably remove them. This cycle continues through the Cold War but can clearly be seen during the 1930s.

As War Approaches

American regional leadership was bolstered by the specter of international war in the late 1930s. The US envisaged the 'Monroe Doctrine' as a regional alliance against the duel threats of European fascism and Japanese militarism. This was clearly self-interested as it increased the economic dependence of Latin America upon the US. The Germans waged a campaign for "minds, materials and markets" in Latin America during the 1930s which the US sought to actively counter.[234] In an attempt to create hemispheric solidarity, the Inter-American States convened in 1936 in Buenos Aires, Argentina.[235] This conference demonstrated a renewed faith in American foreign policy. Roosevelt was revered throughout the region for his domestic New Deal and foreign Good Neighbor Policy. Hull sought a binding inter-American alliance in 1936 to ensure hemispheric solidarity and security against European, and Japanese, aggression. Seventeen of the twenty republics supported this resolution. Only Argentina, Chile and Mexico opposed. Hull again sought to establish a "regional league of nations" during the 1938 conference in Lima, Peru.[236] Argentina was the only country to vote against the binding security resolution, which would have seen the hemisphere committed to war following the Pearl Harbor attack of 1941. The transition of Washington's image in Latin America between 1933 and 1938 was an astounding success. While Argentina continued to hold out of this alliance, many nations moved closer to the US in their alliance against European fascism.

Japan's undeclared war upon China had expanded from Manchuria into the mainland during 1937. This closed export markets throughout much of northern Asia while regional exports into Europe were also being threatened by fascist expansion. Moreover, the Western Hemisphere became isolated from global trade between 1936 and 1939, which made regional security interdependent. This interdependence was recognized by Sumner Welles, who declared the US would "assure [Latin America] that [it] was in a position to defend [Latin America] from all aggression from whatever source it may arise, and [wished that Latin America would be] prepared to join with fellow democracies of the New World" to prevent any attack on the region.[237] While threats to Latin American security were limited to sporadic attacks on Brazilian shipping, Washington's commitment to regional defense was significant. The US extended its security personnel to bolster Latin American defenses under US command. These assurances depended on a Latin American declaration of war, should the US be attacked. Latin Americans, primarily Argentina and Chile, rejected the

US' conditions. The 1938 Declaration of Lima was not a formal unilateral security alliance. Instead it expressed a desire to "defend the peace of the continent".[238]

From 1936 until 1945, the US expressed their concerns about hemispheric defense. This was in response to fascist infiltration in Brazil, Argentina and Chile. The threat seemed especially real in Argentina, which continued to trade with the Axis powers throughout the war, albeit at a declining rate. Following the attack on Pearl Harbor in 1941, the US joined the war. Nine Latin American republics declared war on the Axis after Pearl Harbor.[239] Their motives for war were determined by "geography, internal politics, intra-Latin American relations, economic factors, history, and a host of other variables".[240] In early 1942, the inter-American states convened in Rio de Janeiro to consult on wartime policies.[241] In Rio, the US demonstrated that there was a significant threat to the hemisphere. Accordingly, 18 of the 20 sovereign Latin American states severed relations with the Axis. They were also encouraged to monitor fascist activity at home. Only Brazil and Mexico committed troops to WWII, aiding in the invasion of Italy in 1943.[242] Hemispheric defenses were also bolstered by US personnel during WWII. The US declared that Latin America's role in WWII was to defend itself from foreign aggression, thereby allowing US troops to fight in Europe. The limitation of Latin forces, though, meant that 100,000 US troops were stationed in the region throughout the war. Jesse Jones of the State Department remarked, "we shall thus have for the first time the ammunition to deal with South America".[243]

Economic dislocation from Europe defined Latin America's role in the allied victory in WWII. The region experienced a structural readjustment to service the US war economy. The US prioritized Latin American trade because of the decreased access to the economies of Eurasia. In November 1939 the US, represented by Welles, established the Financial and Economic Advisory Committee (FEAC).[244] The FEAC and the War Resources Board controlled the political economies of most Latin American states throughout WWII. The FEAC's stated intention was to "provide long-term solutions to increase inter-American trade and seek ways to stimulate Latin American growth".[245] However, "no long-term planning was given serious consideration".[246] The FEAC absorbed excess Latin exports formally destined for Europe. The US gave special priority to essential war materials, to keep them out of Axis hands. The other significant element was keeping Latin American states as primary exporters. By committing to the purchase of goods, the US maintained the existing political-economic structure of the hemisphere. According to Henry Wallace, this dependency should be further enhanced through the establishment of more complimentary trade. In 1939 Latin America only provided US$16 million of the US$236 million of "tropical imports".[247] The US Congress committed US$500,000 to research technologies to create goods, such as rubber, in Latin America.[248]

During WWII Latin America postponed economic diversification in order to assist the US war economy. The production of cash crops and the extraction of minerals temporarily enriched the oligarchic classes. This situation was temporary, however. Many Latin American states were committed to an Allied victory in order to receive their share of development aid as a reward for their economic contribution. The US was poised to become the global hegemon, and the Latin American leaders believed a close relationship would grant them a better position in the world order. The years 1945-1948 revealed this was not their intention. Wallace remarked,

> It is a rather disturbing thought that we in the United States can maintain a deep interest in Latin America only so long as we think we have something to gain by it. I hope…during the next few years that Latin America will feel that we are really her friend and not merely a friend for expedient purposes in time of great need.[249]

Wallace's wish was not fulfilled as WWII increased Latin American dependency upon the US; it was never intended to drag Latin America out of poverty in the process. The fallout from this misinterpretation of US commitments to regional development defined the diplomatic conflicts of the immediate post war period.

Chapter Three

'Justice and Humanity to Order'

Democracy thrived in Latin America in the aftermath of World War II. Many Latin Americans were inspired by the Atlantic Charter commitments to freedom, prosperity and safety for all members of the human race. Guatemala is emblematic of this trend. A nation that had never experienced any of those virtues in its history, saw its people demand democracy and development at a rapid pace. Their first popularly elected President, Juan José Arévalo, commented in March 1945, "We are going to begin a period of sympathy for the man who works in the fields, in the in the shops, on the military bases, in small businesses…We are going to add justice and humanity to order, because order based on injustice and humiliation is good for nothing".[250] This was a period of optimism. Democracy to the majority of Caribbean nations and plans for the overthrow of the long-term dictators of the Dominican Republic and Nicaragua were put into motion. This democratic revolution had its roots in the social democracy of Haya, Grau, Gaitán and Betancourt, with these stalwarts returning to their respective national stages. It also witnessed the expansion of this philosophy within the national revolutions of Guatemala and Costa Rica in 1944 and 1948 respectively. This democratic revolution was predicated on a lenience from the US in the immediate aftermath of WWII, with a preference for constitutional reform over pro-fascist authoritarian regimes in the hemisphere. While short-lived, this period provided a framework a democratic Latin America.

Pan-American Commitments

Franklin Delano Roosevelt reframed the Pan-American relationship during World War II. He stated, in 1939, "that is a new approach that I am taking to these South American things…Give them a share. They think they are just as good as we are and many of them are".[251] This was a major reversal in Roosevelt's Latin American policy. Roosevelt renounced the language of racism and imperialism to forge a bond of good-will during a time of mutual need for the two continents. This rhetoric was extended throughout the War. The Atlantic Charter of 1941 was designed to convince the occupied people of Europe, Africa and Asia that the US-led system would offer self-determination, prosperity and safety after WWII.[252] Yet Latin Americans were not the targets. The Atlantic Charter justified US global leadership under the auspices of a moral crusade. The US sought to attain this global moral leadership through its professed commitment to democracy, human rights and economic development, claiming to be an unwilling participant in WWII, that had fought only for the betterment of human kind.[253] This allowed it to establish a new global political and economic order following the war based on the Atlantic Charter and Roosevelt's Four Freedoms speech, with its naked appeals to the oppressed peoples of the world.

Roosevelt described an idealized society to appeal to those peoples living under fascism, communism and European imperialism. It promoted self-determination and an end to exploitation between nations. Roosevelt declared the aims of the Allies as humanitarian and based upon 'four freedoms'. The first "freedom" included the independence of speech and the press to appeal to all oppressed people as it gave way to political activism in the developing world.[254]. The second "freedom" was of religion and was in response to the horror of the Jewish holocaust.[255] The third "freedom" guaranteed against "want" to appeal to the impoverished people of the colonial and semi-colonial world.[256] The fourth, and most significant "freedom" was from "fear" as the US committed to ending dictatorial rule over the globe".[257] While history has proved these claims to be propaganda, they were very powerful in convincing peoples and states to join the American led world order. Latin Americans took two points from Roosevelt's humanist appeal, that democracy and self-determination were going to be unilaterally supported following WWII and that the US was going to provide development assistance to alleviate regional poverty. Unfortunately, for those social democrats that based their movements in the promises of Roosevelt's words, this was never the American intention.

Roosevelt did not author the Atlantic Charter or the Four Freedom Speech. Rather, this was orchestrated by the secretive 'Council for Foreign Relations' (CFR).[258] Preceding WWII, "the [CFR] saw the purpose of post-war planning as the creation of an international economic and political order dominated by the United States".[259] The CFR's membership was intertwined with US State Department, which included Sumner Welles, Hamilton Fish and Adolf Berle.[260] Its membership also included influential economists, executives and intellectuals. It redefined the future of American imperialism by asserting committing to internationalism. Given the dominance of the Germans in Europe, the CFR proposed to integrate other areas of the world economy into a US-led political-economic bloc. Resource-rich Latin America was designated within this bloc. However, Latin America did not yet have sufficient internal markets to support the US industrial economy. The CFR also sought to integrate the British Empire and much of decolonized Asia into their "Grand Area".[261] This meant war with Japan, and in order to wage war, a degree of idealism was necessary to combat Japanese propaganda. CFR recommendations shaped the State Department's conception of war, as Roosevelt fondly referred to the CFR as "my post-war advisors".[262] Their aims in 1941-42 were to convince the American people to fight WWII, and to leave the international community mystified by its actual motivations for war. The organization asserted that the: "formulation of a statement of war aims for propaganda purposes is very different from formulation of one defining the true national interest".[263] The Atlantic Charter and the Four Freedoms served this purpose.

The US claimed to fight the war for moral reasons. They declared that Nazism and Japanese militarism were 'evil', and that the US had a moral obligation to end them. While the American people, and soldiers, were at war for those reasons, the aims of its leading diplomats did not fulfil this rhetoric. The protracted decline of the British and French empires in the inter-war period created a void in global leadership, which Roosevelt and his advisors sought to claim for the US. The CFR's vision of the post-war economic system reveals US foreign policy in the immediate aftermath of the war. The CFR divided the world into economic regions. Within this division of regions came a vision of permanent division of labor. The CFR argued that the tropical economies of the world were to remain resource producers, with limited economic development.[264] Along with most of Latin America, South and South-East Asia, the Middle East and Africa were seen as dependent economies to be controlled by Western powers. The industrial regions of Europe and North-East Asia were seen as industrial manufacturers. These CFR plans were largely initiated after WWII; Europe and North-East Asia were given large development funds, while Latin America remained underdeveloped.[265] The Atlantic Charter and Four Freedoms Speech concealed the economic aims of US foreign policy behind its moral crusade. This was one of the most successful utilizations of propaganda in US history. In March 1945, with the war largely won, the

Latin Americans pressed the US on the issues of post-war development during the conference, at the ancient Mayan city, of Chapultepec.[266] They were encouraged to remain patient for that assistance. But after six years of delayed development in the service of the US war economy, regional patience was waning.

Taking Their Share

WWII was a contradiction for most Latin Americans. They professed commitment to a war against fascism in Europe and militarism in Asia while fascist and authoritarian regimes still dominated their region. The reciprocal trading and tariff arrangements of the 1930s had formed police states throughout Central America and the Caribbean. The long-term dictators included the Guatemalan Jorge Ubico (1934-1944), the El Salvadoran Maximiliano Martínez (1931-1944), the Honduran Carías Andino (1933-1949), the Nicaraguan Anastasio Somoza (1936-1956), the Cuban Fulgencio Batista (1934-1944),[267] and the Dominican Rafael Trujillo (1930-1961).[268] Less formal military rule was also conducted in Panama and Haiti.[269] The only regional nation with a somewhat democratic system was Costa Rica; however, with limited suffrage, the political economy was tightly controlled by a landed oligarchy.[270] In 1944, conservative military leaders, many of whom resembled European fascists, dominated Central America and the Caribbean. The future Guatemalan president, Juan José Arévalo asserted that the "Nazism of Central and South America was intrinsic with [the] Police-State rulers, ideologically and in practice".[271] The citizens of the region enjoyed few of the freedoms pronounced by President Roosevelt. Roosevelt's promises, in part, motivated the regional change that came to threaten US dominance. Betancourt stated, Roosevelt "gave hope to the oppressed people of Latin America".[272] The region's social democratic leaders were in exile. Circumstances, however, returned them into the political fold. Democracy returned through a wave of enthusiasm to Cuba, Venezuela, and Peru between 1944 and 1945 bringing the social democrats to the forefront. The Colombian leader, Gaitán, also reemerged as a presidential candidate during 1945, while the influence of these movements inspired revolution, to varying degrees, throughout the Caribbean region.

The US State Department realized these desires and temporarily took a backseat in Latin American domestic politics. This era of American leniency is best defined by the career diplomat, ambassador and eventual Undersecretary for Inter-American Affairs, Spruille Braden. Charles Ameringer suggests, "Braden was a firm believer in positive action to attain the goal of democracy in the Americas".[273] The US State Department was more concerned by Nazi infiltration than by the coming Cold War against the USSR between 1941 and 1946.[274] The pro-Nazi and anti-American nationalists of Argentina were a more urgent concern to American foreign policy than moderate social democratic revolutions. While Ambassador to Argentina, Braden organized a coalition of moderate and conservative democrats against the military populist Juan Domingo Perón.[275] The US also convinced the Brazilian populist Getulio Vargas to cede power through democratic elections in 1946.[276] In order to legitimize these two elections as a consistent part of US policy, they avoided interfering in the democratic revolutions of the era. This era of US policies has retrospectively been referred to as "Bradenism".[277] Indiscriminate preference for democratic rule over authoritarian rule that resembled their fascist enemies. The US were still fine-tuning their ability to influence those elections as the anti-American Perón and Vargas' hand-picked successor Eurico Gasper Dutra won power In Argentina and Brazil respectively.[278] Nevertheless, the brief interlude would make Latin America more democratic than it had ever been.

Cuban democracy ostensibly began in 1940, however, the military dictator, Batista, was returned to power. Grau was re-elected Cuban President in June 1944, which his colleague Eduardo Chibás, defined as "the glorious journey" for the Autentico Revolution.[279] Grau remained wary of Batista's ambitions to retain the presidency but took assurances when in July, Batista removed the Chief of Police who was conspiring to oust Grau as the democratic president.[280] Grau was willing; however, to soften his stance towards Washington. On their first meeting in August, Roosevelt quipped, "And to think that I did not recognize you eleven years ago".[281] Roosevelt was assured by Braden that Grau "was not the same man" as the alleged revolutionary that Welles had conspired to remove in early 1934.[282] However, Grau wished to be that man and fulfil the Authentic Revolution. He claimed that the government was "the will of the people" and that the "Cuban people are going to rule their own destiny".[283] He also claimed, "the economic and social imperatives of contemporary democracy" centered upon education, health and the raising of revenues to support those ventures.[284] Grau was very the eloquent and populist politician Eduardo Chibás while president. Chibás' weekly radio announcements drew mass appeal and protected the democratic regime from the military. Grau's fear of another Batista led coup led to his support armed groups, called 'pisteleros', who had resisted the Machado and Batista regimes and were now given free-reign.[285] Cuba became a haven for exiled leaders of social democratic parties including Betancourt and the Dominican Juan Bosch. Unfortunately for Grau, his social policies were completely dependent on sugar revenue which fluctuated on price and quota – and was largely controlled by the US market. This meant that the proposed social revolution never took place. The lack of revenue and the violence of Grau's militant supporters, drew the ire of Chibás who withdrew his support, and supporters from the Autentico party in 1946.[286] Claiming to be the true means to the Cuban Revolution, Chibás' Ortodoxos began criticizing Grau's government and recruiting young Cuban students, including Fidel Castro.[287]

American pro-democratic rhetoric also had a significant impact upon Peruvian politics. The authoritarian regime of Manuel Prado y Ugartheche faced civil discontent during 1944.[288] The strikes were led by students and workers who sought material gains and social change. Prado believed that the US, under Braden's leadership, had become pro-democratic and the ageing despot stepped away from the Presidency. In a calculated move, however, APRA was legalized after the opportunity to field a presidential candidate had passed.[289] Haya still wielded significant power in Peru and APRA won around a third of the congressional seats.[290] Haya sought to use his 'king-making' voting bloc to achieve much of the APRA agenda from 1931. He ultimately gave APRA's support to José Bustamante who was elected as President in 1945. While Haya's supporters "saw [APRA] as a vehicle for anti-Imperialism, agrarian reform and economic planning, Haya was not president and only some aspects of the APRA program were initiated by Bustamante".[291] He unsuccessfully pressed Bustamante to implement APRA policies given that they had gotten him elected. Nevertheless, the support for Haya and APRA increased between 1945 and 1948 and the path towards this social democratic revolution was opened through the liberalization of Peruvian politics that occurred due to the softening of US regional policy. It would, however, be short-lived and the APRA program would go unfulfilled.

Rómulo Betancourt also took the rhetoric of the Atlantic Charter literally and initiated a democratic revolution in Venezuela. Venezuela had limited experience of constitutional government with tyrants dominating their twentieth century history. The military also played a defining role in the 'democratic revolution' again in 1945. They had become dissatisfied with the military regime of Isais Medina.[292] AD had pressured Medina and the oligarchy to hold open elections through the early 1940s, which culminated in protests and strikes throughout the nation.[293] Ultimately, the military removed Medina on October 18 and turned to AD to gain legitimacy for their civilian junta.[294] Betancourt was elected President in 1945 and initiated his program to nationalize the oil wealth and to reinvest it into economic diversification and social services. Betancourt ensured that he included rural peasants in this movement by providing investment, reform and services in the countryside. AD remained the popular choice of peasants over the coming decades due to this commitment. The AD candidate Rómulo Gallegos was elected in 1948, demonstrating the success of these programs and the popularity of AD philosophy. Unlike Mexico, for instance, there were strong opposition parties including the liberal democratic URD and the conservative COPEI.[295] Venezuela initiated a thriving and competitive democratic system in just three years. Ultimately, the softening of Washington's position on democracy invited this generation of social democrats to assert themselves on their national stages and to provide material support to their allies overseas.

The New Wave

The expansion of democracy in post-war Latin America was not isolated to those nations with established social democratic movements. The demands for democratic reform were, in fact, loudest in Central America, where popular democracy had never been initiated, at the conclusion of WWII. The first such action occurred in the small nation of El Salvador. Since its independence, El Salvador was tightly controlled by a small oligarchic class which used its monopolization of land to control the disgruntled agrarian class. Many members of this class had been inspired by revolutionary movements such as that of Emiliano Zapata in Mexico and Augusto Sandino in Nicaragua. However, their one large insurrection of recent history had ended with the brutal execution of 30,000 poorly armed peasants in 1934.[296] The man responsible, President Maximiliano Martínez, remained in power in 1944. 10,000 students converged on San Salvador in March of 1944. The "strike of the fallen arms" remained a non-violent appeal to the military to replace Martínez.[297] The military agreed to their demands but did not move towards democratic elections. In May of 1944, this wave of protest spread to Honduras. The union of united banana workers staged strikes for improved pay and conditions.[298] When the military moved to break up the strikes, the sentiment quickly turned against the dictator, Carias Andino. This movement was put down by the military and Andino remained in power until 1949.[299] While these two movements are mere footnotes of history, they stirred the demands for improved quality of life throughout Central America.

Guatemala's 1944 revolution is well-known. It was the movement that placed Juan José Arévalo and eventually, Jacabo Árbenz, into power and into conflict with the US and the UFCo. However, its roots are not unique; they are consistent with those movements in neighboring Honduras and El Salvador. The regime of Jorge Ubico had become increasingly hostile to any protest during 1944. In June of 1944, the regime killed a group of dissident schoolteachers.[300] Word of this action brought 100,000 campesino laborers to strike and protest the continuation of Ubico's rule.[301] Guillermo Toriello, a future diplomat under Árbenz, proudly read Roosevelt's Atlantic Charter to the protestors, envisaging a democratic revolution and an end to Ubico's rule.[302] Ubico acknowledged that he had to resign and called an election for September 1944. In that election, the reported results were 45,000 for Ubico's Chief Lieutenant Ponce Vaides and 3,000 votes for popular public intellectual Juan José Arévalo.[303] This was in a nation of three million people that limited voting to the oligarchic minority. When the results were released in October, three young generals, Francisco Arana, Jacabo Árbenz and Jorge Toriello, shot and killed Vaides.[304] They called elections for January 1945 and extended voting to all literate males. The election was won by Arévalo in a landslide.[305]

Juan José Arévalo was born in September 1904. He was a middle-class Guatemalan who became a primary school teacher at the age of 18.[306] In addition to teaching, Arévalo was a gifted writer of literature and political philosophy. He earned a scholarship to Argentina in 1927 to pursue a doctorate in the philosophy of education. After six years he received his doctorate and sent 150 copies of his book "Viajar es vivir" back to Guatemala.[307] Unfortunately, there was little market for philosophical literature in the small agrarian republic. He approached the government for support in publication but was humiliated when he was refused and offered a mid-level post in the ministry of education. Sincerely offended and unable to achieve the work that he coveted, Arévalo left Guatemala in 1936. He later claimed that he had fled in protest of the dictatorship, however, it seems that his personal feelings toward Ubico's inability to see his vision for Guatemalan education had been the true motivation. In 1944, after his second long stay in Argentina, he was invited back to Guatemala to head the "teacher's party" and to contest elections against the dictator.[308] Piero Gleijeses claims that he was anonymous to most Guatemalans, which was advantageous as "he could be all things to all people".[309] Upon his return, he became a populist in Guatemala. His message was vague. He spoke of practical reform and spiritual socialism. He claimed that the de-emphasis of materialism would bring the Guatemalan people the maximum happiness. He won 85 per cent of the post-revolutionary vote and represented the success of the October Revolution.[310]

Arévalo's political triumph masked the extent of the challenge. The 1945 constitution made Guatemalans as politically 'free' as North Americans. It allowed all citizens to vote, express themselves, organize unions, establish political parties, protest, and engage in all of the free activities of a civil society.[311] However, these freedoms masked a Guatemala that was severely underdeveloped. In a nation that committed 75 per cent of its labor to agriculture, they could not produce enough food for consumption.[312] This was due to the export of two cash crops, coffee and bananas. Two per cent of the population owned over 72 per cent of agricultural land and effectively owned the people who worked for them.[313] Illiteracy was endemic. There was no protection for labor, no social security, a tiny industrial sector and no meaningful health system. It was amongst the poorest countries in the world and required a major economic revolution. Arévalo's first major initiative a sweeping labor code in 1947. Modelled on article 123 of the Mexican constitution, all Guatemalans were subject to the 40-hour working week and a four-fold minimum wage increase to 20c per day.[314] While these were small measures in Arévalo's task to "make men equal to men", he did earn a lot of enemies both within and outside Guatemala.[315] The largest landowner, the US owned UFCo, viewed his government as a threat to their enterprise.[316] Towards the end of his presidency, Arévalo survived dozens of coup attempts against his government due to the loyalty of the army and his commitment to let power go at the next election.[317]

The Caribbean Legion

The Caribbean Legion was an informal alliance of social democratic governments to extend democracy to their neighbors. Gleijeses identifies that term as a US media invention and never used in Latin America.[318] They worked closely with the exile communities that fought against the vestiges of authoritarian rule. While successful democratic revolutions had displaced the authoritarians Ubico in Guatemala, Batista in Cuba and Gómez in Venezuela by 1945, other dictatorships included Trujillo in the Dominican Republic, Somoza in Nicaragua and Andino in Honduras.[319] Hence, their mission was incomplete. For as long as those tyrants remained in power, they would support anti-democratic exile communities. Guatemala's Arévalo held the joint objectives of "Central American federation and the elimination of dictators".[320] Therefore, Arévalo, Cuba's presidents Grau, and his successor Prio, and the Venezuelan Betancourt provided material support to the exiled revolutionaries that sought to bring down their neighboring dictators.[321] Their motivations were complex. Firstly, all of these leaders had once been exiled by authoritarian regimes in their homeland, most commonly in Mexico. They had received material support for their movements by overseas friends which made their ascent to power possible. Hence, they felt an obligation to assist their fellow revolutionaries. Secondly, the dictatorships were volatile and posed a threat to their own political survival. In the 'regional civil war', the dictatorships in Nicaragua and the Dominican Republic had just as much power to fund anti-democratic coups and were willing to use it. Finally, the idea of a central American community was significant to Arévalo and his fellow democrats. He stated,

> The democratic alliance of the Caribbean will constitute an indivisible bloc in all international crises. Its fundamental aims will be to strengthen democracy in the region; … [and] to act as one in defense of our common economic military and political interests.[322]

This, in theory, would permanently protect their movements from counter-revolutions within the region. This ambitious goal required military action to remove the enemies of democracy in the region.

The exile community was correct to work urgently towards the liberation of their nations. The brief lull in repression from the US State Department caused by the policies of 'Bradenism' offered the brief opportunity to reclaim their nations. Braden and the US State Department demonstrated open hostility towards Trujillo from 1946 and even imposed a ban on the sale of weapons.[323] During 1947, the Dominican exiles living in Cuba began to organize their assault on Trujillo. The movement that included a young Juan Bosch and his Dominican Revolutionary Party, began their preparations in Cuba.[324] The Cuban government worked closely with the exiles, ensuring their ammunitions purchases and allow them free movement in Cuba. Trujillo's protests to Grau, Haiti and the US began to derail the operation. Grau distanced himself from the invasion by moving the Dominican training to the remote island of "Cayo Confites".[325] Meanwhile, Haiti's leader, Dumersais Estime, who had been enthusiastic about the downfall of Trujillo, succumbed to international pressure.[326] Fatally, a civil conflict between the 'pistoleros' and the Cuban military highlighted the Cuban involvement in the plot to overthrow Trujillo to the US State Department. The US put pressure on Grau to abort the operation.[327] From there, the Dominican exiles scattered, and the Caribbean legion's center moved from Cuba to Guatemala. The Dominicans met up with leaders from Nicaragua, Honduras and a young enigmatic José Figueres of Costa Rica to plot their future actions.

José Figueres Ferrer was born in September 1906. His parents migrated from Spain to the remote coffee hinterland of San Ramón, Costa Rica, in the months prior to his birth.[328] His father was a physician, specializing in electrotherapy. The young Figueres felt school in San Ramón did not sufficiently challenge his intellect and the family moved to San José for his high schooling. Figueres, found the social aspects of school difficult and even attempted suicide after the first year of senior studies.[329] Determined to escape these pressures, Figueres travelled to Boston before technically finishing high school. The Massachusetts Institute of Technology (MIT) placed additional barriers to his study so he opted for self-education in the Boston library. Once there, he read about political philosophies, including socialism, which "set his mind on fire" and started him "dreaming of a perfect world".[330] He then moved to New York where he worked as a translator and continued to study both electrical engineering and the classics at Columbia University. After years of unstructured study in the US, Figueres returned home in 1928. In Costa Rica, he began operating a run-down farm that he called "The endless struggle".[331] He adopted modern technology to produce electricity, ensure irrigation, and begin the production of ropes and coffee bags. He continued his love of literature and claimed a desire to be a "renaissance man".[332] Through the hard years of the depression, Figueres kept the business alive. He also developed a strong relationship with labor ensuring their education and empowering their communal efforts. His version of socialism was based upon his own self-education.

Costa Rica's movement for social democracy began in the early 1940s. Several sectors sought to fill the political vacuum created by the ageing liberal generation of 1889. Rafael Angel Calderon Guardia attempted this, through populist measures. However, corruption and cronyism had earned him the distrust of the oligarchy, the student movement and Figueres who was initially inserting himself into national politics. Figueres was exiled in 1942 for his criticism of Calderon, eventually arriving in Mexico.[333] In 1943, he wrote "Worn-out words" and sent it back to San José as a protest.[334] In it, he proposed a socialist economic order based on merit and contribution to society. He became part of the exiled Central American community and learnt of the struggles faced in the region. He argued that dictatorship must be eradicated from Central America, convincing the Nicaraguan Exile Dr. Rosendo Arguello that Costa Rica should be the first stage of the attack due to its relative weakness. Figueres remained in exile through the violent 1944 election of Teodoro Picado. In Figueres' opinion, the election of 1944 was corrupted by the military and government. Figueres committed the next four years to seizing power and taking government. Figueres led the national opposition in the interim period and began preparing for the military action against Picado. With limited arms arriving through the Caribbean pact, Figueres chose to observe the results of the 1948 election. The election was won by the socialist Otilio Ulate, but the government refused to accept the result and arrested the elected president.[335] Meanwhile, Figueres and a small guerilla cadre prepared for an armed assault. He had told Ulate that he would "back their votes with guns if necessary".[336] Costa Rica's small army of 300 men was easily defeated by the well-armed guerillas. By May 2, 1948, José Figueres had gained control. After a short juncture as head of the revolutionary Junta, he returned power the elected government of Ulate, but remained active in Costa Rican politics.[337]

April 9, 1948 was the turning point of the Cold War in Latin America. It became the moment when the US would no longer accept democratic revolutions within its sphere of influence. The events of April 1948 would reverse the legacy of 'Bradenism' and install a generation of regional anti-Communism. In 1950, the US State Department described the Caribbean legion as "one of the principal causes of unrest and instability in the Caribbean". In the face of US hostility, the legion became rudderless. Figueres, who had received the support of regional allies under the premise of continued support for pro-democratic rebels, withdrew his support almost immediately. Trujillo had been playing the 'communist card' since 1947. However, after 1948 these warnings were taken more seriously by Washington. As will become evident in coming chapters, the US removed their support for democracy and gave preference to stability. In this context, the Caribbean Legion was a threat to security and the Somoza and Trujillo regimes were important allies. Those governments in Cuba, Venezuela and Guatemala that had funded regional instability would be swiftly dealt with over the coming years. While the Caribbean Legion continued to exist into 1950, and Arévalo continued his diplomatic appeals for regional democracy, the high point for democracy in Latin America had passed. On April 8, 1948, the region was largely democratic, and those ageing despots were outliers. The Cold War would destroy regional optimism and witnessed a return to tyranny throughout the hemisphere.

Chapter Four

'Silence Pervades Politics'

In August 1934, upon leaving the Colombian Liberal Party, Jorge Eliécer Gaitán exclaimed: "nothing has changed in the republic… Our phrases to the multitude were nothing more than electoral hoax…A barricade of conventionality…[while] silence pervades politics".[338] Colombian electoral politics, according to Gaitán, was a manipulation of the masses for immediate personal gain. For those masses, Gaitán was the one voice of hope. During his time inside, and outside, of the Colombian Liberal Party, he spoke with a truth that was absent in oligarchic politics. For Gaitán, politics was a means to social, economic, and political improvements for the urban and working poor. Gaitán was the one Colombian who challenged the oligarchic monopolization of political life during the 1930s and 1940s and held a large following of loyal 'Gaitánistas'. On April 9, 1948, he was killed outside of his Bogota office.[339] This chapter will demonstrate how national, regional, and global events converged in his assassination that has conventionally been explained as the act of a single 'mad-man'; Juan Roa Sierra. It will demonstrate how the assassination and subsequent civil conflict created: a Colombian Cold War between the oligarchy and Gaitán's supporters; a regional Cold War between Latin America's social democrats and their militaries, oligarchies and US supporters; and made Latin America part of the global Cold War through the false accusation of George Marshall that Colombian Gaitánistas were in fact Communists who threatened the security of the region. No single event had a greater impact on Latin America in twentieth century history. The Bogotazo of 1948 created the Latin American Cold War theatre to the detriment of several regional democratic regimes. While Gaitán had effectively ended the silence within Colombian politics, the aftermath was a violent civil war that has been fought in various iterations for the past seventy years. Much of this can be attributed to Marshall's calculated response.

The Global Cold War

World War II provided a brief respite in the rivalry between American capitalism and Soviet communism. The US had harbored anti-Soviet views since the Russian Revolution of 1917. In the lead up to World War II, there was legitimate debate over whether communism or Nazism was the greater threat to US global interests.[340] Despite this, Franklin Roosevelt and Joséf Stalin were close and effective allies for the duration of the war. They combined to defeat the duel threats of European fascism and Japanese militarism in the vacuum that was created by the protracted decline of the British and French empires. Through their alliance; however, there was competition for global political and economic dominance. Both allies planned for the fall of Germany and Japan in 1945. During the war, both nations focused on occupying the regions that they sought post-war control over and the creation of a post-war order. For the USSR, this meant creating communist regimes around their borders in Eastern Europe and in Central and Northern Asia. For the US, it meant securing vital trade routes and strategic centers of the fallen British and French Empires. At the conclusion of the war, the world was divided into two clear 'spheres of influence'. Within the Soviet bloc, the people were encouraged to rebuild their lives through communism. In many places, this was peaceful and popular. In other places, the Soviets used their military to ensure communist control.[341] Within the American bloc, the people were encouraged to rebuild their lives through capitalism. In the wealthier parts of Europe this was easily achieved. But in the devastated regions of Southern Europe and much of Asia, the calls for revolution grew louder. The US took the reins of British imperialism to prevent pro-Soviet communist revolution in Greece and Turkey during 1946 and 1947.[342] The story of the Cold War is not simply defined as good versus evil. Rather, it was two superpowers attempting to stabilize their spheres of interest while simultaneously destabilizing their opponent's sphere for political, economic and strategic gain.

The conceptual Cold War was institutionalized by 1947. George Kennan's 'X' article in Foreign Affairs provided an Orwellian vision of Soviet-dominated Europe.[343] Former British Prime-Minister Winston Churchill fanned the flames of distrust by claiming that an "iron-curtain" had descended upon Eastern Europe.[344] Reports of the spread of "red fascism" necessitated response from the US.[345] Meanwhile, the US was grappling with the challenge of administering global decolonization. President Franklin Roosevelt had envisaged the United Nations (UN) as a global forum for the preservation of peace.[346] An idealist by nature,

Roosevelt believed in the Wilsonian "liberal-internationalist" culture of American policy, which promoted the universal extension of American values in "free-trade, political democracy, and the rule of law".[347] The UN also sought to maintain Washington's globalist stance in the post-war world. The collapse of the League of Nations (LoN) had led to WWII, which demonstrated the importance of US global leadership to ensure global peace and economic stability. The rapid decolonization of the European empires would provide lucrative opportunities to US businesses. The only significant threat to this global expansion was the communism of the USSR. The UN Security Council was composed of the victors of WWII, four of whom were capitalist. Russia's optimism about the global forum was crushed during preliminary talks between newly inaugurated US President Harry Truman and Russian Foreign Minister Vyacheslav Molotov.[348] Truman's demands upon Russia's administration of Poland not only defied promises made by Roosevelt; they revealed the underlying intentions of the UN as a pro-US organization designed to administer conflict during the Cold War.

The US was in a powerful position in the Cold War by 1947. It held a roughly equal share of Europe; the vast majority of Japan's colonial territory and it had planned to bring all of the ex-colonies of the European empires into their sphere of influence. However, during 1947, Europe was rocked by a series of strikes led by pro-communist unions.[349] Communists competed in European elections with some success. Moreover, the American dominance in the Cold War was made vulnerable by the poverty of the Europeans. To counter this sentiment, the US Secretary of State George C Marshall composed the largest aid program in history. The 'Marshall Plan' committed US$13.015 billion in economic and technical assistance to Europe.[350] A proportion of this money was channeled into supporting pro-capitalists in democratic elections securing the American sphere of influence.[351] Eastern European states, and even the USSR, were invited into the program on the condition that they renounce communism and hold democratic elections. The Soviet Foreign Minister Molotov forbade the Eastern Europeans from joining and offered them the far inferior 'Molotov Plan' for their redevelopment.[352] Marshall aid rapidly rebuilt war-torn Western Europe. It also committed those nations to US led capitalism. Significantly, the US could use the withdrawal of Marshall aid as a strategic threat when the Europeans got out of line on international issues. Congress also allocated 5 per cent of Marshall aid to the CIA to support pro-American resistance movements in Eastern Europe.[353] Marshall stated, "they wanted to be able to act quickly in an emergency".[354] The US won Western Europe through aid and political manipulation rather than through war or repression.

Marshall's focus upon European alliances cost the US the most populous nation on Earth. Mao Zedong's Communist Revolution in China globalized the Cold War.[355] The US had largely neglected Asia as they did not foresee a major revolution in the East until it was too late to change directions. The Chinese Revolution came in an era of European decolonization. Britain relinquished control over its Indian territories in 1947 and the vast majority of Asian peoples were independent from European rule by the 1960s.[356] Each of these new states were vulnerable to communist Revolution due to their extreme poverty and the conditions by which Europeans held productive assets within these economies.[357] The 'domino theory' was popularized during the Korean War (1950-1953) to explain that if any additional state turns communist they will influence their neighbors.[358] Accordingly, from 1949, Truman committed to the 'containment' of communism at all costs. The conceptual Marshall plan was extended to Japan, South Korea and Taiwan to secure those strategically important points.[359] Meanwhile, a series of alliances including the North Atlantic Treaty Organization (NATO), the South East Asian Treaty Organization (SEATO), and the Australia, New Zealand, United States (ANZUS) alliance were concluded to globalize this containment line.[360] 1949 also saw the first successful test of the Soviet atomic bomb.[361] This meant that war between the two states would ensure mutual destruction and potential extinction of humanity. US actions towards Latin America between 1945 and 1950 should be interpreted through their fixation on the international Cold War. They were attempting to secure Latin America as their 'sphere of influence' with minimal attention or economic investment.

Latin America in the Cold War

The wartime collaboration between the USSR and the US increased the prestige of global communism. The May 1943 dissolution of the Comintern was seen as an abandonment of the Soviet policy of world revolution.[362] The US encouraged diplomatic ties as a demonstration of wartime unity. Fulgencio Batista, for example, was encouraged to include Cuban communists in his government and to expand diplomatic ties with the USSR.[363] Several more regional communist parties were established during WWII.[364] US policy did not immediately change at the conclusion of hostilities in 1945. The US communists continued to be led by Earl Browder who utilized the temporary US-USSR and his support of the Roosevelt administration and raise the prestige of communism.[365] Between 1944 and

1945, the peak membership of the Communist Party of the USA (CPUSA) was 100,000.[366] The Latin American communists also supported the Allied campaign against the Axis. This led to a temporary détente in which the US did not actively prevent Latin American communism between 1945 and 1947. The number of Latin American communists increased from 100,000 to approximately 400,000 between 1940 and 1947.[367] However, this must be kept in context. The approximate population of Latin America in the late 1940s was 180 million.[368] Communists represented 0.22 per cent of the Latin American population at their peak.

A survey of Latin American communism from 1945 to 1948 demonstrates its limited impact. The most significant national communist movement was in Brazil with a claimed membership of 150,000 and temporary freedom to participate democratically.[369] The Cuban communists thrived during the Batista period as their membership grew to an estimated 150,000 in 1944.[370] In Uruguay there were approximately 50,000 communists.[371] In Chile, the Communists participated in the Popular Front alliance with socialists and radicals. However, their membership and influence were miniscule in greater Latin America. In Colombia, the party possessed less than 4,000 members.[372] Mexican communism only had 13,000 members in 1946, well below the requirements to form an electoral political party.[373] In tiny Guatemala, fifty 'communists', including former members of Arévalo's PAR government formed the Democratic Vanguard in 1947. This evolved into the Guatemalan Communist Party in 1949, with a peak membership of 4,000 in the early 1950s.[374] Communism was a peripheral movement in Latin America that did not have the ability to stage a revolution. They were, however, quite vocal and were an obvious target of pro-American loyalists.

WWII led to an unprecedented military engagement between the US and Latin America. The continental mobilization against the duel threats of Germany and Japan allowed the US the most extensive access to Latin America's military in its history. Latin America was significant to US security during WWII on three fronts: the region's productive capacity of raw materials; the region's ability to protect itself from external threats; and vocal support for US moral leadership over the war effort. Each of these areas would remain significant in the post-war period. The US was maintaining a permanent wartime economy. During WWII, the US supported the increasing military capacity of Latin America in three ways: financial assistance, arms sales and personnel training. Each of these measures were continued into the Cold War era. In 1949, wartime military assistance was evolved into the Military Assistance Program (MAP).[375] Prior to WWII, the US had only a small share of military sales to Latin America. However, the US replaced Germany as the primary arms supplier to Latin America, through the Lend-Lease policy of WWII.[376] The process was accelerated after the war, with US manufacturers monopolizing supply. In addition to arms sales, the US also sought to dominate military training during WWII. During WWII, the US sent attachés to most Latin American countries.[377] The US also sought to continue this process into the Cold War. Accordingly, the US established the Latin American Ground School (LAGS) in 1946.[378]

Latin American support for US moral leadership at international forums was also significant. During WWII, the US had committed to both the Atlantic Charter and the Four Freedoms. The UN adopted these ideals. Following 1945, the Latin American nations continued to condemn any system that opposed the Atlantic Charter. In the Cold War context, this meant the USSR. The dominating ideology of the UN threatened the significance of regional organizations; this in turn imperiled the inter-American relationship. According to former Secretary of State Hull, "there will no longer be the need for spheres of influence, for alliances, for balance of power or any other of the special arrangements which, in the unhappy past, the nations strove to safeguard their security or to promote their interests".[379] By 1945, however, the geopolitical climate had changed. Regionalism became the priority of the US at the UN. The Latin American voting bloc was significant at the UN, as they comprised twenty of the fifty foundational UN members.[380] This support made them valuable allies. Articles 51-54 of the UN Charter undermined Hull's vision by allowing the formation for regional organizations.[381] The US and the USSR were able to maintain their respective spheres of influence through multilateral political, military and economic alliances. The Latin American delegations vociferously supported these resolutions. They foresaw the OAS as a mechanism for economic development, and regionalism as a guarantee of financial assistance.[382] While this was not the uniform view in Washington, Marshall wanted a regional organization to protect American interests.

The US cemented its influence in Latin America in two forms: protection against 'external' enemies and protection against 'internal' threats to US regional interests. The 1947 Rio Pact was the most extensive inter-American military alliance in history.[383] The official 'Inter-American Treaty of Mutual Assistance' brought the entire Western Hemisphere into the US security zone. The only viable threat to hemispheric defense, the

USSR, was concerned with security in Eurasia and lacked the capacity for a long-distance attack.[384] With the exception of Mexico, Argentina and Uruguay, Latin American leaders had ended diplomatic relations with the USSR.[385] The other component, the OAS, was a forum to discuss political and economic developments in the region. While the US and the Latin Americans saw the importance of a regional economic alliance, their visions of its purpose were quite different. While Latin America foresaw significant technical assistance from the US, the US sought to maintain the economic status quo through its UN agencies. The conference in March and April 1948 saw these two visions collide. Once there, the Marshall declared that there would be "no Marshall Plan for Latin America".[386] To quell the region's outrage, he gained congressional approval to increase the EXIM lending capacity by US$500 million.[387] However, many Latin American leaders were reluctant to link their political futures to Washington without a significant economic commitment. Fortunately for Marshall, the *Bogotázo* would recast the political dialogue of the OAS.

Marshall wanted a broad anti-communist coalition in Latin America at the OAS meetings of March and April 1948. Anti-communism was a long-term policy objective that predated the violence in Bogota. On April 8, the day prior to Gaitán's assassination, Ambassador Baulac held preliminary discussions with Colombia's foreign minister Laureano Gómez regarding the potential anti-communist declaration of the OAS.[388] While Gómez enthusiastically supported Washington's position, he identified a number the reservations of the Latin American delegations in Bogotá. Gómez identified that the progressive governments would condemn an anti-communist declaration as interventionism.[389] A foreign power dictating the eradication of a peripheral movement would not be acceptable to them to leaders like Betancourt and Arevalo. Another reservation he identified was economic.[390] The Latin American governments wanted economic assistance in return for this diplomatic support. The Chilean and Uruguayan delegations also expressed their reservations against US-led intervention of any kind. According to Gómez, the Latin Americans sought to modify the target of the declaration to the USSR specifically, rather than communism generally.[391] However, this was the exact distinction the NSC sought to undermine. The USSR was an external enemy with no power to invade the Americas. Communism, on the other hand, could be interpreted in many ways, which made it the ideal pretext. The Latin Americans required visual evidence of the communist threat, which the *Bogotázo* provided.

Mataron a Gaitán

On April 9, 1948 Juan Roa Sierra shot and killed Gaitán outside his Bogotá office.[392] The official story stated that Sierra was the nephew of a man convicted by Gaitán's law firm.[393] However, further investigation questions this rather innocuous assumption. After firing the shots, Sierra took refuge in a local pharmacy. As the crowd began to multiply, Sierra spoke to a sole policeman. In response to the policeman's request to "tell me who ordered you to kill, for you are going to be lynched by the *pueblo*," Sierra replied, "Oh *senõr*…the powerful things I cannot tell you".[394] Within fifty minutes of the assault both men were dead and Bogotá was left on the brink of civil war. The true motivation for Gaitán's death remains unresolved. While some have asserted US complicity, Herbert Braun's analysis, stating that "his death was inevitable" is the most penetrating.[395] Gaitán "was too dangerous and too feared by both parties".[396] While Gaitán posed some threat to US interests in Colombia, the threat to the local oligarchy was far greater. However, the case arguing American previous knowledge of the attack and subsequent protests is compelling. The human rights lawyer Paul Wolf, in attempting to account for the origins of the Colombian Civil War, took both the CIA and FBI to court for defiance of the Freedom of Information Act (FOIA).[397] While the court ruled in his favor, many documents pertinent to Gaitán were omitted or concealed.[398] It is unlikely that the CIA or FBI killed Gaitán. However, their prior knowledge would have given Marshall the opportunity to plan their post-*Bogotázo* reaction in advance.

The Colombian *Bogotázo* was a violent protest that cost fourteen hundred lives in forty-eight hours.[399] It was a direct response to Gaitán's assassination. Those who witnessed Gaitán's death quickly mobilized the masses by spreading the message "Mataron a Gaitán" which translates to, "they have killed Gaitán".[400] The ambiguity of the word "they" led to uncontrolled violence throughout the city. The mob's first action was to lynch Sierra inside the pharmacy. This small group of followers then dragged Sierra's mutilated corpse outside and began marching towards the center of Bogotá. As word spread, the crowd grew larger. Within two hours the mob had grown to approximately 200,000.[401] The protesters assumed "they" – those who had killed Gaitán – was the conservative government of Ospina Pérez. Accordingly, their march headed to the Presidential palace. Civil order quickly declined as the Bogotá police were amongst Gaitán's most loyal supporters, and they too joined the march. Liberal politicians unsuccessfully sought to moderate the rage. The military were prepared at the presidential palace. They aggressively suppressed the protest, killing those who would not leave. The following forty-eight hours saw aggressive street battles between Gaitán loyalists and the Colombian military. The *Bogotázo* was the catalyst for the rapid expansion of the Colombian Civil War, *La Violencia*.[402] It gave an urban theatre to the ongoing rural civil war. The *Bogotázo* was not a communist conspiracy, as there is insufficient evidence of communist involvement and it did not serve the interests of communists. While there were young nationalists, including Fidel Castro, in Bogotá protesting the formation of the OAS, their role in the *Bogotázo* was extremely peripheral.[403] Castro even sought refuge as the fighting grew more severe. Rather, The *Bogotázo* was a spontaneous reaction to the assassination of Gaitán.

US intelligence did not believe that Gaitán or his followers were affiliated with international communism. However, the FBI and State Department were aware, and cautious, of the effects of Gaitánism on the Colombian political system. The FBI was responsible for regional intelligence during WWII and the early Cold War period.[404] Prior to the initiation of the CIA in 1947, the FBI had vast regional networks. Its director, J. Edgar Hoover, identified the "threat" of Gaitán and his "manifestation" prior to the May 1946 elections.[405] While linking Gaitán to European fascists, Hoover argued, "collaboration between the *Gaitánistas* and the communists has been terminated".[406] Further FBI documents reveal that the *Gaitánistas* had persecuted communists in rural Colombia in competition for *campesino* support. State Department informer Joseph Ray indicated that Gaitán "was the worst enemy of communism".[407] The FBI and the State Department both compiled summaries of the political history and policy of Gaitán's movement. No document argues that Gaitán was a communist or under the influence of communism. In the immediate aftermath of the *Bogotázo*, the CIA claimed not to know of Gaitán's movement or the motivation for civil unrest.[408] This symbolized a failure for the newly instituted CIA. Nevertheless, Marshall's State Department was fully aware of Gaitán, Gaitánism and the origins of the *Bogotázo*. In the five days prior to Marshall's accusation of Soviet interference, he was in contact with Willard Baulac, the US ambassador to Colombia, who possessed this intelligence.[409] Baulac saw communists and "left-liberals" as synonymous.[410] Marshall concluded that 'communists' were responsible for the Colombian *Bogotázo*, despite the evidence provided by their staff.

Marshall blames Reds

Despite the intelligence of the US State Department, Marshall used the violence of the *Bogotázo* to initiate the Cold War in Latin America. The Secretary of State was in Bogotá attending the first meeting of the OAS. During the violence, Marshall sat solemnly in a hotel room as many of his fellow delegates sought a panicked evacuation. Marshall saw the events in Bogotá as "concrete evidence…of the vitality of hemispheric communism and the need to ensure security against it".[411] As the violence subsided, on April 14 Marshall ordered the delegates to return to work. Addressing them, Marshall stated:

> This situation must not be judged on a local basis, however tragic the immediate results to the Colombian people…It is the same definite pattern to events which provoked strikes in France and Italy… In actions we take here…we must keep clearly in mind that this is a world affair – not merely a Colombian or Latin American [one].[412]

Marshall made direct and intentional reference to the global Cold War. His comment demonstrated the violence of 'communism' to the region's oligarchs, which motivated compliance regarding US anti-communist policies in the region. The Latin American Cold War was then sold to the international community. The New York Times' front cover on April 15, 1948 read: "Marshall Blames Reds in Colombia; Secretary Tells Conferees That World Communism Set Off Revolt in Country".[413] Marshall intentionally fabricated the relationship between the Bogotázo and the international Cold War to further US interests in Latin America.

The Conservative Colombian President Ospina Pérez echoed Marshall's accusation. Events in Bogotá exacerbated Colombia's Civil War. Many peasants had rallied to the promises of a Gaitán-led Colombia. Gaitán's social program had promised to drastically improve their livelihood, despite his reluctance to promote permanent land redistribution. His death fueled the violence in rural Colombia for two reasons. Firstly, the peasants protested more actively immediately after the *Bogotázo*.[414] Secondly, and more significantly, the conflict between landlords and peasants was reframed within the Cold War. Pérez "pointed to popular insurrections in certain towns as incontrovertible evidence of a larger predicted communist plot to seize control of Colombia".[415] Pérez furthered Marshall's claim of urban communism within the *Bogotázo* to define all class struggle in Colombia as a communist insurrection. As part of the global Cold War it justified military intervention. Pérez sent the military to those rural departments with peasant unrest, predicating the massacre of peasant 'armies' throughout Colombia.[416] Peasants who had illegally squatted on oligarchs' lands in protest were viewed as 'insurgents'. The perceived threat of communism in rural Colombia justified the systematic genocide of the Indigenous population. Those who remained became increasingly docile in the face of oligarchic demands. 'La Violencia' ultimately cost approximately 200,000 lives between 1948 and 1958.

The Latin American Cold War theatre was a fabrication created through the statements of George C Marshall. This is clear for three reasons. Firstly, the USSR played no role in the Colombian Bogotazo. There was no significant communist presence in Colombia before, or during the 1948 Bogotazo. The insurrection did not serve the interests of communists as there was no attempt to seize power. In fact, their interests were hindered by the Bogotazo as the minute Colombian Communist Party was forced underground and into exile due to Pérez's anti-communist rhetoric.[417] Secondly, the Bogotazo demonized a non-communist left-liberal movement as a threat to regional security. Gaitán's followers were seen as 'communists' and persecuted as such. But for those without the means to relocate, such as Gaitán's rural supporters, they faced the full brunt of military action. Thirdly, the interests of the US and the Latin American oligarchy aligned to the detriment of regional democracy, liberty and human rights. The US abandoned the liberal ideology of Bradenism, favoring military leaders who could ensure the stability, security, and pliability of the region. This situation aligned the interests of the military, the moneyed oligarchy and US business interests throughout the Caribbean. This was all achieved through Marshall's calculated response to the Bogotazo.

Anti-Communism

Marshall's anti-Communist accusations convinced Latin America's leaders of the threat of hemispheric Communism. While this was built upon a false premise, it was an effective tool. The leaders of most Latin American countries were still upper-class property owners that feared revolution from below. Their lives were threatened by the Bogotazo and they feared the spread to their nations. Marshall was committing to protect their safety and economic interests. The OAS signatories condemned international communism for its 'role' in the Bogotázo. A document entitled 'The Menace of communism' condemned any organization operating in the Western hemisphere that was antithetical to US interests. It stated,

By its anti-democratic nature and its interventionist tendency the political activity of international communism or any other totalitarian doctrine is incompatible with the concept of American freedom, which rests on two undeniable postulates: the dignity of man as an individual and the sovereignty of the nation as a state.[418]

This declaration effectively outlawed the Latin American communist parties. While many nations outlawed communism prior to the Bogotázo for domestic reasons, full eradication was expected after this document.[419] The OAS also committed to condemn the USSR at the UN. Any government who "suppressed political and civil rights" was to earn the condemnation of the OAS at the UN.[420] In order to ensure unanimous support, an increase in the "standard of living" was set as a goal in the war against communism, yet no practical measures were proposed or carried out.[421] The final commitment imposed upon the OAS members was the "full exchange of information" regarding Indigenous communist organizations.[422]

Latin American diplomats distanced themselves from US intelligence during WWII. The pervasiveness of Hoover and the FBI undermined their sovereignty. Domestic Latin American issues had no legitimate potential to threaten the security of the US. Accordingly, Latin American affairs served no 'security' purpose against an external enemy. The CIA inherited a difficult intelligence landscape. Despite Washington's Cold War with the USSR, the states of Latin America protested against the foreign surveillance of their domestic politics as irrelevant and intrusive.[423] Many in Latin America did not realize that the US was not protecting itself from external enemies; rather, it was protecting its sphere of influence from internal enemies. In this respect, intelligence was the most powerful weapon in its arsenal. By guaranteeing a 'full exchange of information', the CIA was given access to Latin America intelligence for the first time.[424] Communism was the pretext that justified this. Firstly, the CIA could force Latin Americans to outlaw communist parties and extradite its leaders. Secondly, the CIA could monitor the actions and policies of governments and political parties, which would report directly to the NSC, of which the CIA director is a member, on which leaders were the most desirable in individual nations. Thirdly, the CIA could provide support to preferred political movements and leaders, leading to the dozens of the military coups which define the Cold War in Latin America. Finally, the CIA could eventually act unilaterally, with "plausible deniability" of US action, to eliminate unsavory political actors.[425] While it took several years for the CIA to become fully operational, its access to Latin American politics would not have been as extensive without the Colombian *Bogotázo* and the anti-communist declaration.

Colombia has effectively been engaged in Civil War since the assassination of Gaitán in April 1948.[426] Through its several iterations, the Colombian Civil War has cost hundreds of thousands of lives and created millions of internal refugees.[427] Gaitán's vision for a liberal and democratic Colombia was symbolic of much of Latin America during the Cold War. The increased political participation invariably leads to increased standards of living and rights for the masses who had never tasted freedom or prosperity. One can view the violence of the Cold War as a response to the failure to the meet rising expectations of the masses. They were sold a promise for a better political and economic future by Gaitán and the other regional leaders. The US and the oligarchy sought to both silence and demonize these leaders to return the masses to the suffering of the status quo. But Gaitán and his colleagues had stirred something significant in the Caribbean. A unique Latin American version of social democracy that spoke to members of the disenfranchised social classes was proposed. When that was violently taken from them, many in the region sought to fight to reclaim it. Gaitán had claimed that "silence pervades politics".[428] By the end of his life, he had unleashed the vociferous calls for humanity, not just in Colombia, but throughout the region. Whether he was a spectacular person or simply the man who tapped into decades of frustration is open for debate. Nevertheless, Gaitán left an irreversible legacy upon the people of Colombia and broader Latin America.

Chapter Five

'No Interest Whatsoever'

The introduction of a Latin American Cold War changed the political layout of the region. The optimism for democratic governance and economic development was subdued by the American emphasis on confronting regional communism, as exemplified by the violence in Colombia. The focus on communism was paradoxical due to its limited impact on regional politics. In fact, the outlawing of Communist Parties was only a small factor of this redirected US position. Anti-communism infiltrated the US State Department position on each Latin American government. The language of McCarthyism created a regional purge of all 'communists' and those who could be labelled as 'communist sympathizers', or 'vulnerable' to an alleged communist influence. This was a new kind of war that blurred national borders and questioned sovereignty. Washington looked to assert its control over the politics and economies of Latin America despite the lack of physical threat to hemispheric security emanating from Stalin's USSR. The US National Security Council (NSC) and State Department looked at regional democracies as weak points in their hemispheric military alliance. They fostered the loyalty of dictatorships to create stability in the region through their pretext of anti-communism. The US increased economic and military assistance to the dictatorships of Nicaragua and the Dominican Republic. They also created incentives for other militaries to remove the rhetorical communist threat. This led to the military coups in Peru, Venezuela, Colombia and Cuba, each of which were predicated upon an alleged 'communist threat'. This new attitude towards 'communism' and democracy led the deposed Venezuelan President Rómulo Betancourt to comment that the US had "no interest whatsoever" in protecting democracy in Latin America.[429] He identified this contradiction between their rhetoric of freedom in different parts of the world. This chapter will outline how anti-communism became the source of American foreign policy in the aftermath of the Bogotazo.

McCarthy and the American Cold War

Communism became a pretext to bring about more pliable military leadership in Latin America, which advantaged their regional interests. However, this was not the cause of anti-communism for most American diplomats or the broader US population. Following the fall of China, in 1949, and the onset of the Korean War, in 1950, the US engaged in a global Cold War against communism.[430] Hence, the accusations that political unrest in Bogota, or elsewhere in the region, was 'communist' caused a deep psychological impact on the American public. The evolving domestic attitude towards communism and progressivism had a direct impact upon American foreign policy abroad. President Truman's victories over the progressive New Dealer, Henry Wallace, during 1947 and 1948 was a victory for globalism, the Cold War and the military industrial complex.[431] Then, following the perceived failure of Truman in China, the 1950 Republican congressional victory increased suspicion, paranoia and anti-Communism. Steinberg argues,

> The paradox of the communist issue during the Cold War was that American communists were almost universally defined as representing no danger to the United States, but their presence was used to fabricate a sufficient hysteria to create an American mental straight jacket on both domestic and foreign policy.[432]

This was ultimately a defeat for free thought in American foreign policy towards Latin America that had dire consequences for the region.

Wisconsin Senator Joseph McCarthy led the campaign against free thought in the US. McCarthy tapped into the feeling, that many Americans held, that they were losing the Cold War. Schrecker states, "McCarthy attracted attention precisely because of his outrageousness".[433] McCarthy reasoned that the US had lost China and allowed the Soviets to develop a nuclear bomb because of the disloyalty of individuals in the US government who had placed their loyalty to 'communism' above the American people. This sentiment was popular and gave McCarthy the national spotlight. In his most famous speech he stated,

> The State Department is infested with communists. I have here in my hand a list of 205 – a list of names that were made known to the Secretary of State as being members of the Communist Party and

who nevertheless are still working and shaping policy at the State Department.[434]

McCarthy claimed that these people within the State Department were disloyal to the US due to their 'communist leanings' and needed to be removed and possibly detained. In an attempt to appease the McCarthy's paranoia, President Truman initiated the loyalty-security program, which examined "communist sympathy or affiliations".[435] The definitions were vague and the program lacked safeguards for those accused of communist links. McCarthy even gave their names to the US media on one occasion in what became a 'witch-hunt'.[436] McCarthy himself was an unremarkable politician. But he created a climate of fear, paranoia and uncertainty. Within this climate, members of the State Department were not willing to question assumptions about communism or be sympathetic to leaders that the media had accused of communism. While McCarthy focused on American life and politics, he had an irreversible impact on American foreign policy through the 1950s.

Every Latin American leader was expected to follow McCarthy and the US State Department in their universal condemnation of Communism. This began with the eradication of the official and doctrinaire Communist Parties. As mentioned in the previous chapter, the US had encouraged a positive image of the USSR and Communism in the region during WWII, which led to a surge in party membership to approximately 400,000. By 1947 many nations foresaw the shifting American attitude and began outlawing their Communist Parties. Other populist forces began scapegoating Communist Parties to improve their electoral position. Most notably was the Brazilian outlawing of the Communist Party led by Carlos Luis Prestes.[437] But for most nations, the Bogotazo created the incentive. In 1948, the Chilean Popular Front excluded their Communist Party allies and banned the movement through the "Law for the Permanent Defense of Democracy".[438] There were also domestic motivations for the ban, as the Communists had made significant electoral gains during 1948.[439] The Cuban Communist Party was also banned by President Carlos Prío in 1950, much to the derision of Ortodoxo leader Eduardo Chibás.[440] The violent overthrow of the governments of Colombia, Venezuela, Paraguay and Peru led to the outlawing of regional communism in the late 1940s and early 1950s.[441] Guatemala's decision to allow political freedom to the miniscule Communist movement earned them the enmity of the US State Department, that will be examined in the following chapter.[442] Only Mexico and Uruguay allowed for the legal operations of their Communist Parties through the 1950s.[443] Unsurprisingly, neither party were of any threat to those popular democratic governments.

Most US citizens and diplomats were convinced that communism was a profound threat to national, regional and global security by 1950. George Kennan was sent to Latin America to export this assumption. Kennan was not a regional expert. He admitted his ignorance on the region in a 1948 survey of global communism.[444] Hence, Marshall's decision to send Kennan to Latin America held only one possible outcome. Attempting to fit regional events into this 'Cold War' paradigm, Kennan stated, "most people who go by the name communist in Latin America are a somewhat different species than in Europe".[445] He also identified "anti-Americanism" as a large regional manifestation, linking it to the appeal of Communist movements.[446] He acknowledged that the immoral actions of US corporations had caused this anti-Americanism. Kennan continued,

> People will not be inclined to believe that communist penetration bears serious dangers for them, as long as there are no tangible evidence in that direction…[and that]…if the countries of Latin America should come to be generally dominated by an outlook which views our country as the root of all evil and sees salvation only in the destruction of our power…[the American global political program]… could not be successful.[447]

Kennan saw the threat to US interests in the region as threefold. Firstly, he identified the communist use of anti-Americanism as posing the threat of internal revolution. Secondly, he identified US businesses as creating the circumstances for these revolutions through their treatment of labor and government. Finally, he claimed that the US must starve the USSR of Latin American resources by prohibiting trade. To overcome these challenges, Kennan advised Truman to "create…incentives which will impel the governments and societies of the Latin American countries to resist communist pressures".[448] As a result, the US significantly increased their financial and military support of unconstitutional governments who staunchly opposed communism. Many of Kennan's proposed program become government policy during the 1950s.

The Miller Doctrine

Domestic politics influenced the US State Department in the era of McCarthyism. Anti-communist paranoia created a climate where all of Latin American politics were seen through the Cold War terms. Preference was taken from democratic rule and granted to regional dictators who could ensure stability against the supposed threat of communism, and the more immediate threat of independent social, political and economic development in the region. Washington's global priorities were given precedence over the reality of the situation in Latin America. In response to this perceived 'threat' of global communism, Truman defined his foreign policy as the "support [of] free peoples who are resisting attempted subjugation by armed minorities or by outside pressure".[449] This rhetoric was towards Eastern Europe and did not apply to Latin American. In the Americas, Truman created a coalition of military regimes of 'armed minorities' who were subjugating free peoples with the support of 'outside pressure'. Truman entrusted this radical evolution in foreign policy to Edward Miller, who sought to undermine all legacies of the Good Neighbor Policy of 1933 by refuting the Montevideo treaty on non-intervention. In his opinion, the crises of communism necessitated such action. By 1950, internal and external threats to Latin American security were blurred. According to Miller, the use of 'collective force' to combat communists "far from representing intervention…is the alternate to intervention".[450] The 'Miller Doctrine' committed the US to protecting the status quo of conservative military rule in Latin America. Through anti-communist propaganda, the US could intervene in any sovereign state that challenged its political, economic or military dominance in Latin America. This intervention could be direct, as in Guatemala, or indirect assistance for military rule, as in Peru, Venezuela, Cuba and Colombia. But from 1950, the US took control over regional affairs.

To explain this contradiction, the US State Department official Louis Halle published anonymously in the influential *Foreign Affairs* journal in 1950 under the pseudonym "y".[451] The 'y' telegram provided an examination of Latin American politics during this reversal of American policy. Halle supported the US preference for dictatorial regimes by arguing that Latin American countries were not 'ready' for democracy. Halle examined the rise of radicalism, particularly communism, within democratic states, by stating,

> The ferment of new ideas – ideas of economic and social democracy, ideas emphasizing emancipating from the United States among other sources – contributes to [Latin American] instability, as it also does to their progress.[452]

Until the Latin Americans could operate a political system that de-emphasized economic and social democracy, the US should cease to promote civilian rule. That is, Latin America was only entitled to democracy if they resisted the popular demands of their people. For Halle, security and "stability" were more important than idealist policies promoting liberal and social democracy.[453] Halle's view was supported by Policy Planning staff member Francis Truslow, who made a distinction between "a dictatorship such as Somoza's, which involves autocratic rule and totalitarianism, which we define as autocratic rule plus total absolute control of economic life, as for example communism".[454] Hence, the value of economic trade and investment was placed above human rights. With no clear critique from the US public or its politicians, these statements formed government policy.

The US gave physical support to their rhetoric from 1949. The proposed economic development assistance was directed to those nations who closely followed the anti-communist position.[455] This gave the US significant leverage over developing nations. For example, Cuba would not have banned the Communist Party in 1950 without the promise of economic assistance during a downturn in global sugar prices. This leverage also provided them the power to solidify new regimes and military coups through recognition and assistance. Of even greater significance, though, was the direct military aid. The expansion of the Military Assistance Program (MAP) from 1949 effectively armed their allies. It should be noted though, with the exception of Colombia's role in the Korean War[456], the Latin Americans were not fighting a foreign enemy, or even each other. These arms were designed to protect the pro-US governments from 'insurgencies' of all political persuasions. The US had expressed their frustration that the leaders of Venezuela, Guatemala and Cuba launched attacks on pro-US dictators in Nicaragua and the Dominican Republic under the 'Caribbean Legion'.[457] That they bought arms from the antagonistic Perón regime made matters worse. The MAP armed their allies to an unprecedented level and made them more capable of resisting revolution, whether it be democratic or communist. It also gave them the ability to fund military coups against their antagonistic neighbors, as was the case in Guatemala. Nicaragua received the most MAP funding during the program's first five years.[458] Hence, they were solidifying their regional allies, while also providing incentives for military groups under the leadership of democratic governments.

The "Communist Line"

The contradiction between wartime promises and US actions was highlighted during the early stages of the Bogota conference in 1948. The US had promised to reward wartime sacrifices with post-war economic development assistance. But any assistance that industrialized Latin America, and decreased their focus on raw material exports, would be opposed to US economic interests. It would also decrease their dependence on industrial finished goods. The CFR determined that much of Latin America would remain as dependent raw material producers and US actions in Bogota made this evident.[459] By stating there would be "no Marshall Plan for the Western Hemisphere" and that "European recovery…was a prerequisite for Latin American development", Marshall confirmed the US position.[460] Hence, several Latin American nations sought independent economic development. Mexico had begun to construct barriers to foreign investment and trade in the 1930s, attempting to create a self-sufficient economy. Mexico experience rapid growth from the 1930s until the 1970s through their protectionist policies. Mexican policies posed a significant impediment to US economic leadership in Latin America. This is exemplified by the historian Stephen Niblo, who states that the US,

> Inadvertently revealed the real importance of the communist Party in Mexico by shifting their reports from party activity to what they called the communist line, that is to say any radical ideas they disapproved of.[461]

Any policy of economic nationalism was objected to by the US. This economic nationalism provided the greatest obstacle to US globalism. But to outright state this, would be an admission that US leadership was detrimental to Latin American economic and political development. Hence, any policy that resembled economic nationalism was labelled as 'communist'. It was a convenient pretext that would continually echo throughout the continent and justify any, and all, US positions.

The concept of economic nationalism is based upon the control of commodities, labor and markets. Commodity control involved: the expropriation of foreign-owned mineral reserves; the predetermination of economic activities through government-initiated industrial or agrarian development; and price manipulation through government control of commodities, such as coffee. Labor control involved the improvement of working conditions in domestic and foreign-owned industries. Mexico set the precedent of a modern 'labor code' in the 1917 constitution. After WWII, other Latin American leaders sought to offer increased wages and conditions in exchange for electoral support. Market control involved the regulation of commodities entering the domestic markets. This involved collaboration between state and private sectors, which was most prominent in Mexico and Argentina. Both nations attempted to grow their economies through protectionism.[462] This decreased their participation in the global capitalist economy, again conforming to the notion of the 'communist line'. Economic nationalism challenged US trade and investment in Latin America through its efforts to improve the lives of its citizens. Anti-communism justified the Washington's crusade against it.

The US established global institutions to ensure its pre-eminence following WWII. These institutions stood in direct conflict to the economic theories of the Bretton Woods Conference and its chief theoretician Lord Milton Keynes. Keynes foresaw a world economy with maximum employment in every nation. He advocated a global economy based on thirty key resources, including oil, gold, other mineral extracts and agricultural products.[463] The creation of a fixed value for all goods would stabilize the exporting economies of the developing world. Nations could plan their export output – for example of sugar and coffee – on the assumption of a fixed price for commodities. The US resisted this plan as it imposed regulation on an unrestricted 'free' global economy.[464] As the US had triumphed in WWII, it possessed a free hand in designing the post-war global economy through the institutions of the International Monetary Fund (IMF), the International Bank for Reconstruction and Development, later called the World Bank (WB), and the General Agreement on Tariffs and Trade (GATT). Each plays a role in the maintenance of US ideology within the world economic system. The IMF regulates currency and holds at its core the US dollar. The IMF discourages inflationary economic policies that threaten trade. As most development policies require at least a modest devaluation of the currency, the IMF was designed to maintain the status quo of economic relations. At its core, the IMF and the WB were "mutually complementary" as they assisted states with a "short-term balance of payments" and the "longer-term flow of credit".[465] The WB is modelled on the US EXIM bank. It is designed to encourage 'development' programs that promote international trade. Only nations with 'responsible' free market economies are eligible, ensuring the pliability of the developing world. The GATT is designed to promote global free trade. The US set about creating a global Open-Door Policy as the victor of WWII. Marshall, and his colleagues, determined that Latin America was to remain a raw material-producing appendage of the global capitalist economy. The global economic institutions lacked a mechanism to normalize global commodity prices. While coffee remained at US88c per pound in 1953-4, the rapid decrease to US36c per pound in 1958 demonstrated the vulnerability of Latin American states.[466] Industrialization, especially ISI, could shelter Latin Americans from the full effect of this crisis. As many countries were dependent upon foreign food, their currency exchange was exhausted prior to any capital investment.[467]

Washington's political economic position was codified by the NSC under the republican Eisenhower administration. The NSC document 144/1 identified the source of US opposition. It states,

> Cardenás in Mexico, Árevalo in Guatemala, Figueres in Costa Rica, Gaitán in Colombia, Betancourt in Venezuela, Haya de la Torre in Peru, Ibanez in Chile, Perón in Argentina, Vargas in Brazil, Grau in Cuba, all achieved their political power by promising change. [Yet, many were] immature and impractical idealists [who] not only [were] inadequately trained to conduct government business efficiently but also lack[ed] the disposition to combat extremists within their ranks, including communists.[468]

This group of leaders are quite disparate. Juan Domingo Perón, Getulio Vargas and Carlos Ibanez were populist military leaders who made naked appeals to the industrial labor unions to ensure their personal power.[469] Cardenas was also a former military leader who sought to rebuild Mexico under a new form of constitutional social democracy. While Haya, Gaitán, Grau, Betancourt, Figueres and Arévalo were all civilian democrats that sought to apply differing versions of social democracy. The common threat was not political, rather, it was economic. Each leader sought to generate popular support and federal revenue by altering their place in the US led global economy. Through nationalist economic development they sought to improve the quality of life for their people. But in doing so they were limiting the control exerted by the US over their economies and setting a precedent for domestic development for their neighbors. Hence, their policies, according to the Americans, were following the 'communist line'. It was irrelevant that communism was outlawed in most of these countries. It was also irrelevant that many of these leaders opposed and often persecuted the official Communist Parties in their nations. What mattered were their economic policies. Hence, through thinly concealed paternalism, the US labelled them as "immature and impractical idealists" and began creating the circumstances for their demise.[470]

Coup d'états

The Miller Doctrine had reversed the US State Department preference for democracy in Latin America. It also provided justification for US support provided to military regimes that emerged in the wake of this era of coup d'états, under the pretext of anti-communism. The governments associated with the parties of Haya, Betancourt and Grau were seen as hostile to US interests through their commitment to economic nationalism. Their focus on internal social, political, and economic development undermined US control of their nations. Additionally, their association through the Caribbean legion, created the additional threat of precedence. These 'impractical idealists' became the focus of US policy following the Colombian Bogotazo of 1948. For the US, it was preferential for them to fall and be replaced by regimes that closely resembled the Somoza dynasty in Nicaragua. US intelligence did not directly overthrow these governments, as was the case in Guatemala. It did not need to. Rather, the US State Department condoned the steps away from constitutional rule and towards militarism. Each of the militaries of Peru, Venezuela, Cuba and Colombia used the pretext of anti-communism to remove democratically elected governments between 1948 and 1953. This pretext ensured that the US continued to provide support throughout their tenures. In doing so, they continued to reiterate the necessity of their position. That is, they used the communist accusations towards their democratic opponents as proof of the necessity of their actions. This directly created a pro-military climate through their actions and rhetoric during the second Truman administration.

Haya de la Torre remained in a tenuous position throughout the democratic interlude of 1945 to 1948. APRA's support for Bustamante had grown increasingly difficult as conservatives pushed back against some of the more substantial social policies. APRA continued to be the most popular political movement in Peru and was in the position to take the presidency at the next election.[471] However, many APRA supporters grew frustrated by the slow rate of change. Many Peruvians lived in poverty and demanded immediate action. Hence, in October 1948, a dissident APRA group staged a "mutiny" against Bustamante.[472] Haya publicly condemned the actions of this small breakaway group. However, this was the evidence of disorder that the military of General Manuel Odria had been waiting for. In an attempt to reassert control, Bustamante "reorganized his cabinet to exclude [APRA] members".[473] Bustamante believed this would calm the military. Unfortunately, "this move, however, backfired; for without their support, he could not check a revolt by [Odria] who had been his minister of the interior".[474] The unrest of October 1948 caused "the moneyed aristocracy [to turn] to Odría as if he was their savior".[475] In power, Odría described the *Apristas* as "communists in disguise" and his mission "was to save the country from *Aprista* plots and political poisoning by leftists".[476] From November 1948, the Odría regime arrested and imprisoned *Apristas*, communists, unionists and social activists, many of who 'disappeared'.[477] Odría "kept the ghosts of APRA's menace alive" by exaggerating their influence within the Bustamante government and blaming them for the economic crisis.[478] The death Penalty was initiated for the ambiguous crime of "political terrorism" in 1950.[479] From November 1949, Odría opened the Peruvian economy to increased foreign investment and trade, which spurred a temporary boom in employment based on liberal trade with the US. Meanwhile, the unions were undermined, and real wages plummeted.[480] Odría's war against APRA, interpreted as anti-communism, also won him a US Legion of Merit award in 1953.[481]

Venezuela's brief democratic experiment brought substantial social and economic progress. Venezuela is distinct in Latin America due to its oil wealth. The oil nationalization programs of Betancourt and Gallegos generated federal income that had the means to establish social security and basic infrastructure. However, the social policies also challenged longstanding class distinctions. The oligarchy complained that "the government was trying to do too much, and go too far, too fast".[482] Meanwhile the Catholic Church labelled AD as sectarian.[483] Despite this, AD was hugely popular, winning 75 per cent of the presidential vote in 1948.[484] AD represented the poor and middle-class sectors of Venezuelan society and engaged in a program of rapid change. Given his immense popularity, Betancourt attempted to limit the political powers of the military.[485] This led the military leaders into an alliance with the opposition. The chief conspirator, Pérez Jinimez, claimed the military acted "to prevent the creation of a new oligarchy...a sectarian minority with a failed ideology".[486] He purposely likened Betancourt's attempt to increase civilian controls to the ideology of communism. Prior to the 1948 coup, Venezuelan communism was irrelevant, and its small membership could not compete with that of AD.[487] Nevertheless, the military assumed power in 1948 and Jiménez rose to the leadership in 1950. From 1948 the 'Gestapo like' secret police eradicated AD.[488] Its leaders fled to Costa Rica and Mexico. Venezuelans existed in a state of terror for a decade. Social security was also eradicated during this period. Venezuela was one of the few nations globally to suffer a decrease in childhood literacy during the 1950s.[489] Throughout this period Venezuela exported 6.185 million barrels of oil, primarily to the US.[490] Yet none of this revenue was sown back into the nation. In fact, Jiménez's pilfering of the economy, in addition to wasteful spending, meant that in 1958 Venezuela owed foreign creditors US$500 million.[491] He also signed long-term oil contracts, which handicapped his post-1958 successors. For these achievements Jiménez was also awarded the US Legion of Merit in 1954, for his struggles against a 'communist' threat which never existed.[492]

The Colombian situation worsened following the 1948 Bogotazo. The Conservative President Ospina Pérez became increasingly authoritarian during 1949. His declaration of martial law during April 1949 was followed by the dissolution of the Colombian Congress later in the year.[493] In his Civil War against the landless peasants, Pérez turned increasingly to the military and regional militias known as the 'paramilitary'. As the conflict worsened, the peasants organized into insurgent groups to protect themselves and to reclaim agricultural land. By 1953, the conflict had grown increasingly violent and Pérez's grip on Colombian politics was fading. Therefore, the military sought to take control. The US gave tacit support to the Colombian General Rojas Pinilla to take power in 1953.[494] The Pinilla dictatorship used US-trained, and funded, military to destroy peasant insurgencies thought to be 'communist'.[495] When the peasants retaliated, the accusations of communism increased. Colombia waged a war on its own citizens during La Violencia. This was justified through domestic and international policies of anti-communism.

Cuba had proven unsuccessful in creating a social democratic revolution. Its economic dependence upon the US for sugar exports was a major disadvantage. Although Ramón Grau had easily won the presidency in 1944, he did not control the Congress. As a result, the PRC-A were forced to rule by decree. Cuba was "locked in a strait jacket economy dictated by sugar".[496] His attempts to limit US control over the Cuban economy were handicapped by declining sugar exports and the associated revenue. Despite Grau's economic failures, Cuba was freer than at any other point in its history.[497] Power was transitioned to Carlos Prío in 1948 without incident. However, Grau and Prio's failure to fulfill the Autentico revolution in Cuba led many to follow Eduardo Chibás.[498] Prio's decision to ban the Cuban Communist Party (PSP) in 1950 was seen as particularly egregious.[499] The long-term military president, Fulgencio Batista had placed pressure on the two Cuban Presidents during the eight years of PRC-A rule.[500] Eventually, in 1952, with the shifting American attitude towards democracy, Batista reclaimed power through a military coup and dissected the Autentico Party.[501] Following Grau and Prio's demise, and the public suicide of Chibás, the stage was set for a more radical era in Cuban history.

Latin America had changed course following 1948. The enthusiasm for democratic and progressive politics had been eradicated by the Colombian Bogotazo. Those governments that had promised, and in some cases delivered, social reforms were interpreted as weak links in the international Cold War. Though not necessarily 'communists' themselves, they had given haven to more radical elements within their movements. This is most directly evident within the case of Peru. Without the violent mutiny of the renegade APRA supporters, then the military would not have been able to use that specific pretext to turn on both Haya and Bustamante in October 1948. Once that pretext was tested in Peru, it became widely applied. The military and the oligarchs wanted control of Latin American politics and wished to suppress the types of reforms that were demanded by masses. In the immediate aftermath of WWII, Spruille Braden had encouraged them to allow democracy and reform. However, in the Peruvian incident specifically and in the concept of the 'Miller Doctrine' broadly, the US was clearly saying that the era of Bradenism was over. It did not want the social democratic revolution because it was in direct contradiction to their regional interests. While the US did not directly overthrow the governments of Peru, Venezuela, Colombia or Cuba, in the way that can be observed in the following chapter on Guatemala, it did clearly signal its new preference for militarism under the pretext of anti-communism. These four nations remained isolated from the international cold war. However, the use of the term 'communism' was utilized to impact their national politics to the detriment of the great majority.

Chapter Six

'The Example of Guatemala'

Dwight Eisenhower was elected president, in 1952, by riding the wave of anti-Communism led by McCarthy.[502] Eisenhower was elected to win the Cold War and accordingly saw the world in Cold War terms. By this time, however, any war designed to "roll-back" Soviet territory became virtually impossible as both superpowers held the nuclear technology.[503] Eisenhower's focus shifted to the decolonizing 'third world', and Latin America. In these 'developing' nations, Eisenhower could claim victories against 'communism' without confronting the Soviets or risking devastating nuclear war. Eisenhower expanded the responsibilities of the Central Intelligence Agency (CIA) and began framing every regional struggle in the context of the Cold War. He continued the Truman policy of befriending dictators and providing diplomatic support to unconstitutional regimes, but in Guatemala, those methods did not yield the desired results. Therefore, the Eisenhower regime followed the lead of the United Fruit Company (UFCo) in labelling Árbenz as a Communist and formulated a CIA plot to overthrow the regime. The democratically elected Jacabo Árbenz commented upon his June 1954 overthrow,

> The United Fruit Company in collaboration with the governing circles of the United States is responsible for what is happening to [Guatemala]…They have used the pretext of anti-Communism… [Their motivation] is to be found in the financial interests of the fruit company and other US monopolies which have invested great amounts of money in Latin America and fear the example of Guatemala would be followed….[504]

This chapter examines the 1954 CIA operation against the democratic Árbenz government. Rather than treating it as an errant outlier in US Cold War policy, it will characterize it as the pinnacle of America's anti-

Communist crusade that targeted any government that diverged from US interests. Their goal was to install a hemisphere of compliant military regimes who were dependent on the US. Guatemala differs in approach, not in motivation. It also served as a warning to like-minded liberal regimes in the region.

The South America Problem

Eisenhower adopted a stern approach to Cold War affairs. He ended the conflict in Korea through the nuclear threat of 'brinksmanship'.[505] He also asserted control in East Asia through his strategy of Mutually Assured Destruction during in the Taiwan Straits crisis of 1954.[506] However, this bluster failed to 'rollback' Communism. Eisenhower sought a cheaper answer to expanding US influence.[507] Hence, he expanded the intelligence role of the CIA to an operational arm of US foreign policy. By funding factions opposed to 'problematic' regimes in the 'third world', Eisenhower could cheaply buy allies while maintaining the veneer of 'plausible deniability'.[508] Following the success of the CIA operations led by Kermit Roosevelt in overthrowing the nationalist Iranian government of Mohamed Mossedegh, Eisenhower swiftly turned to Latin America.[509] For Eisenhower, "the time to deal with the South America problem [was] now".[510] The 'South America problem' was one of social democracy, military populism, and any form of independent government. The United States were engaged in a Cold War that extended from Europe to Asia. They wanted all of Latin American to fall in line, in the way that they had done during WWII. However, unlike WWII, there was no prolonged military conflict and no threat to hemispheric security. Therefore, many regimes ignored this 'threat' of communism and focused on their independent political and economic development. Each regime that did so were labelled communist in the 1950s.

By late 1953, the "South America problem" was reduced to Árbenz in Guatemala, Juan Perón in Argentina, and Getulio Vargas in Brazil. While Perón and Vargas ideologically differ to the social democrats of the Caribbean region, US policy towards them was consistent: to oppose and eventually overthrow. Perón had been an opponent of US regionalism since his 1946 election. He ambitiously advocated an Argentinean led redevelopment assistance scheme in 1948, but lacked the capital to fulfill his rhetoric.[511] As an industrial state, though, Perón's Argentina looked to form their own sphere of influence with its less developed neighbors in Paraguay and Uruguay.[512] As his downfall approached, Perón attempted to expand this into a trading bloc with Chile and Brazil.[513] This independent bloc would have disadvantaged US investment throughout the 'Southern Cone'. Meanwhile, Vargas returned to the Brazilian Presidency democratically in 1951.[514] He earned the support of the union movement by claiming that foreign capitalists, including the US, had been "bleeding" Brazil.[515] He substantially increased the minimum wage in 1952 and again in 1954 leading to inflation.[516] He also targeted foreign capital by capping profit remittance at 8 per cent of initial investment annually.[517] In his most drastic move, Vargas established a cartel of coffee producing nations to inflate the international price.[518] He stockpiled large supplies which increased prices. Both nations were acting independently of the US. While their economic policies provided mixed results for their people, and their records of human rights were questionable, they were standing up to the Americans through their independent actions.

Both Perón and Vargas were removed by anti-communist accusations and the collective pressures of their national militaries. The US ambassador to Brazil, Herschel Johnson commented to Edward Miller "if it had occurred that Vargas might not be able to finish his term?", and that "Vargas might abandon his conservative connections and seek to establish a labor-leftist regime".[519] Further State department reports had claimed that "Brazilian ultra-nationalists, abetted by communists, have secured the passage of a law prohibiting the participation of foreign capital".[520] By 1953, the US State Department viewed Vargas as an enemy and wanted to replace him. Vargas had been heavily criticized by conservative journalists like Carlos Lacerda since 1951.[521] But after Vargas was blamed for an attack against Lacerda, on August 5, 1954, this criticism spread to the military.[522] Vargas took his life on August 24 to prevent a military coup and preserve democracy.[523] His suicide notes blamed "international economic and financial groups" for his death.[524] Meanwhile in Argentina, Perón's popularity declined after the death of his wife, Eva, in 1951. His inability to communicate his message coincided with a severe economic downturn.[525] By 1953, Perón turned to the US and their businesses to salvage his regime. He invited Standard Oil of California to explore and produce vast oil reserves and took EXIM loans from the US.[526] Despite this, Eisenhower's State Department still feared him. In March 1954, it stated "Perón now dominates Argentina more completely than ever before" and that he "has sometimes adopted polices advocated by the Communists".[527] In reality, Perón had lost both the nationalists and the military and was eventually overthrown in September 1955. America's economic war and close diplomatic ties to the conservative military were factors in his downfall.

In Guatemala, Communism had existed in a limited form after the 1944 Revolution that brought about Arévalo's democratic rule. However, the small literate class of reformers gave unanimous support for Arévalo's PAR, knowing the foreign and domestic obstacles standing in their way. In 1947, a small group of PAR politicians formed the "Democratic Vanguard", a socialist arm of the PAR that diverged from Arévalo, primarily on economic issues.[528] In 1951, the election of Árbenz's, this group evolved into the Guatemalan Communist Party (CPG).[529] Significant Guatemalan Communists include: José Manuel Fortuny and Victor Manuel Gutiérrez. Fortuny was an original member of the PAR and a founder of both the Vanguard and CPG.[530] He was not, however, able to translate that into a seat in the 1951 Congressional elections. Gutiérrez emerged in the union movement. This broad support led to his election and an expanded role in international communism. He visited East Berlin for the World Federation of Trade Unions in 1952.[531] Several other CPG members had visited the Eastern bloc; however, reciprocal visits were rare, and no substantial Soviet presence existed in Guatemala. Ultimately, the height of Guatemalan Communism saw a peak membership of 4,000 members and 3 of the 54 congressional seats.[532] The PAR was extremely popular in Guatemala, which made it difficult for the CPG to attract members. It was not a threat to Guatemalan security or its place in the OAS at any point prior to 1954.

Arévalo brought political freedom to Guatemala for the first time. The 1945 constitution allowed for the free organization of political parties, except for those "of a foreign or international character".[533] While Arévalo was a liberal and opposed to communism, he was ideologically against political persecution. His disagreements with the US extended into international affairs, as he was a chief opponent of the 1948 anti-communist declarations as he foresaw the reemergence of the dictators. The former US ambassador to Guatemala, Richard Patterson, claimed several members of Arévalo's government were communists. He once remarked that if something looked and sounded like a "duck" then it much be a "duck"; therefore, if politicians made leftist remarks, they must be "communists".[534] These claims that Guatemalan politicians and public servants were "communist", are rife with paternalism, racism, and Cold War paranoia. They did, however, shape the view of Guatemala within the US government. The UFCo had claimed that Guatemala was on the verge of communist revolution since 1946. This was due to the "nearly continuous strike actions" of exploited banana workers against their employer.[535] Arévalo empowered unionism, which was detrimental to UFCo operations. The anti-UFCo sentiment was representative of the anti-Americanism that Kennan described. Workers voiced their grievances for the first time in Guatemalan history. Arévalo, for his part, only gave limited support to workers and distanced himself from the communists. His successor took a different approach.

Jacabo Árbenz Guzmán

Árbenz was elected as the President of Guatemala in 1951. While Arévalo had led Guatemala through six years of political reforms, Árbenz inherited a nation where 68.1 per cent of the population worked in agriculture, but was not self-sufficient in food production.[536] The creation of huge agricultural plantations for the production of coffee and bananas absorbed both land and labor. 2.1 per cent of the population owned 72.2 percent of the arable land.[537] While the UFCo were the largest agricultural land holder, wealthy Guatemalan coffee producers also held excess quantities of land. To compound matters, the Guatemalan government had limited resources implement their policies. There was no income tax, while tariffs had slowly been eroded by reciprocal trading deals. Árbenz appealed to the masses throughout the election by proposing,

> To convert [Guatemala] from a dependent nation with a semi-colonial economy into an economically independent country to convert Guatemala from a country bound by a predominately feudal economy into a modern capitalist state; and to make this transformation in a way that will raise the standard of living of the great mass of our people to the highest level.[538]

This program required economic nationalism. As a hero of the October 1944 Revolution, that killed Ponce Vaides and brought democracy to Guatemala, Árbenz was popular among the peasants.[539] He also received support from the majority who provided protection from his domestic enemies. From 1951, Árbenz enacted a social revolution to change the place of Guatemala in the international capitalist economy. Much of his program emulated the actions of Lazaro Cardenas in Mexico. But as his predecessor, Arévalo, had warned, this would provoke "the hidden force against himself and the revolution".[540]

The US sponsored coup against Árbenz in 1954 was predicated upon exaggerated accusations of communist infiltration within his government. Like other regional social democrats, he did share some association with communists prior to the election in 1951, making him vulnerable to these accusations. Arévalo had ensured the legal protection of the tiny Guatemalan Communist Party which provoked the Americans.[541] Árbenz's wife, Maria Christina Vilanova, was sympathetic to communism. Vilanova was an El Salvadorian expatriate from the ruling oligarchic class.[542] She opposed the treatment of the peasantry and expressed sympathy to the communist position in the wake of the 1934 massacre of peasants by Maximiliano Martínez .[543] She brought these ideas to Guatemala and commonly associated with leading Communists included Victor Manuel Gutiérrez.[544] Árbenz did associate with Guatemalan communists through these social settings. He also took their limited support in the 1951 election. However, this should be kept in context. Guatemalan communists did not form an armed insurgency that threatened to seize power. They also lacked the political power in Congress. Therefore, the communists existed. They even spent time in the Árbenz residence. They surely shared their ideas on the development of Guatemala. However, they did not pose a threat to Guatemala and did not justify the response of the US CIA.

Árbenz fast-tracked his land reform program, Decree 900, during 1951. The program redistributed land from large landowners to small peasant farmers without negatively impacting the coffee or banana exports. The National Agrarian Department targeted the uncultivated land.[545] This land was monopolized and kept away from peasants to ensure a constant, dependent and cheap labor force. The threat to large landowners was not the immediate government purchase of their land. Rather, it was the loss of cheap labor, which impacted the profitability of their production. 20 percent of the nation's arable land was redistributed to 24 per cent of the population within fourteen months.[546] This was a rapid redistribution of land. Árbenz stated his intention to "eradicate feudal property in rural areas" and did so quite quickly. However, Árbenz lacked capital. Land costs money. The peasants also needed money to develop their land. The government lent small amounts of capital to settle peasants with accommodations and agricultural equipment.[547] These small loans were proven to be successful with 90 per cent repaid in a year.[548] They also created stable food supply which limited the need for food import from the US. While this was an economic success, his decision to focus on peasant loans would prove fateful. The government had every legal right to purchase the land at its taxable value. However, their choice to stall payment through long-term government bonds earned the ire of large landowners, including the US owned UFCo.

Decree 900 seized 178,000 acres of land from the UFCo. They were compensated US$525,000 based upon the taxable value.[549] While they had avoided federal taxes for four decades based on this valuation, their protests were twofold. Firstly, they demanded immediate cash. They also claimed that the actual value of the land was US$16.5 million.[550] Decree 900 did not impact the business of growing bananas. But it did limit their access to cheap labor. They characterized Guatemala as communist in order highlight their economic interests. UFCo executives convinced the US State Department, and the CIA initiated Operation PB Fortune to remove Árbenz in 1952; however, Truman and Acheson aborted the plan.[551] Fortunately for the UFCo, Eisenhower was elected US President in 1952. His administration held many personal UFCo connections. Eisenhower was a personal friend of UFCo public relations director Edmund Whitman and employed Whitman's wife, Anne, as his secretary.[552] Secretary of State John Foster Dulles was a corporate lawyer for Sullivan and Cromwell and directly worked on UFCo affairs.[553] CIA director Allen Dulles served on the board of directors for the Schroeder Bank, handling UFCo finances.[554] Undersecretary of State for Inter-American Affairs, John Moors Cabot and the UN Ambassador Henry Cabot Lodge were both large UFCo shareholders.[555] The interests of the UFCo and the US government became inseparable during 1953. While Árbenz pushed forward with his economic nationalism, the campaign to remove him was well underway.

Land was not the only impediment to Guatemalan development. Guatemala was also dependent upon US companies for transport, electricity, financial services and export exchange, which made the Guatemalan government susceptible to foreign economic warfare. The World Bank report of 1951 highlighted Guatemala's economic dependence upon US corporations and advised the Árbenz regime to establish domestic competition in the fields of transport, naval ports and energy production.[556] The internal transport of Guatemala was controlled by two US firms, the International Railways of Central American (IRCA), which was a subsidiary of the UFCo, and Grace Lines. Monopolization prevented the affordable internal distribution of goods and persons as US interests were routinely prioritized. The UFCo also owned Guatemala's only deep-water port, Puerto Barrios, which controlled trade along the Caribbean coast. Furthermore, energy production was monopolized by the US General Electric Company, leaving Guatemala unable to control their energy distribution. The lack of government revenue impeded its economic development. With negligible tariff earnings, and no income tax, the Árbenz government was powerless to fulfil its electoral promises regarding health, education and infrastructure. Árbenz was unable to expropriate US holdings or motivate domestic competition. Accordingly, Árbenz developed a pragmatic nationalistic platform to improve the Guatemalan economy.

Árbenz faced several obstacles during his presidency. He sought to develop a modern 'capitalist state' through advanced economic development. Arbenz commissioned the construction of the deep-water Puerto Tomás by the US company Morrison Knudsen in 1953 at a cost of US$4.8 million.[557] Árbenz also advocated a 700-mile network of paved roads and motor vehicles to replace the monopolized rail system.[558] Árbenz's government began the construction of the link between Guatemala City and Puerto Tomás during 1954. Guatemala also began construction on a large hydroelectric plant. The 28,000-kilowatt plant in Juras, Escuintla, was estimated to cost US$6 million to decrease consumer electricity costs and oil dependency.[559] The final tenet of the reform program was the establishment of an income tax. The progressive income tax was approved by the Congress on June 7, 1954 and would have gone into effect on July 1, 1954.[560] Árbenz began to create a more self-sufficient capitalist economy to improve the lives of Guatemalans. The reforms were less radical than the New Deal, the Mexican Revolution, or post-War policies in Western Europe. Despite the protestations of the US corporations, Guatemala's reforms posed a miniscule threat to the broader US economy. It was one of many dependent plantation economies in the Western Hemisphere. Árbenz indicated as he left office in June 1954, the precedent of Guatemalan development was the true threat to US interests.[561] If several nations could develop without US assistance and begin to alter their place in the global capitalist economy, the position of the US in the Western Hemisphere would diminish. Accordingly, Árbenz had to go. The US would use all necessary means to ensure his demise.

Operation PB Success

According to the declassified CIA report, Operation PB Success was a multi-faceted plan to demonize, alienate then remove Jacabo Árbenz from the Guatemalan Presidency.[562] The CIA had little experience in regime change. Guatemala was their second attempt after a successful operation removed the democratic Iranian government of Mohamed Mossadegh.[563] The first phase to characterize Árbenz as communist was initiated by the UFCo. Its public relations director, Edward Bernays, had initiated a program to influence the US government and general public. The government was targeted when Bernays paid the influential conservative Republican John Clements US$35,000 to produce the "Report on Guatemala".[564] The report claimed, "communism had already gained a foothold in Guatemala [and that] the next objective of Árbenz and his regime was to seize the Panama Canal".[565] This report, composed of exaggerations and fabrications, was distributed to 800 leading conservatives.[566] Bernays also accelerated his anti-Arévalo campaign following the 1951 election and subsequent decree 900. In 1952, he hosted a press tour to Guatemala in order to demonstrate the threat posed to US business. Bernays carefully controlled the information fed to the journalists and shaped their opinions.[567] Bernays was related to the NY Times director Arthur Hays Sulzberger through his wife.[568] He took pride in his ability to feed stories directly to the top US news agencies as "fillers".[569] Some included, "Guatemalan exiles in anti-red fight: Group in Mexico unites to undermine Árbenz and land reform", from June 22 1952, and, "Ideas of Red held ruling Guatemala: Ideologies wear a nationalistic cloak but observers see a Kremlin program, from May 21, 1952.[570] The CIA directed their agents to coordinate "the collection of evidence, fabrication of same, [to] be attended to accordingly".[571] The documents also show dialogue between Allen Dulles and Sulzberger. The CIA took over this campaign from 1953 and accelerated their 'communist' characterization of Árbenz.

The US required a consensus amongst their public, politicians and the OAS in order to overthrow Árbenz. By 1954 the US public and politicians had been convinced. They called an emergency session in May 1954, in Caracas Venezuela. The meeting saw the US Secretary of State, John Foster Dulles, claim that Árbenz was both a communist and a traitor to the region.[572] He argued, "anyone travelling in the interests of communism is in fact part of the whole subversive program of international communism".[573] To which the Guatemalan foreign minister, Guillermo Toriello replied,

> The plan of national liberation being carried out with firmness by my government has necessarily affected the privileges of the foreign enterprises that are impeding the progress and economic development of the country...They wanted to find a ready expedient to maintain the economic dependence of the American Republics and suppress the legitimate desires of their people, cataloguing as communism every manifestation of nationalism or economic independence, any desire for social progress, any intellectual curiosity, and any interest in progressive and liberal reforms.[574]

Given that Árbenz's last regional ally, the Costa Rican José Figueres, had boycotted the meeting due to its location, the task for defending the Guatemalan position fell to Mexico. The Mexican foreign minister compared the Guatemalan case to their own revolution under Cardenas and made the point that the US would have claimed that they would be "guilty of some subjugation to foreign influence".[575] Only Mexico and

Argentina abstained from the vote that condemned Guatemala.[576] The OAS concluded that, Árbenz was a communist and that "the domination or control of the political institutions of any American states by the international communist movement…would constitute a threat to the entire hemisphere and would require appropriate action".[577] This provided the US with a green light to initiate their paramilitary campaign.

The US waged economic warfare against Árbenz from the late 1940s. This process was accelerated under Eisenhower. The first part of the economic warfare was the arms embargo, in place since 1948.[578] The Guatemalan government was unable to manufacture arms domestically, hence, it looked elsewhere. Arévalo had bought weapons from the Argentine Juan Perón.[579] However, after the failed Caribbean Legion invasion of Santo Domingo, Argentina ceased arms shipments. As the invasion was imminent, Árbenz reached out to the Eastern Bloc, but had no personal contacts there. In his one brief correspondence with Joseph Stalin, Stalin requested a shipment of bananas as a sign of goodwill.[580] Árbenz was forced to reply that the UFCo owned the bananas and he had no power to give them to Russia.[581] Nevertheless, he acquired outdated arms from Czechoslovakia in May 1954. The CIA was aware of the cargo of the Swedish freighter Alfheim.[582] This transaction provided the final condemnation of the Árbenz regime, and rhetorically confirmed all of their previous accusations. The CIA also sabotaged foreign exchange by reducing Guatemalan coffee imports.[583] This propelled Decree 900 and the role of domestic food production to national importance.

The paramilitary campaign against Árbenz was not a 'covert action'. The CIA armed, planned, funded and executed the coup in Guatemala in 1954.[584] The US chose Castillo Armas, who the NY Times described as a "stupid man", to lead the coup.[585] Armas was a follower subject of Francisco Arana, who had been killed by Árbenz loyalists in 1949 for planning a coup against Arévalo.[586] Armas also attempted a coup in 1950 and evaded execution by escaping. The CIA had been working with Armas since the thwarted PB Fortune of 1952. PB Success began in June 1954.[587] The invading force of a few hundred Armas loyalists were stopped just inside the Southern border with Honduras was underprepared.[588] CIA propaganda attempted to convince the nation of the coming invasion through radio and leaflets.[589] However, the army remained loyal to Árbenz and by June 15 the coup had failed. Allen Dulles requested additional US military support. Under presidential orders, the US began bombing Guatemala City on June 20, 1954.[590] The city was defenseless since Árbenz had mistakenly grounded his air force due to fears of espionage.[591] Árbenz's final attempt to save his government was peaceful. He requested UN observers to Guatemala to witness the US war against his democratic government. The UN was initially open to this. The delegations of France, Britain, Lebanon, Denmark, New Zealand and the USSR supported the action.[592] Lodge was instructed to use the first ever US veto should the resolution go through. Fortunately for Lodge, Britain and France were dependent upon US aid and support to sustain their empires. Eisenhower threatened his two greatest allies to stay out of Latin America.[593] They did. With this last effort defeated, Árbenz, believing that the war was against him and not his revolution, resigned on June 27, 1954.[594] Árbenz left the presidency to his revolutionary colleague Carlos Enrique Díaz. Díaz allowed Árbenz to address the nation before leaving. In his address, Árbenz blamed the fruit company for his demise. However, "the fear that the example of Guatemala would be followed by other Latin American countries" was greater for the US than for UFCO.

In the Aftermath of Caracas

The OAS meeting in Caracas indicated the first serious departure from the 1933 treaty of Montevideo. Any government following 'the communist Line' required 'appropriate action' to reinstall pro-US regimes on behalf of the OAS. Interventionism was again an acceptable part of US policy. However, many questioned whether this interventionism was in the regional interests. The last bulwark of the social democratic revolutionary period was José Figueres. The Costa Rican President had watched the demise of his social democratic allies throughout Latin America. Figueres' had advocated for the eradication of regional dictatorships. By the time of the Caracas conference of 1954, 12 of the 20 Latin American Republics were under authoritarian rule.[595] After the coups against Árbenz and Perón in 1954 and 1955 respectively, Costa Rica's was one of just six democratic governments in Latin America.[596] While Perón was by no means a champion of political or social rights, he was a democratically elected leader deposed by his military after a decade in power. That case also demonstrates links to an anti-communist Pretext. Figueres represented the new minority in Latin America. Washington's decision to hold the May 1954 meeting of the OAS in Caracas, Venezuela, was insulting to Figueres. The Venezuelan leader, Pérez Jiménez, had ruthlessly dismantled AD and Rómulo Betancourt was living in exile in Costa Rica. US policy towards anti-communist dictators under Eisenhower was also alarming for Figueres. Jiménez and Peru's Manuel Odría were awarded the US Legion of Merit for their repression of internal democratic elements under the auspices of anti-communism.[597] These factors led to Figueres' boycotting of the meeting.

Guatemala's tragic twentieth century history began on June 27, 1954. Following Árbenz's resignation, 200,000 peasants were killed and over 1,000,000 internal refugees were created between 1954 and 1990.[598] Castillo Armas was promoted to President by the end of July.[599] He revoked Decree 900 and returned all land to the UFCo He ended development programs and returned Guatemala to IMF policy. Armas' 1957 assassination brought more corrupt military leaders to power and the US continued to provide military aid to ensure that no renewed revolutionary activity would be possible.[600] Democracy did not return to Guatemala until 1994. As violence decimated Guatemala through the 1970s one US official quipped, "what we'd give to have an Árbenz now, we are going to have to invent one but all the candidates are dead".[601] The US destroyed a democratically elected regime because it inconvenienced the economic interests of a handful of its citizens and set a precedence for peaceful political and economic development in the third world. It is also revealing that this is not how they interpreted events in the years following. Eisenhower's brother Milton remarked, "we breathed in relief when forces favoring democracy restored Guatemala to its normal place in the American family of nations".[602] The insanity of the age was now evident. US policy supporting repression was called "democracy"; social democratic governments were called "communist" and even "totalitarian". Any lack of real outrage over Guatemala from within the US or the region motivated Eisenhower to go further, and successive administrations to continue this path. Historians have characterized Guatemala as a Cold War anomaly, in which the corruption of the UFCo convinced the US to invade a democratic government. However, this Cold War conspiracy did not end in Guatemala; it was just the beginning. But in doing so they were creating more dangerous and more radical enemies through the region.

Chapter Seven

'People Cannot Spit on Foreign Policy'

Latin America was firmly within the US sphere of influence after 1955. The post-war democratic interlude was ended by the fall of eight democratically elected leaders over the previous seven years, which left only six democratic Latin American governments, while none were populist or progressive. The Caribbean region was dominated by despots who suppressed individual political freedoms and economic nationalism. Many Latin American people blamed the US for their position. The Guatemalan invasion instigated a regional backlash of anti-Americanism and more radical solutions in the anti-dictatorial struggle. This was symbolically, and physically, directed at the US Vice President, Richard Nixon, during his tour of 1958. While the US supported militarism, it would be unpopular in the region. In an address to the US Congress, José Figueres stated,

> I deplore that the people of Latin America… have spit upon a worthy public officer… [However,] I must speak frankly because… the situation demands it: the people cannot spit at a foreign policy… But when they have exhausted all other means of trying to make themselves understood, the only thing left to do it spitting…[603]

This chapter will explain the evolution to the social democratic movement in the aftermath of the Guatemalan invasion. It will firstly demonstrate the American position towards economic development through the 1955 Rio Economic Conference, and the Latin American rejection of their policies. It then overviews the renewed democratic push of 1956-1959, and its implications for the anti-dictatorial left in Latin America. It will conclude with an examination of the Nixon trip of 1958 and the lost opportunity to embrace democracy and avoid the imminent Cuban Revolution.

The Rio Economic Conference

The OAS met in Rio De Janeiro in 1955 to discuss programs of economic integration and development. The Latin Americans had called for the meeting since their 1945 resolution at Chapultepec and John Dulles had committed to the conference in exchange for regional condemnation of Guatemala.[604] Despite regional optimism, Dulles claimed "an economic treaty [was] not necessary to further [US] objectives in Latin America".[605] NSC 144/1 stated US economic policy in Latin America as, "Encouraging Latin American governments to recognize that the bulk of capital required for development can best be supplied by private enterprise... [and the] reduction of trade barriers under the Reciprocal Trade Agreements program...".[606] Neither Eisenhower, nor Dulles, rejected the need for the economic assistance proposed by the Latin Americans. This position was unpopular amongst the Latin Americans. However, that did not seem to matter. Military dictators ruled the majority of Latin America. The US economic agenda was passed without the consent of the region. Under-Secretary of State, John Moors Cabot "worried about the vast disparities of wealth in Latin America, with the upper classes exercising an almost feudal control".[607] Cabot was replaced by corporate lawyer Henry Holland in 1955.[608] From that year, Holland led a major decline in EXIM loans to Latin American leaders.

The 1955 Rio Economic Conference, once again, witnessed the collision of two conflicting economic philosophies. While the American position remained dominant, the Argentine economist Raúl Prebisch posed an alternate vision. Prebisch, and the Economic Commission for Latin America (ECLA), identified three steps to revive the Latin American economies.[609] Firstly, Latin America needed to absorb US$1 billion annually to counter the capital drain of profit remittance to foreign companies.[610] Secondly, Latin America required immediate economic diversification to create internal markets.[611] Finally, Latin America needed price stabilization of key export commodities to create a secure price for exports.[612] These policies were defined as "developmentalism," and were in conflict the US.[613] Dulles did not travel to Rio with congressional approval for increased aid. Rather, he sought to institutionalize the economic policies of NSC 144/1. Stephen Rabe demonstrate that in 1958 Latin America received US$113.5 million in economic assistance.[614] 54 per cent of that was military assistance; 35 per cent was granted to US companies operating in Latin America; and the final 11 per cent was economic aid afforded to Guatemala, Bolivia and Haiti.[615] In Guatemala and Haiti this aid strengthened the position of allied dictators. In Bolivia, the humanitarian aid assisted the reconstruction of Bolivia's export economy, especially in oil. Nevertheless, America's military allies ensured their economic policies. Dulles noted privately, "[it] was sometimes a bit embarrassing to win votes by a margin of one, along with the despots of the region".[616] While Dulles considered Rio an astounding success, the State Department's Latin American specialist, Roy Rubottom, considered it "one of the worst failures of any conference we've ever had".[617]

Washington's economic agenda in Rio attempted to further liberalize Latin America. The Latin American governments who had expected more from Rio "were deeply disappointed [as] they had been waiting ten years to discuss economic cooperation with the United States".[618] The Brazilian delegation, led by João Carlos Muniz explained,

> During World War II, Latin Americans had believed that the vast resources of the United States were going to be brought to bear on wide and rapid economic development in Latin America- but since the war there has been an intense process of disillusionment throughout Latin America.[619]

That independence was outlined by Brazilian President, Juscelino Kubitschek who proposed a change in inter-American relations in the aftermath of the 1958 protests. In a private letter to Eisenhower, Kubitschek claimed that the Caracas protests were the "product of years of neglect".[620] Kubitschek exaggerated the communist menace to place Brazilian development within the context of the Cold War. This was a calculated move where he claimed that the "continued economic development of the Western Hemisphere is vital to the winning of the Cold War" and that no military would protect the region should "the great masses in Latin America continue in poverty and disease".[621] In an attempt to persuade Eisenhower to grant economic assistance, Kubitschek worked with the Argentine Arturo Frondizi, the Colombian Alberto Lleras and the Peruvian Manuel Prado. They proposed Operation Pan-America (OPA), in 1958, as an economic alliance that required external economic assistance.[622] OPA attempted to acquire assistance by demonstrating the threat of poverty to hemispheric security.

Kubitschek advocated OPA as an investment program for the Americas. However, the US had little intention of providing that investment. Kubitschek's stated that OPA would "Obtai[n] a level of living per-capita, which permits the beginning of a process of a cumulative and autonomous growth with local resources, to a satisfactory level, without brusque or institutional alterations".[623] Kubitschek stated that Brazil alone required an investment of US$3.5 billion, however, Dulles disagreed. According to Kubitschek, "Foster Dulles showed himself as a tenacious arguer, intransigent, almost incapable of reaching agreement. He put forth his points of view, and from there was no way out".[624] Eisenhower and Dulles' stubbornness led to a resurgence of independent economic nationalism in Brazil and Argentina, characterized as 'developmentalism'. Kubitschek promised "fifty years' progress in five".[625] From 1956, he initiated a "targets program" which emphasized "a monetary and budget program, an exchange reform, and an investment plan".[626] This plan centered on the expansion of the energy, transport and manufacturing industries in both Rio de Janeiro and São Paulo. Developmentalism was also advocated by Frondizi, who declared after the 1958 election, "Our triumph will be a great step forward in the struggle against colonialist imperialism and native oligarchies who throughout the continent have always blocked national development and the fraternity of the people of the Americas".[627] In his first year, Frondizi also established a 'targets program'. American economic leadership was viewed as a negative influence among the large South American democracies from the late 1950s.

Eisenhower's intransigence towards Latin American affairs was motivated by a doctrine of military supremacy. He began his second term by implementing NSC directive 5613/1, which stated,

> If a Latin American state should establish with the Soviet Bloc close ties of such a nature as seriously to prejudice our vital national interests, be prepared to diminish government economic and financial cooperation with that country and take any other political, economic, or military actions deemed appropriate.[628]

Eisenhower reinforced the hegemonic relationship with Latin America. This approach, however, defied the realities of time. Ten anti-communist allies fell during Eisenhower's second term. Dulles commented, "if we carry out our theory too rigidly the practical result would be that many friendly governments would collapse and communism would take over".[629] The ageing Secretary of State acknowledged the changing role of Latin America in the face of revolutionary anti-Americanism in Cuba and elsewhere. In 1959, Christian Herter replaced him due to declining health.[630] Between 1955 and 1959 regional military assistance was increased from US$54 million to US$160 million.[631] Washington's refusal to participate in OPA was fueled by a belief that regional security was best served through alliances with conservative, and often despotic, regimes.

However, military strength led to hubris. The Latin American people began to call for democratic and economic reform during 1956. The turning tide of regional politics forced the US to reconsider its image in the region.

The Tide Turns

The Latin American people reacted to their military leaders between 1956 and 1960. However, this movement began in earnest in Nicaragua. On September 20, 1956 Rigoberto López Pérez shot Anastasio Somoza García in the town of León.[632] Somoza's personal guard killed Pérez instantly. In his last testimony to his mother, Pérez said

> I have always been involved in everything concerned with attacking the dismal regime, which rules over our fatherland. In view of the fact that all attempts at making Nicaragua once again a free country, without stain or dishonor, have failed…I have decided to try to be the person who will begin the end of this tyranny…This is not a sacrifice but a duty I have been able to fulfil.[633]

Des Eisenhower's personal physician was sent to attend to Somoza, however, he died nine days later. The US ambassador, Thomas Whelan, labelled Pérez's actions a "communist conspiracy hatched in El Salvador".[634] Whelan acted against further revolutionary and pro-democratic activities through the approval of the Nicaraguan Congress to install Luis Somoza as president the following day. Pérez' actions had failed. The military received increased funding from the US.[635] Anti-communism led to the persecution of moderate opponents of the government. Many liberals, including the now elderly Emiliano Chamorro, were arrested as they attempted to flee Nicaragua, despite there being "no visible connection with left-wing conspiratorial activity".[636] While the effort to remove the military government of Nicaragua failed, they foreshadowed more significant events throughout the region.

Peru had suffered under military rule since 1948. Haya had spent five of those years held up in the Colombian embassy due to the intense persecution of APRA.[637] APRA's repression led Peruvian workers into more radical movements, which led to cyclical strikes which often turned violent. On one such occasion, in 1956, the military crushed an industrial strike on behalf of the employer and the Odria government.[638] Progressive military officers protested their role in this event. The military moved against Odría "in protest of [its] oppressive role" upon society.[639] They saw the inappropriate use of military force on workers as against the best interests of the nation. Despite surviving the military action, in this context, Odria was encouraged to step down and called elections for late 1956.[640] APRA had again been active in Peru since late 1954, but again, their recognition was only de-facto so they could not run a presidential candidate in 1956. Haya and Odria organized a treaty that would allow APRA full legalization in 1961 and a clear path for Haya to the presidency.[641] Accordingly, Haya and his APRA followers endorsed Hernando de Lavelle for the Presidency.[642] Many within APRA saw this alliance as a betrayal of Haya's original mission for social democracy, leading to the eventual schism between the older APRA followers and the more militant youth.[643]

Venezuela had also suffered under militarism since 1948. However, their tyrant, Pérez Jiménez was more violent and better funded by the national oil wealth. The human rights abuses carried out by Pedro Estrada's secret police and the continuing poverty of the Venezuelan population motivated revolutionary resistance.[644] This resistance had been building as conditions continued to deteriorate throughout Venezuela. In 1957 events turned against Jiménez. A series of strikes throughout Caracas culminated in the Catholic Church withdrawing their support in May 1957.[645] In December of 1957, Jiménez ordered a plebiscite which asked the Venezuelan people, "should General Marcos Pérez Jiménez continue as President of the Republic during the next Presidential term?".[646] This was designed to sure up power but ultimately backfired. State employees were forced to vote yes.[647] The vote was not secret; it was enforced by the military to ensure total compliance.[648] According to the historian Robert Alexander, "from the day of the vote, the regime was harassed by street demonstrations, plots and disturbances, ending, only a few weeks after the plebiscite, in the fall of the dictatorship".[649] On January 22, 1958, a Revolutionary Junta replaced Jiménez and committed to presidential elections.[650] While the military was purged of pro-Jiménez elements, the military continued to undermine the junta in July and September. Several progressive elements supported the actions against Jiménez. The 1958 elections were tightly contested. The AD party of Betancourt resumed leadership of Venezuela in 1959 by narrowly defeating both the Christian Left Copei Party and the Socialist-dominated Democratic Republican Party.[651] The "Betancourt Doctrine" survived, with Venezuela remaining democratic throughout the remainder of Cold War.[652]

Colombia was also returned to constitutional rule during 1958. However, it was under very different circumstances. Colombia's longstanding Civil War, 'La Violencia', had been raging for twelve years and had cost approximately 200,000 lives.[653] The peasantry was hardest hit by the conflict as forced evictions and indiscriminate 'anti-communist' raids by paramilitaries swept through rural Colombia.[654] The two political parties whose disagreements had led to the Civil War and five-year dictatorship of Rojas Pinilla, sought to return governance to civilian rule. In March 1957, at the behest of an ageing former Liberal President López Pumajero the two major parties formed the "joint manifesto of the Liberal and Conservative Parties".[655] Pumajero suggested that to remove the dictatorship, the Liberals endorse Conservative Presidential candidate Guillermo Leon Valencia.[656] On May 1, 1958, Pinilla detained Valencia and cancelled the upcoming election.[657] Mass civil unrest ensued throughout Bogota with students, workers and peasants taking to the streets. The military killed at least 20 civilians on the first days of protests.[658] On May 7, students took refuge in a Catholic Church and the religious leaders condemned the actions of the regime. Defying an age-old covenant of religious protection, Pinilla's military bombarded the church with teargas.[659] The military deposed Pinilla for his actions and scheduled civilian elections for August 7, 1958.[660] The Conservative Lleras was subsequently elected and the oligarchy returned to control the political system.[661] Those who had demanded substantive change remained on the outside of the political system and turned to more radical paths over the following decade.

This period of democratization offered mixed results. Venezuela can be considered a success in implementing social democracy. The return of Rómulo Betancourt brought a renewed emphasis on economic development, oil nationalization and limited social reforms. Meanwhile, Colombia and Peru reinitiated representative governments during this period, they remained bound by oligarchic rule. Dictators were executed without the attainment of democracy in Nicaragua in 1956 and in the Dominican Republic in 1961, as will be explained below.[662] Additionally, elections were held in Haiti and Honduras during 1957, where the corrupt regime of François 'Papa Doc' Duvalier replaced the dictatorship of Paul Magloire.[663] In Honduras, the moderate Liberal Ramón Villeda Morales was elected.[664] Finally, in Cuba, the revolution of Fidel Castro sought instant and radical change. Moreover, the late 1950s witnessed a resounding surge towards 'democratic ideals' against the right-wing dictatorships. Yet, the regimes of the late 1950s offered far less hope to the people of Latin America than those of the 1940s had done. Many social democratic leaders had lost their positions of dominance within the progressive movement. While Betancourt's success was resounding in regional areas, the margin was far closer in Caracas. In many cases, this new path was more radical than social democracy, as was evidenced in Cuba from 1959, as old leaders lost moral authority.

The social democrat movement was formed during the anti-dictatorial struggles of the 1920s and 1940s. They were led by middle-class intellectuals who created coalitions of workers, peasants, and urban professionals modelled upon the Mexican Revolution and Constitution of 1917. Their weakness; however, was their inability to prevent military coups or protect their populations US interests. That is, due to their civilian origins and opposition to military leaders, many could not protect their people or defend the popular will. The ageing social democrats were increasingly viewed as ineffective against militarism and foreign interference. The new left modelled their ideology on that of the social democrats, however, their strategy was much more aggressive. Ernesto Guevara had recommended that the Guatemalan Árbenz government arm its citizens to protect its democratic institutions from the impending US led intervention in 1954.[665] This was unprecedented for a democratic regime and rejected by Árbenz. However, the result of not defending his people from that coup was ultimately tragic. This revolutionary mindset increased during the 1950s. Only Mexico's revolutionary government could reasonably assure their citizens protection from the military and foreign powers due to their own nationalist and military. Other movements took this power into their own hands. The generation of activists that formed in the 1950s demanded immediate change and were willing use violence. In their mind, this would protect their revolutionary governments from outside interference and the powerful domestic interests. The revolutionary coalitions were fragmented between the stalwarts of social democracy who wanted to reclaim the achievements of the 1940s, and the new left who took that movement further.

The new left was forged in the late 1950s. They determined that the old guard had failed and took it upon themselves to fulfill revolutionary ambitions through a violent road. Radicals were given more freedom within these broad revolutionary alliances. This included the revival of the dormant communist movement, especially evident in Colombia, Cuba and Venezuela. But in most cases, the leaders were former members of the social democratic parties. Thomas Wickham-Crowley has reasoned that the leaders of peasant insurgencies were not peasants. He states, "The leadership of guerilla movements was, with few exceptions, drawn from the urban middle and upper classes and from rural elites. In all of these groups university-educated predominated".[666] While this was clearly evident after the Cuban Revolution, they were already evolving prior to the Castro's example. Take the Colombian example, where politicians excluded revolutionary forces, and the left-liberals, from political participation in

1958. The peasants did not have the 'political' path that they may have had with Gaitán. Rather, "peasant republics" were formed to govern the people within the broken state.[667] These were, in effect, self-defense groups during La Violencia and were targeted by the new Colombian government also. This was an evolving civil war between a group of organized insurgencies in Colombia that predates the Cuban Revolution or the establishment of the quasi-communist FARC. Again Wickham-Crowley states, "Guerilla movements are not best understood as the response of oppressed peoples to government repression…Rather they better fit Theda Skocpol's concept of marginal political elites, heretofore excluded from full power, who turn to revolutionary organizations".[668] That is, the jaded members of old revolutionary movements took a new road.

Castro's Revolution is one part of a regional revolution to surpass the ageing social democrats. This guerilla movement was also slowly fomenting in Venezuela, Peru and Bolivia during 1958 and explains the rapid rise of "insurgencies" in the immediate aftermath of the Cuban Revolution. This also addresses the issue of Castroist and Communist leadership of these insurgencies in that period. Those insurgencies would have formed without the assistance of Cuba or the philosophy of communism. It is also clear that their rapid rise was motivated by the success and example of the Cuban Revolution. While Latin America in this era was 20 individual republics, ideas, strategies and concepts did cross borders. The remote philosophy of communism was no difference. But that does not make it the central tenet of these movements. The people of Latin America had rising expectations after WWII. They thought that their lives would improve and the social democratic politicians began fulfilling that. When those promises were cruelly taken away, and life became worse, hostility and the armed struggle were a natural reaction. The United States, naturally, became the target for much of this anger.

The Nixon Trip

The US ignored the political change in Latin America between 1955 and 1958. Economic interests dictated their policies and they reasoned that the new Latin American regimes could be controlled through political, economic and, if necessary, military means. The 1958 granted the US State Department insight into the views of the Latin American masses. When Eisenhower asked Nixon to lead a goodwill tour throughout Latin America, following the Argentine presidential inauguration, he expected it to be "the most boring trip [he] had ever taken".[669] According to Nixon's memoirs, "the CIA warned that although the Communist Party had been officially suppressed in most South American countries, [the Vice President] might have to face occasional demonstrations".[670] The trip began peacefully in Argentina, where the military effectively suppressed the Perónist opposition, allowing Nixon a relatively quiet time in Buenos Aires. The small protests were led by 'Perónists' who opposed the dictatorship.[671] Nixon viewed this critique of the US and its military allies in Latin America as communist propaganda. Latin American military leaders who were indoctrinated to anti-communism reinforced this view.

In Lima, the demonstrations grew more vocal and violent. Peruvian officials warned Nixon not to go to San Marcos University, fearing a direct confrontation at the spiritual home of APRA. During the 1948-1956 persecution of adherence of APRA, San Marcos had been targeted by Odría's military, with several students detained on suspicion of 'communism'.[672] The San Marcos student union was hostile to militarism and the foreign policy of the US in Latin America. As Nixon's motorcade approached San Marcos on May 8, 1958, the crowds were shouting "Fuera (go home) Nixon" and "Muera (death to) Nixon".[673] Nixon approached the crowds and declared, "I want to talk to you, why are you afraid of the truth".[674] A barrage of projectiles, primarily stones, met Nixon as he approached the crowd. One projectile injured a secret service officer, who forced Nixon back to the motorcade. Nixon sought the refuge of his Lima hotel, yet demonstrators blocked his entrance, with one spitting at the Vice President.[675] US media coverage of the Lima protests, however, undermined Nixon's characterization of the protesters as communists. According to the New York Times, "the event cannot simply be dismissed as communist inspired. This is a mistake that is too often made in Latin American affairs".[676] Nixon and the Eisenhower administration ignored such advice.

Nixon then travelled to Bogotá where the CIA warned of protests organized for Caracas. The CIA advised Nixon not to enter Venezuela. Nixon defied their warning and flew to Caracas on May 13, 1958. An estimated 5,000 demonstrators awaited him at Caracas airport.[677] As Nixon exited his aircraft, meeting with the provisional military junta, the demonstrators began throwing projectiles and spitting at him.[678] The Americans hurriedly entered a motorcade destined for the US embassy. On route, the Venezuelan foreign minister explained to Nixon that, "The Venezuelan people have been without freedom so long that they tend now to express themselves more vigorously...we do not want anything that would be interpreted as a suppression of freedom...".[679] To which Nixon replied, "if your government does not have the guts [to suppress mob activity] there will soon be no freedom for anyone in Venezuela".[680] As the motorcade travelled to the US embassy a large group of protesters blocked the main route. The motorcade drew to a halt. While it was stopped, the cars were kicked, shaken, stoned and pummeled.[681] This was horrifying for both Nixon and his wife Nancy. After twelve minutes the driver of the lead car took the desperate option of forcing his way through the large crowd, striking several protesters. The entire motorcade arrived at the embassy safe. However, the ordeal had a significant impact on America's relationship with South America.

Nixon was irate at the US embassy. He met with the head of the military junta, Wolfgang Larrazábal. As he chastised the Venezuelan leader, he demanded that the car be kept at the embassy as physical evidence of the events that had transpired. Nixon stated,

> It's time that [Latin America] sees some graphic evidence of what communism really is... The men and women who had led the riots could not be loyal to their country because their first loyalty was to the international communist conspiracy... Those mobs were communists led communists, and they have no devotion to freedom at all.[682]

Upon learning of the events in Caracas, Eisenhower contemplated an invasion to rescue the Vice President.[683] He stationed four naval divisions in nearby Puerto Rico to be prepared for military intervention. However, the military junta controlled the situation. It declared martial law throughout Caracas. In an act of symbolism, Nixon left Caracas via the same road he had been attacked on. This time, however, the streets were empty with a thick haze of tear gas.

The US struggled to grasp the motivations of the residents of Lima and Caracas. Nixon's anti-communist paranoia was compounded by his experiences in May 1958. Nixon was convinced that the Soviet Union had incited the protest against him. Meanwhile, the US Congress was concerned by the events of May 1958. Democratic Congressman Charles Porter invited Figueres to help understand why these protests had occurred.[684] Figueres testified before the Inter-American Affairs Sub-Committee on June 9, 1958. In consultation with his close ally and personal friend Betancourt, Figueres sought utilize the events in Caracas to re-determine the direction of US policy in Latin America. Figueres asserted that Latin Americans had been demanding a change to US policy since WWII.[685] The Latin American people had only met intransigence and indifference in return. The people were frustrated and lacked options. Hence, they turned to anger, and the action of spitting upon US foreign policy. Figueres continued with an indictment of the US' foreign policy towards Latin America since WWII. His first critique was over US policy towards dictators, stating "you have made certain investments in the American dictatorships".[686] Anti-democratic US policies were a result of the imperial system, rather than an aim in and of itself. Figueres also addressed US policy regarding human rights and economics. In a critique of US indifference to human rights in Latin America, Figueres said, "when American boys have been dying, your mourning has been our mourning. When our people die you speak of investments".[687] He questioned the dehumanized pragmatism by critiquing the US economic policy that condemned much of the region, stating "we want to be paid a fair price...when we provide a product needed by another country".[688] According to Figueres, that fair price was "enough to live, to raise our own capital and to carry on with our own development".[689] Figueres was offering Washington the opportunity to redevelop their Latin American policy.

Anti-Americanism became a call to revolution throughout the Eisenhower's second term. The resurgent Latin American left had identified US action in Guatemala as symbolic of its imperial interests. Eisenhower's closeness to the military Odria and Jiménez regimes, in Peru and Venezuela, labelled the US as an enemy of regional democracy. Fatally, the US under Eisenhower and Dulles refused to cooperate with the moderate democratic leaders who proposed OPA and sought the redevelopment of their national economies. Communism continued to act as their pretext. Eisenhower's estimation that the 'revolutionary' forces of Latin America could be controlled through military alliances with dictators had proven to be mostly correct by 1955. However, by 1958 regional momentum was changing. Democracy had returned and the coalitions in the new states had become increasingly fractured. By refusing to work with non-communist democrats, the Eisenhower was empowering those who he most feared. The US held the opportunity work with the social democrats in promoting regional development. However, they again neglected this option. Meanwhile, in Cuba, an expanding revolutionary front was moving towards Havana. The Cuban Revolution would redefine the relationship between the US and Latin America. A nationalist revolution would turn communist and confirm all of Eisenhower's previous accusations. While the threat would change, US policy remained the same.

Chapter Eight

'A Bad Friend, A Bad Democrat and a Bad Revolutionary'

The Cuban Revolution altered the course of history for all of Latin America between 1959 and 1962. Fidel Castro's defiance in the face of US political, economic, and ultimately, military aggression endeared Cuba's version of revolutionary nationalism to many within the hemisphere. He proposed a new path towards social progress for the masses who yearned for change. This drive towards regional leadership, however, would ultimately lead towards Cuba's isolation from the hemispheric community. Castro's revolution had begun within the social democratic tradition of liberation from autocratic rule. But in fostering a revolution of rising expectations, Cuba required instant benefits for the masses. When José Figueres suggested that Cuba should commit to the idea of democracy above immediate economic action, and should side with the US in the global Cold War against the USSR, Castro accused Figueres of being "a bad friend, a bad democrat and a bad revolutionary".[690] Castro continued by claiming that Costa Rica had never experienced a revolution and that Figueres had personally betrayed his citizens by continually yielding to US demands.[691] Castro's experience confirmed previous evidence that the US opposed nationalist social democratic development in the hemisphere, and that Cuba's only option was to stand defiantly against the US. Cuba ultimately achieved independence from the US, ironically, by committing its dependence to the USSR. This chapter will document the evolution of the "Castroism" from the Moncada assault to the missile crisis. It will demonstrate that US aggression pushed Castro from nationalism and towards the declaration of Marxism-Leninism and the political, economic, and military alliance with the USSR. Despite the obvious US complicity, the events of 1962 demonstrated the threat of Soviet aggression to Latin America's leaders. For many, this confirmed the anti-communist pretext that America had been building since the 1920s and paved the way for further US economic and military engagement throughout Latin America.

Castroism

Fidel Castro was born into considerable wealth. His family, of Spanish heritage, owned significant property in the sugarcane region of Southern Cuba. He was afforded a private boarding school education and progressed to Havana University in 1945. Castro arrived at Havana University during the violent conflicts between Grau's pisteleros and the military, which verged upon Civil War. During this time, Castro entered student politics while studying Law. An average student, Castro became more interested in politics than his education. In 1946, he delivered a speech that condemned both US imperialism and the failures of the Grau government, raising his national profile.[692] Castro became increasingly involved in regional democratic action. He joined the aborted 1947 Caribbean Legion invasion of the Dominican Republic.[693] He also attended the 1948 Bogotá conference of the OAS, which saw the death of Gaitán and the subsequent Bogotázo. He was involved in the anti-US protest movement, but took refuge once the violence increased. The origins of Castroism lie within the ideological progression of the young Fidel Castro. By 1947 he had chosen his political and philosophical path, as a young Ortodoxo and a follower of the politician Eduardo Chibás.[694]

Chibás was a leader the anti-Machado student resistance and an active advocate of the PRC-A program for Cuba.[695] He was elected to the Cuban Congress in 1940, where he remained until his death.[696] However, Chibás grew frustrated with the inability of Grau and Prio to enact reform. On May 11, 1947, Chibás declared the establishment of the Ortodoxos as "he claimed that Grau had abandoned the ideas and programs of the PRC-A".[697] Chibás unsuccessfully ran for the Cuban Presidency in 1948. He was prominent as a radio host, and his weekly broadcast had a loyal following throughout Cuba. During those broadcasts, he routinely accused the government of both corruption and intransigence. Cuba moved quickly to the right under Carlos Prío.[698] Chibás claimed that the PRC-A abandoned their ideological commitment to the Cuban people. Benjamin notes "under the charismatic leadership of Eduardo Chibás, the Ortodoxos held together in growing tension the forces of moderate political reform and those of political purification".[699] In fact, support for the Ortodoxos grew significantly between 1947 and 1951. Fidel Castro was an Ortodoxo. He later formed the Ortodoxo Radical Action (ARO) group within Chibás' movement.[700] Castro considered himself the "intellectual descendent" of Chibás, and prepared for the 1952 elections, in which he contested a Congressional seat.[701] However, Castro's life took an unexpected turn in August 1951. Chibás had caught wind of a plan to overthrow the constitutional government to prevent what he perceived as likely Ortodoxo victories in key offices.[702] To create political impact, Chibás committed suicide on air on August 5, 1951.[703] This was followed by Batista's coup in early 1952. Constitutional options were seized from Castro and the Ortodoxos.

A small group of revolutionaries set to reestablish democracy in Cuba through an armed assault on the Moncada Barracks in 1953. Following their failed attack, Castro laid out his revolutionary philosophy. Benjamin asserts that "the thesis of 'history will absolve me' followed the moral reformism of Eduardo Chibás and drew inspiration from the utopian egalitarianism of José Martí".[704] Castro cited Chibás' forewarning of Batista's militarism within his 1953 speech. He then laid out four revolutionary 'laws' that 'would have' come into effect if Moncada had succeeded.[705] They included: the reinstatement of the 1940 constitution; extensive land reform; fairer distribution of profits to industrial and agricultural workers, by way of wages; and the expropriation of properties attained through government fraud.[706] He continued to state that he possessed majority support in Cuba and that "history will absolve" his actions. The revolution, until 1959, was fought by the Cuban people for these revolutionary principals built upon the platform of "nationalism, socialism and anti-Imperialism".[707] It was important that Castro's message was consistent and appealing to the Cuban people. A communist revolution would have lacked that appeal and would have failed accordingly. The Cuban communists of the PSP did not have the appeal to stage such a revolution.

Castro's ideological relationship to 'communism' has been heavily scrutinized. Castro committed to Marxism-Leninism came almost three years after the fall of Batista, in December 1961.[708] He did so to procure Soviet economic and military assistance against the aggression of the US. However, this ideological orientation is a defining legacy of the Cuban Revolution. That is, Fidel Castro staged a 'communist' revolution. However, there is little evidence to indicate that Castro was a 'communist' prior to 1959. The Cuban Revolution did not follow 'Leninist' strategy, as power was handed to conservative allies for much of 1959. The Cuban people were not indoctrinated towards socialism or Marxism prior to 1961, nor did the Castro cadre make any public proclamation of Marxism until then. However, given that Marxism is an ideology, there is no way to prove that it did not influence Castro's thinking prior to the revolutionary victory. All that can conclusively be said is that Castroism is a unique version of socialism and the result of Fidel's ideological progression between 1945 and 1962. The Cuban communists of the PSP did not directly influence him. Castro opposed the sedentary nature of their organization.[709] The small group of 37,000 collaborated with the Batista dictatorship and publicly condemned both the Moncada assault and the Sierra Maestra campaign.[710] They were the only progressives omitted from the pact of Caracas in 1958 and Castro.[711] Moreover, Castroism and communism were distinct. According to Aguilar, Castro's Marxism "has been generally limited to vague declarations or sporadic quotes often aimed at justifying pragmatic political decisions".[712] His version of Marxism was designed to gain the necessary amount of domestic and foreign support for his revolution to ensure its longevity. While it eventually evolved into a form of communism, this was due to political factors, and does not reflect the ideological development of Fidel Castro or his movement.

Castro's political philosophy was also influenced by Cuba's political and economic situation under Fulgencio Batista. Castro looked to the indentured agricultural population as the key to his revolution. More so than any other Latin American nation, Cuba was an economic satellite of the US. Under Batista, "Americans owned forty per cent of the Cuban sugar industry, eighty per cent of Cuban utilities [and] ninety per cent of Cuban mining".[713] The Cuban economy was dependent on sugar sales to the US, however, the decrease in world sugar prices between 1955 and 1958 left Cubans increasingly impoverished.[714] This poverty was felt disproportionately in rural areas. The top 20 per cent of Cubans, primarily urban professionals, took 62 per cent of the national income.[715] This figure accounts for the average annual wage of US$374, which was second in the region behind that of oil-rich Venezuela.[716] The importation of US$777 million of US consumer goods affected the real purchasing power of the Cuban people.[717] Meanwhile, "nearly 60 per cent of the total labor force languished permanently in conditions between unemployment and underemployment," due to seasonal labor in the sugar economy.[718] Cubans wanted to replace Batista. However, the urban opposition was unable, and unwilling, to wage a long-term war against the well-trained and armed Cuban army. Hence, rural poverty became the greatest source of revolutionary ferment in Cuba. Without government intervention, this poverty was set to increase. Between 1956 and 1958 150,000 Cubans reached working age, while only 8,000 urban jobs were created.[719] Accordingly, the children of rural peasants would mature into rural peasants. The PRC-A, while ideologically committed, never enacted meaningful land reform in Cuba. These factors made revolution in rural Cuba inevitable.

The Sierra Maestra

Latin America held a longstanding tradition of progressive revolutions against authoritarian regimes. These began within the military or amongst urban elites. While the Cuban Revolution represented a unique strategy, the class origins of the leading cadre were consistent with other anti-dictatorial movements in Latin America during the twentieth century. It is also consistent with Cuba's 1933 anti-Machado movement that was stifled by Batista and the military. No civilian movement can permanently protect itself from the military without the physical support of the great majority of the people. Even with that support, the revolutionary leaders must be willing to utilize that support by arming the citizenry. Ernesto 'Che' Guevara's observations of Árbenz's downfall in Guatemala indicated the perils of the constitutional road. Guevara's experience in Guatemala convinced him "that the struggle against the oligarchic system and the main enemy, Yankee imperialism, must be an armed one, supported by the people".[720] Moreover, the Cuban Revolution was a departure from the moderate social democratic revolutions. It was also distinct from 'communism', which had taken the constitutional road until this point. The Cuban Popular Socialist Party (PSP) criticized the Moncada assault as a "desperate action which may be regarded as an adventure...," asserting that such action could "lead only to failure".[721] The Sierra Maestra strategy was both unique and an evolution in the Latin American anti-dictatorial struggle. Batista's conventional army and police force were ill-equipped to counter this new form of 'insurgency'.

Castro attempted to land a small revolutionary army in the Sierra Maestra in Southern Cuba. His revolutionary cadre would need to gain rural support through revolutionary propaganda, financial incentives, education and Guevara's ability as a medical doctor.[722] The revolutionaries had significant financial backing from sympathetic wealthy Cubans, urban Cuban anti-Batista politicians, Cuban expatriates throughout the Western Hemisphere and members of the social democratic movement, including Betancourt and Figueres. The Granma departed from Mexico in November 1956, taking 82 Cuban exiles to Playa Las Coloradas.[723] The landing was a disaster, as it missed the beach and the rebels were forced to make their way through mangrove swamps.[724] Batista's troops were onsite to prevent the majority of rebels from reaching the Sierra Maestra. Approximately 20 of the 82 participants survived to continue the revolution.[725] Significantly, the survivors included the Castro brothers, Guevara and Camilo Cienfuegos. Once in the mountains, the rebels had to regroup. They had lost the majority of their equipment, supplies and Guevara's asthma medication.[726] Over the following months, the rebels integrated their movement into rural communities and began the task of overthrowing the authoritarian Batista regime.

The expansion of the Cuban Revolution was dependent on the support of the peasantry. The small revolutionary cadre was poorly armed and lacked basic provisions. It needed to expand and strengthen in order to succeed. However, by January 1957 most Cubans outside of the Sierra Maestra believed that Castro was dead.[727] Castro expanded his revolution through propaganda. Given that his revolution was dependent on national and international support, Castro reached out to the New York Times journalist Herbert Matthews to propagandize the revolution.[728] Matthews travelled to Havana in February, completing significant background work prior to his arranged meeting with Castro. Fidel Castro "controlled the setting, the timing, and to a large extent the content of the interview".[729] His supporters took Matthews into the Sierra Maestra. From there, the interview was carefully staged. Light was limited, the aura of threat was exaggerated, and the power of the revolutionary cadre was overstated. Castro confidently told Matthews that his movement had total support in Cuba and that they were well-equipped to defeat Batista and to create an effective government. He also stated that his movement espoused "nationalism" and "was angry with the United States for continuing to support Batista".[730] The world knew Fidel Castro's name from February 1957. While this was an exaggerated version of Castro, the myth was more significant to the revolution than any realities on the ground as continuing support was dependent on the viability of the M26 as an opposition force. The specter of strength created more supporters in urban areas and brought more foreign financial support.

The Cuban Revolution gained momentum during 1957. As the revolutionaries' message of liberation began resonating with the poor, it expanded to several thousand in late 1957. However, this regional struggle could not succeed in isolation. The M26 were dependent upon support from urban revolutionaries, in addition to foreign assistance. The rebels required resources and ammunition to defeat Batista's army. Guevara acknowledged the support of the urban revolutionary "Ilano" group towards the rural guerrillas.[731] One of the leading theoreticians of the Ilano was Frank País, who was killed in August 1957 by Batista's troops, viewed the aim of the revolution as "To remove, demolish and destroy the colonialist system that still reigns, to do away with the bureaucracy, eliminate superfluous mechanisms, extracting true values and...[to] introduce the values of modern philosophical currents that currently prevail in the world".[732] País and the Ilano had links within the PRC-A and other moderate anti-Batista groups. They raised money inside Cuba to pay for ammunition for the guerrillas. They also had foreign connections within Latin America and within the US. Former President Prío committed US$50,000 to the revolution in 1956.[733] The former Costa Rican president José Figueres raised US$70,000 for the Cuban Revolution.[734] Additional support was procured from Mexico, Venezuela, Argentina and liberal organizations in the US. Batista feared this expansion and launched Operation Verano in June 1958.[735] After two months, Castro's forces prevailed. By this time all progressives were allied under the July 1958 Pact of Caracas.[736] The PSP was not in this alliance until late 1958. Castro asserted his dominance over the revolutionary process in Cuba and he alone would control the peace.

By late 1958, victory for the rebels was inevitable. Batista's military claimed that 90 per cent of Cubans supported Castro's aims.[737] By October, the Americans acknowledged that Batista would be overthrown. Fearing a government led by Castro, they sought to co-opt the revolutionary process. State Department official William Pawley urged Batista "to capitulate to a caretaker government unfriendly to [Batista], but satisfactory to [the US], whom [Washington] could immediately recognize and give military assistance to in order to ensure Fidel Castro does not come to power".[738] By installing a pliable 'democrat', the US attempted to avoid the force of a revolutionary government. While they acknowledged the need for democracy, they hoped there would be no progressive reform in regard to agriculture, economics or international relations. Batista refused to leave and the struggle continued. While conditions in Havana worsened, the three revolutionary fronts of Fidel Castro, Raúl Castro and Ernesto Guevara advanced quickly.[739] On January 1, 1959, Batista fled Cuba via the Dominican Republic, taking US$424 million from the national reserve to impoverish the incoming government.[740] Guevara arrived in Havana on January 2, and Castro followed on January 8. To avoid the condemnation of the US, Castro had appointed the "fiercely anti-communist" Liberal politician Manuel Urrutia as provisional President on January 3.[741] While Castro had defeated Batista, larger enemies would confront the Cuban Revolution in its first months of power.

The Radicalization of Cuba

The US opposed Fidel Castro's leadership of Cuba even prior to the rebel victory in January 1959. While the US did not yet see Castro as a communist, they were attentive to his anti-US rhetoric and that of other, more radical, members of the cadre. Despite the emerging conflict, key US officials questioned Castro's 'communism'. Dulles informed the US Senate that he did not believe Castro to be a communist.[742] Castro also sought to normalize Cuban-American relations. He appointed Urrutia as the constitutional face of the revolution on January 3, 1959. More significantly, he appointed Felipe Pazos and Regino Boti to the treasury to create a moderate economic plan for Cuba.[743] After recognizing Urrutia's Cuba, the US replaced the pro-Batista ambassador, Earl T. Smith, with the liberal Philip Bonsal.[744] While Bonsal was outwardly intellectual, multicultural and progressive, he was also a fiscal conservative. While in Bolivia "he had proved an effective instrument of [US] policy to slow down the revolution".[745] In May, the Cubans began their urban reform designed to lower rents, utility prices and basic consumer goods. While these actions left US investment largely untouched, Castro's anti-US proclamations and his strategy of a "third position" concerned Washington.[746] Similar to Perón in the 1940s, Castro removed Cuba's actions from the context of the global Cold War by claiming neutrality. He extended this neutrality by promising an impartial stance towards both at the UN, when addressing the General Assembly in 1960, and associating with the global non-aligned movement.[747] It was these actions, rather than the early economic nationalism, alerted US officials of the tensions emerging in Cuba. The NSC began discussing how to remove the rebels from power as early as March 1959. If Castro could not be "nudged" towards US interests, they needed a pretext to dislodge him.[748]

Castro controlled the Cuban Revolution. His utilization of liberals was designed to receive a sympathetic American response. However, the revolution's appeal was based on his populist measures granted to the people. The centerpiece of the economic program was agrarian reform. The Agrarian Reform Law of May 1959 applied to all rural properties exceeding 1,000 acres, except for those producing exportable crops, which were permitted to be 3,333 acres.[749] Expropriated land was compensated through government bonds payable after 25 years at the taxable value as of October 1958.[750] The first round of expropriations targeted Cuban landowners. However, by July Americans also faced expropriations. The largest property owner in Cuba was the Kleberg cattle ranch.[751] Richard

Kleberg reacted strongly to expropriation. He lobbied the State Department and even had a private appointment with President Eisenhower, claiming, "Cuba is being dominated and run by the agents of Soviet communism".[752] The sugar industry made similar appeals to the US government. In a meeting with the sugar baron Thomas Mass and Lawrence Crosby of the Cuban American Sugar Council, it was indicated that Castro's actions threatened to destroy the industry.[753] Castro was caught in a difficult position. The US opposed to moderate economic reform in Cuba, as it impacted its private investments. Yet, the Cuban Revolution hinged on the high expectations of the people. If he lost popular support, he would lose control of the revolution. Castro asserted that his agrarian reform was based on the US-led program in post-war Japan. Nevertheless, the modest reforms proposed by the Agrarian Reform Law were enough to convince the US that Castro was opposed to US interests.

The interests of Cuba and the US continued to diverge after October 1959. The US had hoped that conservative democrats would remain at the top of the revolutionary leadership. However, from October, the M26 took control of the Cuban government: on October 17, Raúl Castro became Minister of the Revolutionary Armed Forces; Fidel Castro declared the creation of a popular militia to defend the revolution; and on November 25, Guevara was appointed head of the National Bank.[754] To prevent US confiscation, Guevara hurriedly transferred Cuba's foreign exchange to Canadian and Swiss banks. Castro began ruling by decree as the Cuban Premier, superseding the power of the President of Osvaldo Torrado.[755] These governmental changes solidified the US view of Cuba as anti-American and potentially communist. According to Morley, "sometime during the fall of 1959, officials of the State Department and the CIA initiated discussion that culminated in the President's approval in March 1960 of a covert action and economic sabotage memorandum".[756] The political tension grew as Eisenhower's government ceased its attempts to work collaboratively with the Cuban regime, which in turn, led to further conflict. In January 1960, Eisenhower began the process of reducing, and eventually eliminating, Cuba's sugar quota. This led Castro to initiate trade with the Soviet Union, for without sugar exports the Cuban economy would crumble.[757] In June, US oil properties were expropriated for their refusal to process Soviet crude oil.[758] Eisenhower responded by cancelling the Cuban sugar quota, driving Castro into further dependence upon the Eastern Bloc.[759] America's regional stance at the OAS meeting in San José, Costa Rica, further indicated its hostility towards the Cuban Revolution.[760] Castro vociferously responded through his famed Declaration of Havana on September 2, 1959.[761] This anti-American tirade was directed at the "free people" of the Americas, in response to the North American Declaration of San José. Castro moved further to the left for the duration of 1960. In October 1960, the Cuban government completed the expropriation of all US property, ending all hopes of rapprochement.[762]

The plan to remove Castro was multifaceted under the Eisenhower administration. It intended to demoralize the Cuban people through propaganda, economic sabotage, and ultimately the assassination of the leading cadre.[763] During 1960, Cuba was bombarded with aerial assaults and domestic acts of terrorism. It also faced propaganda efforts through radio and leaflet drops.[764] However, Eisenhower's initial strategy did not generate the required results, leading to his approval of a plan to aggressively invade Cuba on November 9, 1960. Eisenhower approved the Bay of Pigs as the landing site and broke off diplomatic relations with Cuba. This plan to 'liberate' Cuba through the use of exiles was passed from Eisenhower to the incumbent Kennedy administration. Kennedy was elected on a platform of anti-communism. According to Robert McNamara, "Kennedy insisted that the United States cannot allow the Castro government to exist in Cuba".[765] Kennedy approved the CIA plan to invade Cuba with 1500 Cuban exiles.[766] The rebels were trained in Guatemala during 1960. Nicaragua provided the airstrips for aerial bombing. The US also planned to provide aerial support by dropping 500-pound demolition bombs and 750-pound napalm bombs on strategic targets. However, little went to plan. In the months leading up to the April invasion, Guatemalans discovered the poorly disguised training facility.[767] The Soviets also discovered the plan and warned Castro.[768] By this time, Castro was well armed with Soviet ammunition. The initial plan to 'liberate' Cuba covertly had been bungled even before the April 17 invasion. Kennedy was caught between calling off the invasion and the JCS's suggestion of full-scale US involvement.[769] Ultimately, he chose the middle-ground by approving the attack with only minimal visible US support, which left the invading force too weak to pose a credible challenge to Castro's Cuba. The US was seen to be invading Cuba and faced protests at its embassies in Moscow, Warsaw, Cairo, Tokyo, New Delhi, Mexico City and Brasília.[770] Yet its efforts failed to have any impact on Castro's control over Cuba. American foreign policy radicalized the Cuban Revolution.

During the first four years of the Cuban Revolution the United States had isolated Cuba from international diplomacy, removed its traditional avenues of trade, sabotaged its attempts to initiate moderate reform and pushed Cuba closer to the Soviet Union. While these actions were designed to remove the Cuban leadership, they actually pushed the Cuban people further to the left as Castro's accusations of anti-Americanism were continually confirmed by US actions. The Cuban Revolution was not fought for communism. However, by 1961 the Cubans were completely dependent upon the USSR for trade and defense. This led the Castro's to prioritize "national sovereignty against the United States and pursuing social justice for the classes populare" over "democracy, civil liberties and free elections".[771] This allowed Castro to come under the security umbrella of the USSR. On December 1, 1961, he confirmed his ideological commitment to 'communism'. Castro stated that, "I am a Marxist-Leninist and I shall be a Marxist-Leninist to the end of my life".[772] Within this speech Castro made a candid recognition that Cuba was "making a Socialist revolution without Socialists".[773] Following this, Cuba was removed from the capitalist Western Hemisphere. Despite Castro's declarations of communism, it was a deviation of the PSP interpretation.[774] The revolutionary government centralized power within the M26, as it received the support of the people. Moreover, Castro appealed to the Soviet Union through his declarations of communism. He did so because the US was attacked his regime. Nevertheless, his form of socialism was unique from Soviet communism. It was a radical approach to the nationalist desires of the hemisphere. "Nationalism, Socialism, and Anti-Imperialism" were achieved through the armed struggle, and protected through an alliance with the USSR.[775] The revolutionary government went to these lengths because the US would not allow the social democratic goal to be manifested in the hemisphere.

Divide to Conquer

The Cuban Revolution was widely supported by the people of Latin America. Many pro-democratic individuals and governments contributed finances to the revolution. They had also provided refuge for Cuban exiles in Mexico and Venezuela. The revolutionary 'Pact of Caracas' was possible due to active Venezuelan support for Cuba's revolution.[776] This enthusiasm for the Cuban Revolution led to public celebrations in Brazil, Mexico, Argentina and Chile.[777] Celebrations went beyond the traditional political sphere as Castro's movement represented the desires of large populations. These celebrations were not pro-communist as most Latin Americans viewed the revolution as an "autochthonous product of the continent [that had been] aroused in [the Cuban] people" and held the potential to "spread to other Latin American countries".[778] Liberals and social democrats had provided support to this nationalist movement. Additional support was procured from Mexico, Venezuela, Argentina and liberal organizations in the US. Moreover, the revolution was about more than Cuba. This revolutionary potential motivated the euphoria surrounding the Cuban Revolution. Castro's political and economic policies fulfilled the historical desires of this impoverished global region. The tenets of Castroism were integrated into other standing populist political movements, including social democracy. Upon visiting Havana in 1959, Lázaro Cárdenas criticized his successors in Mexico, asking "did they believe in revolutions or didn't they?".[779] The Mexican President López Mateos responded by expropriating and redistributing 16.8 million acres of agricultural land, the largest amount since Cárdenas' presidency.[780] The Brazilian President Jânio da Silva Quadros bestowed the highest military award upon Guevara.[781] His successor João Goulart was criticized by the US for pro-Castro domestic and foreign policy.[782] The regional popularity of the Cuban Revolution posed a critical threat to all other revolutionaries in Latin America. Castro saw himself in hemispheric terms, and initially, the hemisphere agreed.

The ideological divergence between social democracy and Castroism occurred soon after the revolution. Guevara had personally thanked both Betancourt and Figueres for their financial commitment to the revolution in January 1959. Guevara also invited Figueres to tour Cuba. On March 22, 1959, Figueres addressed the 'worker's palace' alongside Castro. Figueres congratulated the revolutionaries but urged them to adhere to two central tenets. Firstly, Figueres promoted democracy, which was "the only source of permanent sovereignty for the people".[783] Secondly, Figueres endorsed support for the West in the global Cold War. As he spoke, the head of the Cuban trade unions, David Salvador interjected with, "we cannot be with the Americans who today are oppressing us".[784] This issue divided the leftist visions. The social democrats idealistically identified with the US global mission, while the Cubans focused on direct US actions. Castro addressed the crowd with a refutation of Figueres' suggestions. He spoke directly of the need to oppose US influence in Latin America. He then turned his attention to Costa Rica. Castro suggested that no revolution had taken place in Costa Rica. Democracy, he asserted, had not liberated the people. In March 1959, "the break between the democratic left and the Cuban Revolution occurred on a public stage".[785] The US sought to exploit this division immediately.

The social democratic leaders of Costa Rica and Venezuela became hostile to Castro during 1959. They sought to undermine Cuba's regional influence. They feared that the liberation of the Dominican Republic and

Nicaragua by Castroist forces would give Castro de-facto leadership over the Latin American anti-dictatorial movement, and create the conditions for regional 'Castroist' revolution in their nations.[786] In the face of these problems, Figueres embarked on a US lecture tour in April 1959 where he met with significant diplomats such as Adlai Stevenson, Richard Nixon, Milton Eisenhower, Nelson Rockefeller and Roy Rubottom.[787] In meetings he suggested that "the resistance to my suggestions for understanding with the United States seems in a large part from communist infiltration, but it is also a logical reaction to the sufferings endured under the dictatorship".[788] Figueres was well-received by both major parties. While in the US, he also addressed the Institute for International Labor Research (IILR), speaking at length with Sacha Volman, who Figueres would later discover that Volman was a CIA agent. IILR gave US$100,000 to Figueres to start the Institute for Political Education in November 1959. The CIA began funding the, rhetorical, expansion of social democratic principles to combat the appeal of Castroism. Figueres was largely a pawn in this process. The Institute sought to mold future leaders and to "determine their ideology in light of their principles, lessons, experiences and achievements of democracy in service of the people".[789] Figueres also worked with the CIA agent Cord Meyer in July 1960 to established the Inter-American Democratic Social Movement (IADSM) as an "effort to help integrate the popular political parties, and the labor and student groups that are fighting the democratic battle in Latin America".[790]

The rift between social democracy and Castroism deepened in 1960 when Guevara addressed a group of Venezuelan students, suggesting that they should organize a Sierra Maestra-type revolution against the Betancourt government. Alexander referred to this as "the final ideological break between the Venezuelan Democratic revolution and the Castro revolution".[791] Betancourt was shocked and denounced the "Fidelista interference in Venezuelan politics".[792] He further suggested the establishment of an Andean Sierra Maestra against several South American governments. These proclamations were influential in the South American decision to remove Cuba from the inter-American community. Support for the Cuban Revolution reduced gradually. The open rift with the social democrats gave the US majority support in its dealings with Cuba. However, Mexico, Argentina, Brazil, Chile, Bolivia and Ecuador protected the Cubans from US-led resolutions in the OAS.[793] Fearing domestic reprisals, even conservative regimes, such as Chile's, refused to be seen as involved in the overthrow of Cuba. Support for Cuba increased following the Bay of Pigs incident but fell following Castro's December adherence to Marxism-

Leninism. On January 21, 1962, Cuba was voted out of the OAS with the six states choosing to abstain rather than to continue defending Cuba and risking their places in the Alliance for Progress.[794] Cuba's aggressive actions in South America accelerated the American program to eliminate the Cubans from inter-American discourse. They distanced themselves from their previous allies, seeing their vision of revolution as the only acceptable course in the Western Hemisphere.

Castro and the USSR

The battle lines between Castro and the US were clearly drawn by 1960. To combat Cuba's dependence on sugar exports to the US, Castro turned to the Eastern Bloc in February 1960. He invited a Soviet trade mission led by Prime Minister Anastas Mikoyan.[795] The Soviets agreed to purchase five million tons of sugar over five years and to provide Cuba with US$100 million credit to combat its foreign exchange crisis.[796] The Soviets provided manufactured goods and minimal US currency to Cuba in exchange for sugar. Castro also signed trading agreements with Eastern European states and with communist China. This infuriated the US and led to further economic embargos and the eventual reduction of the Cuban sugar quota to zero.[797] The Soviets also sent crude oil to Cuba. This both ensured Cuba's energy supplies and further alienated Castro from the US oil companies. By the time of the 1960 expropriations, Castro was completely dependent on the Soviets for trade. The US, which had accounted for the majority of pre-revolutionary Cuba's trade, launched an embargo on it.[798] This US embargo has been in place since this time, and by 1963, Cuba was cut off from the capitalist world. In the space of four years, the Cuban economy went from being a dependent appendage of the American-led capitalist economy, to being a dependent appendage of the Soviet-led socialist economy. Castro's professed desire for 'nationalism' and an independent line between capitalism and communism was impossible given the actions of the two superpowers. While Cuba was economically advantaged through its alliance with the Soviets, it was highly dependent on an alien ideology and interests beyond that of Cuba.

Following the 1961 Bay of Pigs fiasco, Khrushchev committed to defending the Cuban Revolution from American aggression. However, Khrushchev always viewed the Cuban situation within the broader context of the global Cold War.[799] Support for Cuba also helped Moscow with domestic policies as the euphoria over Castro's victory within the socialist world eased the pressure on the Kremlin to directly confront the US. Khrushchev took the opportunity to defend the Cuban Revolution. It was a calculated risk that brought the world to the precipice of destruction. After Cuba declared its communist credentials in April and December 1961 the USSR channeled its resources into Cuba.[800] The Soviets began providing large amounts of ammunition, including MIG jets, tanks and transport vehicles. In September 1962, Castro and Khrushchev signed the Cuban-Soviet Military Agreement, assuring the mutual defense of the Cuban Revolution.[801] To this end, 42,000 Soviet troops were stationed in Cuba by October 1962.[802] The Soviets also constructed nuclear missile sites in Cuba to deter the predicted US invasion. This inspired more direct military responses from Washington. In August 1962, the CIA conceded that the removal of Castro would necessitate a full-scale invasion and a long-term occupation.[803] At this stage, the US was willing to wage war on Cuba. However, American U2 reconnaissance planes identified the missile sites in Cuba on October 26, 1962.[804] Cuba played no role in the resolution of the Cuban Missile Crisis. Khrushchev negotiated the removal of the missiles with Kennedy. Kennedy assured the Soviets that the US would not invade Cuba, in addition to other Cold War concessions in Europe.[805] Castro was furious that the missiles were removed without his consultation. Cuba remained economically dependent upon the Soviets and the Missile Crisis demonstrated the divergent interests of the Cubans and Soviets.

Fidel Castro changed Latin American politics for a generation. He is the most influential Latin American leader of the twentieth century. His legacy surpasses that of Cardenas, Perón, Vargas or Allende because of the international character of his revolution. His achievements within Cuba were modest. However, his impact on the region was immense. The regional political discourse had pegged the oligarchs against progressive democratic and populist movements across the region, with varying outcomes, in the first half of the twentieth century. The strength of the oligarchic and American led position demanded unity and patience within the revolutionary left. Castro's violent revolution shattered this paradigm. By lambasting José Figueres as a 'bad revolutionary' in 1959 and declaring his commitment to 'Marxism-Leninism' in 1961, Castro sent clear divisions through the Latin American revolutionary left. While those divisions had been fomenting for several years due to the cyclical regional militarism, Castro's example demonstrated the possibilities of violent insurgency in the region. This outcome served the interests of the US and the oligarchs by legitimizing their decades of fearmongering and paranoia. The fear of Castroism brought the social democrats sought to move closer to the US. Meanwhile, the insurgencies justified the remobilization and remilitarization of oligarchic rule under the, suddenly plausible, anti-communist pretext. The final two chapters will demonstrate how the US were able to use the threat of Castro's Cuba to fulfill their political and economic leadership of the Americas. It will again be evident that this is a consistent policy of consecutive US governments despite changes in US rhetoric under John F Kennedy.

Chapter Nine

'A Prophesy of Yours'

John F Kennedy won office during the Cuban Revolution's ideological push towards communism. His predecessors had placed limited emphasis on Latin America as it was within the US sphere of influence. Harry Truman had ignored the region and given control to his subordinates in the State Department. Dwight Eisenhower viewed events in Cold War terms controlled the region through military superiority. These policies had ultimately failed when Castro emerged victorious in 1959. Kennedy took on the task of altering the image of American diplomacy without altering the political or economic relations. The Alliance for progress (AFP) claimed to promote a social, economic and political revolution in the Americas. Its statements through the 'Charter of Punta del Este' effectively won friends in the region. José Figueres wrote to his ally Rómulo Betancourt, that "a prophesy of yours is going to be fulfilled, the United States will have to reach an understanding with us, the Latin American liberals, instead of blindly persecuting us".[806] While substantive change failed to manifest, the first year of Kennedy's program was an astounding success for his government's image in the hemisphere. Washington's enemies had been converted to allies through the rhetoric of the AFP, while other governments were bought through the promises of economic assistance. By 1962, Cuba was isolated from the OAS and the threat of 'Castroism' was contained. Inasmuch, the US did not have to fulfill its promises. It did not need to provide support to the social and democratic revolution promoted through the Charter of Punta del Este. It did not need to provide the largescale economic assistance requested by Kubitchek's OPA. Instead it could continue its policies of neoliberal economic engagement through development loans and further acts of propaganda. While this era failed to meet its stated objectives, it ultimately achieved Kennedy's actual objectives within the hemisphere.

Kennedy and the Propaganda War

Kennedy confronted revolutionary anti-Americanism by working with those democratic leaders who opposed the Cuban Revolution. This created support for the American position in the Cold War. The personal attitude of conservative US diplomats towards pragmatic reform was a central grievance against American foreign policy. The anti-communist paranoia that proliferated throughout the Eisenhower administration had led to irrational hostility towards moderate democratic leaders. For Figueres, especially, this needed to change. Figueres and Betancourt viewed US policy as discriminatory against democracy. Figueres stated, "there was little chance for a peaceful revolution in Latin America without a clear and forthright policy change by the United States".[807] Accordingly, Kennedy built upon his "best and brightest" team of Dean Rusk, Robert McNamara, McGeorge Bundy and C. Douglas Dillon with a team of leading Liberals to reformulate US foreign policy in Latin America.[808] These 'New Dealers' advised the young President on Latin American opposition to Eisenhower's policies. Kennedy indicated his intentions through his appointments. For instance, he, and Rusk, appointed Robert Woodward as Under-Secretary of State for Inter-American Affairs.[809] Woodward formed a close friendship with José Figueres while US Ambassador to Costa Rica. Teodoro Moscoso, a native Puerto Rican, was also appointed head of AFP coordination.[810] This gave the AFP a seemingly 'Latin' voice. Additionally, Adlai Stevenson was appointed as Ambassador to the United Nations.[811] The career liberal was less hostile to evolutionary change in Latin America than his predecessors.

This new Latin American team sought to change the American regional image without altering their dominant political and economic position. Samuel Bailey reasons that, "the greatest single task of American diplomacy in Latin America [was] to divorce the inevitable and necessary Latin American social transformation from connection with and prevent its capture by overseas communist powers".[812] That is, to place the US on the side of reform and remove the revolutionary emphasis emanating from Cuba. A Castroist revolution would provide the Soviets increased influence in Latin America at the expense of US trade, investment and security. Kennedy needed to convince Latin Americans that the US would allow non-Castroist revolutions to occur. But of course, this would not have been the case without Cuba. The Mexican agricultural expert, Edmundo Flores argued, "without Castro, few outside Latin America would care about the region's economic stagnation, its political instability, or its undeniable ability to upset the balance of power in Cold War".[813] This is clear through the consistent policies of US administrations towards Latin America. The US did not feel the need to win Latin American hearts and minds prior to the Cuban Revolution. This brief change was an outlier and was not designed to alter the long-term relations between the regions. Nevertheless, Kennedy committed to the sale of the AFP and the new American attitude towards Latin America during his brief Presidency.

Kennedy sought to legitimize the pro-democracy credentials of the AFP by fulfilling a long-held goal of the social democrats and their 'Caribbean Legion'. The dictatorship of Rafael Trujillo in the Dominican Republic had been in place for three decades when Kennedy took office. Trujillo received support from each US President since Franklin Roosevelt.[814] The brief moment of hesitation came from lower ranking State Department officials, including Spruille Braden, who found his regime to be corrupt and offensive. But exploitation of Cold War paranoia reconnected Trujillo to his North American allies. Kennedy sought to confirm that he was different to his predecessors. He would favor the side of democrats, such as Betancourt, over Tyrants, such as Trujillo. Under both Eisenhower and Kennedy, the CIA worked with opposition groups to depose Trujillo.[815] On May 30, 1961, Trujillo was ambushed and assassinated.[816] The US supported the anti-Trujillo opposition and advocated their actions but were also concerned about the consequences of Trujillo's death. The Dominican incident offered insight into Kennedy's thinking on Latin American democracy, "There [were] three possibilities on descending order of preference: a descent democratic regime, a continuation of the Trujillo regime, or a Castro regime. We ought to aim for the first, but we really can't renounce the second until we are sure that we can avoid the third".[817] As the communist movement was extremely weak, the US allowed elections in 1962, bringing the social democrat Juan Bosch to power.[818] In order to avoid a Castroist regime, however, the CIA established a new pro-US police force equipped with advanced counter-insurgency training. This Dominican arithmetic defines Kennedy's handling of Latin American politics generally. The US was unwilling to attempt similar actions against the authoritarians of Nicaragua or Haiti. Nevertheless, Kennedy backed up his pro-democratic rhetoric with action.

Kennedy's rhetoric encouraged the social democratic leaders. His actions in the Dominican Republic demonstrated his sincerity. The idea of an AFP was a significant departure from the foreign policy of Eisenhower. Kennedy was seen to embrace Latin America's liberal leaders on their terms. This was directly emphasized through the "Charter of Punta del

Este". Many of the stated objectives from this 1961 OAS declaration that formed the AFP, were taken from the 1917 Mexican Constitution and the social democratic movement that proliferated from it. The charter committed to agrarian reform, commodity price reform, nationalism, education, women's rights, worker's rights and class mobility.[819] The fact that it was empty rhetoric seemed irrelevant to the social democrats who were desperate for US assistance in their struggle for leadership against the emerging Castroist revolutionary left. The AFP was much more effective than the US initially believed. It was a propaganda program that required little physical commitment. Not only did it "sterilize the example of the Cuban Revolution," it also convinced the Latin Americans that the US was committed to fundamental change.[820] The US ambassador to the UN, Adlai Stevenson, collated the Latin American response to Kennedy's speech in a March memorandum to the President. He informed Kennedy that his speech had "a profound impression in Latin America – the most favorable since Roosevelt's Good Neighbor policy".[821] The US Intelligence Agency (USIA) confirmed this view, identifying one Colombian who called it "the most significant contribution to Pan-Americanism in one hundred years".[822] Moreover, the chief objective of the AFP was achieved in March 1961 without a single dollar of aid or a substantial commitment to altered policies.

The Charter of Punta del Este

The goals of the social democrats were set down by the Americans in the 1961 Charter of Punta del Este. Agrarian reform was a major aim of social democratic revolutionaries in the tropical regions since the Mexican Revolution. It was used to win the support of agrarian peasants, making a key tenet of the "multiclass" revolutions. The US had actively opposed land reform in Mexico, Venezuela and Guatemala during the early Cold War in order to protect its capital interests in the region and ensure reciprocal trading bonds. There was a curious about-face in the 1961 'Charter of Punta del Este', which claimed:

> To encourage, in accordance with the characteristics of each country, programs of comprehensive agrarian reform leading to the effective transformation, where required, of unjust structures and systems of land tenure and use, with a view to replacing latifundia and dwarf holdings by an equitable system of land tenure so that... land will become available for the man who works it as the basis of his economic stability.[823]

This demanded a change in land holdings to the detriment of oligarchic allies, American corporations and the very nature of US trade dominance in the region. Historian Victor Alba asserted, "The landowning oligarchy wants no change".[824] According to Edmundo Flores, the US' position on land reform "is tragic and perhaps absurd: it wishes to entrust what is nothing less than a revolution to the very group…which in its own interest must block it".[825] This meant that no change occurred. While the social democrats were encouraged by Kennedy's language, no concrete steps were taken towards meaningful land reform across the region.

Latin America's dependency upon the revenue derived from their export economies made it susceptible to the global fluctuations of commodity prices. The vulnerability of, specifically, coffee and sugar prices to global depreciation prioritized the concept of commodity price stabilization. The entrance of decolonized Africa and Asia into the global capitalist economy led to the expansion of production in key commodities such as sugar, coffee, meats, iron ore, copper, tin and nitrates.[826] The 'new dealer' Adolph Berle claimed that the US no longer needed Latin American markets and resources, as it had during the 1940s with the increased global supply.[827] This attitude invariably led to price recession that favored developed nations and crippled those of the third world. The comparative advantage of developed goods over raw materials caused a divergence in wealth that followed the division of labor. Latin American leaders, such as Kubitschek, had attempted to create cartels to control the distribution and sale of specific raw materials in Latin America. Accordingly, the AFP granted the Latin Americans' demands for comprehensive commodity price reform through the mechanism of the common market: "To strengthen existing agreement on economic integration, with a view to the ultimate fulfilment of aspirations for a Latin American common market that will expand and diversify trade among the Latin American countries and thus contribute to the economic growth of the region".[828] A Latin American common market was detrimental to US trade and investment, as it would increase the price of primary commodities. In 1968, Covey Oliver, the AFP coordinator of the time, quipped, "to speak of fair prices is a medieval concept, for we are in the era of free trade".[829] The US did not intend to change its economic relations to Latin America despite the rhetoric of increased prices and a common market.

The social democratic revolutionaries also advocated sweeping social reforms in order to alleviate poverty and to increase class mobility. This social program advocated education, healthcare, social security, women's rights, unionization and income redistribution. The US labelled these reforms as 'impractical' and 'dangerous' during the 1940s and 1950s. However, in 1961 the AFP began advocating the following aspects of the social democratic Revolution with various goals, including:

> To eliminate adult illiteracy by 1970....; Comprehensive...national programs of economic and social development...in accordance with democratic principles...; women should be placed on equal footing...; Institutions in both the public and private sectors... including labor unions [should] be strengthened...[so] that social reforms necessary to fair distribution of the fruit of economic and social progress [can] be carried out.[830]

The 'Charter of Punta del Este' was proclaiming a social revolution for all Latin Americans. However, the mechanism for payment was lacking. Institutions such as education, healthcare and bureaucracy, require government revenue through tariffs and taxation. Stronger unions and class mobility require the capitalist class to sacrifice their profits to redistribution. Moreover, the US was rhetorically stating a desire to serve the people of Latin America without the concrete reforms required to achieve this objective. The oligarchs and US corporations were not going to willingly submit to higher taxes or wages. And without those mechanism, the charter's proclaimed goals were practically impossible.

Cuba saw the "Charter of Punta del Este" as a piece of propaganda. They sent a delegation to Montevideo led by Ernesto Guevara.[831] Guevara directly opposed the Charter of Punta del Este. He was forced to ask the delegations of Latin America: is this "our America or theirs"? Guevara specifically opposed to the American utilization of José Martí's nineteenth-century political analysis. Accordingly, Guevara cited Martí's famous "whose America":

> Whoever speaks of economic union speaks of political union. The nations that buys commands; the nation that sells serves... Let there be neither unions of the Americas against Europe, nor with Europe against a nation of the Americas... If the republics of the Americas have any function at all it is certainly not to be herded by one of them against the future republics.[832]

Martí had warned against the collective economic assault on individual republics seventy years earlier. Guevara also took issue with the US State Department White Paper that claimed, "the revolutionary regime betrayed their own revolution" and "The Castro regime offers a clear and present danger to the authentic revolutions of the Americas".[833] Guevara questioned Washington's ability to assess authentic revolutions. He also identified Washington's crimes against the Cuban Revolution and its role in the assassination of Rafael Trujillo.[834] Guevara identified that the AFP was a direct response to the Revolution and would not exist without his revolutionary regime. The US used the AFP politically rather than economically. Nevertheless, following Punta del Este, the Latin American republics committed to the US' position in the global Cold War. Moreover, Cuba had lost its position within the Latin American revolutionary movement.

The social democratic movement effectively ended in 1961. Its proponents had failed to bring their philosophy of 'nationalism, socialism and anti-Imperialism' to Latin America. Those who had tried, had been overthrown, killed, or moderated. The revolutionary impetus in Latin America had passed to the younger generation of Castroist insurgents. The remaining social democratic leaders, including Betancourt and Figueres, aligned their interests with this US rhetoric. Their goals became impossible within this climate. The breakdown of relations between elements of the revolutionary left was also responsible for their decline. Figueres' willingness to host the first meeting of the OAS to condemn the Cuban Revolution in 1960 was highly symbolic, as was the 1961 commitment to the AFP in Caracas, Venezuela. US propaganda played a pivotal role in creating that breakdown of relations between Cuba and the democratic revolutionaries. The US had indicated that the intransigent policies of the Eisenhower administration were over. It filled the Latin American bureau of the State Department with liberals who espoused democracy and social reform. It authored the Charter of Punta del Este, which was a manifestation of the longstanding desires of the social democrats and their supporters. AFP propaganda drove a bridge between the Cuban Revolution and many Latin American governments and political figures. Whether the US committed to that propaganda was irrelevant. It intended to deal with the brief threat posed by revolutionary Cuba. By 1963 that threat had subsided, as Cuba had been painted as the aggressor in the missile crisis and many of the small insurgencies had been defeated. By that time, it was clear that AFP rhetoric had been formulated for political purposes. Alliance for Progress continued through the 1960s, but as an empty vessel of US propaganda.

An Alliance for Progress

Many Latin Americans were enthused by the prospect of American economic assistance. The Charter of Punta del Este was accepted overwhelmingly in 1961. Many Latin Americans believed that the US would commit large amounts of capital and deliver a social and democratic revolution to the region. Despite the weaknesses of Kennedy's AFP, his personal charisma ensured Latin Americans of his intentions. His 1961 goodwill tour was crucial to selling the AFP. Following the Caracas visit, he moved on to Bogotá where he asserted, "The Alianza para el Progreso is a phrase...all of the people of this country...are going to see filling this field in the next months and years".[835] President Alberto Camargo asked Kennedy, "do you know why these people are cheering for you?" to which he explained, "it's because they think that you are on their side against the oligarchs".[836] The peasants were wrong. In Mexico, Kennedy recognized that the AFP was ideologically aligned to the Mexican Revolution as both strove for "social justice and economic progress within the framework of individual freedom and political liberty".[837] Moreover, Kennedy was intentionally aligning the rhetoric of the AFP to the standing revolutionary missions in Latin America. The utilization of his wife Jackie's Spanish language skills in Caracas and Mexico City was a particular highlight.[838] It was a sign of respect to the region. For two centuries, the US had looked down upon Latin America. For the first time, the US had elected a President who would visit Latin America, speak to its leaders as equals while a First Lady spoke fluently in Spanish to the masses. Kennedy's personal charisma ensured regional optimism about the AFP in its early stage.

Secretary of the Treasury, C. Douglas Dillon, meanwhile, was pragmatic about the AFP. He realized the impediments and limitations of US policy commitments. Latin American expectations were at the heart of the propaganda program meaning immediate and obvious progress was necessary. Dillon advocated a modest growth rate of 2.5 per cent per annum throughout the 1960s.[839] While the US provided significant capital investment, the majority was to be accumulated domestically. Latin Americans would need to rely upon "self-help" to achieve significant economic development.[840] As this was a program of propaganda, rather than a long-term solution, immediate effects were required. Dillon envisaged Washington's role in funding small 'visual' projects in 'communist' threatened regions, as "these measures will have greater political ramifications".[841] These visual programs would reaffirm the US' commitment to its rhetoric. While Kennedy's December tour of democratic Venezuela was quite effective, some regions were much more impoverished and vulnerable to Castroism than oil-rich Venezuela. Areas such as Northeast Brazil received the majority of the initial aid, to quell Castroist critiques of Washington's foreign policy.[842] While some positive effects were reaped from the construction of roads, schools and hospitals, the political economic inequality was not addressed.

Kennedy was assassinated in Dallas, Texas, on November 22, 1963.[843] This brought Lyndon Baines Johnson to the Presidency.[844] Johnson was less enthusiastic about the AFP than Kennedy. The greatest security threat to the US global order was now emerging in South East Asia. The Cuban Revolution was contained by the end of 1963; hence, the original objective of AFP had been achieved. Despite Johnson's claims that Latin America was "among the highest concerns of [his] government" and that the AFP sought to "improve and strengthen the role of the US" in Latin America, the region was downgraded to secondary importance.[845] Johnson purged the State Department of liberals and idealists.[846] He replaced Woodward with Thomas C. Mann as Under Secretary of State for Inter-American Affairs and US AID director for Latin America.[847] The unashamed anti-communist installed the 1964 Mann Doctrine for Latin America. The Mann Doctrine highlighted four key points: "(1) To foster economic growth and be neutral on social reform; (2) to protect US private investment in the hemisphere; (3) to show no preference, through aid or otherwise, for representative democratic institutions; and (4) to oppose communism".[848] Mann advocated the political role of economic aid over the humanitarian one. He believed that all US loans should advantage US hemispheric interests. This justified the large loans given to authoritarian governments. Moreover, the Eisenhower foreign policy that caused the Cuban Revolution had quickly returned.

The economic program of the AFP was built upon a contradiction. The US espoused the economic philosophy of 'modernization theory'. Its leading proponent, Walt Rostow, "insisted that the United States could demonstrate in the Hemisphere that economic growth, social equity, and the democratic development of societies can proceed hand in hand".[849] Rostow also called the AFP "a battle of image and identity" Latin America.[850] While enthusiasm for US economic assistance abound throughout Latin America, many people believed that this was a 'Marshall Plan'. It was not. Modernization theory relied upon the openness of Latin American economies to trade and investment. The money committed was also loans which required regular principle and interest repayments. The regional calls for change, however, had espoused 'economic nationalism' and 'developmentalism'. Leading economists and politicians had pointed out that Latin American economies required independent economic development to diversify their economies and fulfil the social revolution.

They reasoned that if Latin America continued to produce cheap export commodities then it would be unable to increase the standard of living for its populations.[851] Herein lies the contradiction. It was in America's interests to maintain the economic status quo of liberal trade in raw materials. Meanwhile, it was in Latin America's interests to diversify their economies lessening their dependence on export commodities. So, while American interests were met, Latin American interests could not be. Hence, it was designed to fail the Latin American economies, which it invariably did.

The AFP was sold as an economic alliance. While it did not seek to alter the economic relationship between the US and Latin America, it did provide a lot of capital. The promises of Dillon were kept. The US lent Latin America US$20 billion over ten years.[852] Special emphasis was applied to Colombia, whose conservative government opposed communism and remained pro-US in the face of the Cuban Revolution and the rise of the FARC. Colombia was provided with US$761.9 million between 1962 and 1969.[853] However, Colombia's embattled economy limited the role of capital in economic development. The decline in coffee prices meant that much of the AID's loans were spent on Colombia's balance of payments and servicing its standing debt accrued during La Violencia.[854] No development could occur in this climate. The US used AID loans to leverage the Colombian economy. It argued that "greater openness in the economy would improve the prospects for US companies hoping to invest" and promote two-way trade Colombia is an ideal case study for the AFP period as its government was not revolutionary.[855] Therefore, its programs of self-help revolved around returning liquidity to the struggling economy, ensuring its ability to purchase US goods and maintain stability through military force. While Kennedy celebrated the social achievements in Mexico and Venezuela, his government would not actively promote them elsewhere. The AID loans became increasingly dependent on "liberalized trade policy and noninflationary fiscal and monetary policies".[856] While these demands ensured stability for investors, they did not address the factors that caused the AFP, making the rhetoric redundant.

The AFP continued the economic philosophy of the Eisenhower administration. The AFP Charter required Latin American states to pursue free-trade economics. Free trade was antithetical, however, to one of the key issues for Latin America – commodity price reform. The US viewed the paying of a fair price for Latin American resources as 'a medieval concept'. The AFP's support of modernization theory increased the export capacities of dependent states. While this could temporarily support employment, and produce government revenues for social services, it did not address the fundamental problem of development in Latin America. In fact, in many aspects the economic problems got worse. Latin American economies were forced to further deregulate their control over commodities in exchange for AFP funding. This further opened their economies, making ISI largely impossible. The vast majority of AFP funds were used for immediate visual 'humanitarian aid' and grants to 'friendly regimes,' with loans for long-term development coming a distant third. Perhaps the biggest flaw of the AFP was the lack of planning. Many states did not produce effective estimates for development projects.[857] Accordingly, the US gave several contracts to US firms to construct visual projects such as ports, rail, road, and to a lesser extent schools and hospitals in the region. These visual projects further enmeshed the dependent economies into the world system. The AFP also failed to address issues of capital flight and Latin American debt, and actively opposed programs of economic nationalism. Far from revising their place in the international capitalist system, the AFP merely reasserted it.

Economic nationalism was advocated as a means of development by several economists, most notably Raúl Prebisch, who argued that the AFP was handicapped by the "failure to strengthen the structure of the Latin American economy so as to withstand external fluctuations and events".[858] The US Congress seized upon the issues of nationalization, regulation and taxation in the case of Brazil. They opposed any deviation from the AFP outcomes. In 1962, the Governor of Rio de Sul nationalized the interests of the American ITT Company.[859] Those actions were questioned by the US State Department. In fact, the US Congress threatened to withdraw AFP funding to all of Brazil if the Governor did not stand down.[860] US contradictions had crippled the AFP. In June 1963, Kubitschek and Camargo emphasized "that the alliance had not been granted sufficient resources and that it had lost the confidence of the Latin American peoples".[861] Camargo asserted that "one cannot see anywhere in Latin America the spirit of enthusiasm" required to achieve the AFP.[862] Kubitschek blamed the US for deviating from the statist philosophies of OPA.[863] The basic contradiction was simple: the US sought to promote Latin American development without jeopardizing its own dominance in trade and development. What it did not recognize was that American trade and investment was at least partially responsible for the underdevelopment of the hemisphere. Without recognition of this point, the AFP could not end the economic stagnation of the hemisphere.

The greatest obstacle to Latin American development during the 1960s was capital flight. The ECLA studied this problem in detail, and demonstrated that in 1962 a disproportionate 61 per cent of the total export earnings of Latin America were absorbed by what it called 'invisible services'.[864] These 'invisible services' included: profit remittance by foreign corporations; the service of foreign debt; foreign funds transfers; and freight, travel and insurance. If one then considered the remainder of its foreign capital, 6 per cent was spent on fuel; 13 per cent on consumer goods and 26 per cent on raw materials including food.[865] Moreover, without spending a single dollar on development, the Latin Americans together had spent 106 per cent of their foreign exchange.[866] Frank called this transfer of capital to developed nations a "cycle of underdevelopment".[867] The total import-export exchange of Latin America in 1962, was US$1.215 billion; however, in actual terms the Latin Americans spent 135 per cent of their foreign exchange.[868] This meant that the 35 per cent would have to be repaid at some stage. Accordingly, in future years 'invisible services' would be considerably higher. While much of the AFP funds were spent balancing the accounts of defunct Latin American regimes, such as in Colombia, no development was achieved. A loan program could not work for Latin America. The money had to be repaid. Latin America required a social revolution. Only then could it alter its place in the global capitalist economy. Kennedy's short-sighted approach to economics condemned Latin America to a problematic future of debt-driven economic crises, which defined the late Cold War period for many states.

The US committed to lend Latin America US$20 billion from 1961 until 1970. While this capital was spent on food aid, military equipment and small-scale public works, that money needed to be repaid. Roddick suggests that by 1987, the Latin Americans had paid US$30.1 billion in interest from these loans.[869] Any good that could be achieved from the loans was undermined by the interest paid. The worst examples of debt accumulation occurred in Mexico and Brazil. During the 1960s Mexico's debt position steadily worsened as a result of the AFP. It culminated in a debt of US$105.6 billion in 1987.[870] The injection of capital into the economy did not alleviate public poverty. Higher capital injections were made throughout the 1970s and 1980s, during a period of increased poverty in Mexico. While Brazil's debt position was onerous prior to the AFP, it worsened during the 1960s. Many of these loans directly increased the capacity of the military, both through grants and 'civic action'. Brazil reached a crippling debt position of US$116.9 billion, leading into the debt crisis of 1987.[871] Given that the AFP did not achieve its stated goals, the regional debt accumulated throughout the AFP era was especially damaging. Moreover, the contradiction of the AFP was its failure to "convert [Kennedy's] good words into good deeds".[872] The US had no obligation to loosen its economic grip on Latin America and, unsurprisingly, it did not.

The AFP was designed to fail Latin America. It was antithetical to US interests to conduct a social and democratic revolution in Latin America. The AFP charter was highly contradictory and in some ways illogical. It advocated extensive land reform without creating incentives for landowners to transfer their land to peasants. It advocated commodity price reform without creating the mechanisms to increase the value of raw materials. It advocated social policies, including education, healthcare, gender equality and income redistribution, without creating the economic incentives to make the ruling class enact these reforms. Most significantly, the AFP advocated democracy without US support for constitutional regimes against military coups. While historians have asserted that the AFP was a liberal aid program, there is little evidence to support this. Economic growth was stagnant during the AFP. The AFP did not follow the recommendations of the ECLA to achieve long-term development, in fact, it actively opposed policies of economic nationalism and did not confront the issue of capital flight. In the end, the AFP period left Latin America with a substantial debt position that crippled the region throughout the 1970s and 1980s. The AFP was designed to fail in Latin America because the success of the AFP would severely handicap the position of US trade and investment in the region. Its success required the US government to act against its own interests. The swift isolation of the Castroist threat de-emphasized the AFP, allowing the US to return to Eisenhower era economic policies under the Mann Doctrine.

The AFP, however, was a success for the US. Within two months of committing to the Charter of Punta del Este, the Cubans were banished from the OAS. The Latin American people were enthusiastic about the AFP. Kennedy was greeted by cheering crowds in Caracas, Bogotá and Mexico City between 1961 and 1963. He was the most celebrated American leader in Latin America, with regional enthusiasm for his polices, exceeding that for Roosevelt's Good Neighbor Policy. The utilization of progressive advisors, strong allegiances to social and liberal democratic leaders, and his wife's Spanish language skills, along with the largest foreign economic commitment to Latin America in history, earned Kennedy astounding prestige in Latin America. This notoriety was achieved without any concrete signs of the social and democratic revolution proposed by

AFP rhetoric. In fact, the enthusiasm reached its pinnacle prior to the beginning of the AFP. UN Ambassador Stevenson and the USIA division in Latin America informed the President in March 1961 that he had made a profound impression on Latin America. By 1963 that impression had changed. However, the Kennedy administration was unfazed. By 1963: the Cuban Revolution was isolated; the majority of the Castroist insurgencies had occurred and failed; the hemisphere began its progression from democratic to military states; the US increased its military influence in Latin America; the philosophical policies of the AFP were institutionalized; leftist and nationalist development policies were eradicated; and the US had created its own version of political and economic stability that allowed US investment to thrive regionally. While it had not met the stated objectives of the AFP, it was a successful policy for the US. The following chapter will explain the parallel political and military events.

Chapter Ten

'In the Grip of a Psychosis'

The Alliance for Progress formed one half of Kennedy's anti-communist strategy for Latin America. The US had won allies and demonized enemies through the "good words", and perceived "good deeds", of the US led aid program for the hemisphere.[873] The Cuban Revolution was isolated in the hemisphere. The anti-communist pretext was, again, used to characterize social struggles throughout the hemisphere. The emergence of insurgent groups was exacerbated by the decline and moderation of the social democrats. With no other outlet for resistance, many progressives turned to armed struggle. These insurgencies, though, were limited in size and scope, during the 1960s, and the response was disproportionate. The US engaged in programs of 'counter-insurgency', 'civic action' and, again, supported a largescale militarization of Latin American politics in response to the limited threat of insurgency. While the anti-communist pretext was confirmed in Cuba, and their example had indeed inspired several small insurgencies throughout the hemisphere, most of Latin America was not under the immediate specter of communist revolution. But by 1965, the region was indoctrinated by anti-communism and the US became fixated on preventing "another Cuba".[874] Speaking to the historian Robert Alexander, the deposed Dominican President Juan Bosch stated, "all of America, with the possible exception of Canada, is in the grip of a psychosis. It's not merely that there is a fear of communism, but there is a fear of anything different".[875] That fear and psychosis justified the militarization of Latin America and the intensification of conflict for the remainder of the Cold War.

Insurgency

Following the failed Bay of Pigs invasion, the Kennedy administration became obsessed with avoiding 'another Cuba'. Kennedy argued that,

133

The free world's security can be endangered not only by a nuclear attack but also by being slowly nibbled away at the periphery, regardless of our strategic power, by forces of subversion, infiltration, intimidation, indirect or non-overt aggression, internal revolution, lunatic blackmail, guerrilla warfare or a series of limited wars.[876]

While Kennedy's prophecy was not solely directed at Latin America, many of these 'peripheral' forces were evident in the region. Kennedy had been warned by Adolf Berle that "eight governments may go the way of Cuba in the next six months unless something is done", prior to in inauguration in January 1961.[877] Berle convinced Kennedy that Moscow was responsible for the region's insurgencies that formed part of a grand conspiracy to attack US interests in the region. Inasmuch, the US claimed that the insurgencies were a new form of externally funded revolution in the hemisphere. However, a closer examination of Kennedy's warning reveals 'threats' that were consistent in Latin America's recent past. Internal revolutions saw power ebb and flow between democratic reform and the military dictatorship. Guerilla warfare was not unique to communism or Fidel Castro. Guerilla campaigns had been conducted for progressive change by Emiliano Zapata, Augusto Sandino, and the Caribbean Legion. Subversion and infiltration were common political strategies. Acts such as blackmail and intimidation were also commonly conducted by the military dictatorships. Moreover, Kennedy was informed that a continuation of the chaotic political life, which the US had contributed to, was clear evidence of Soviet involvement in the hemisphere and required dramatic action.

Insurgency refers to a type of indirect warfare against an established government or social order. This form of military strategy increased in the early 1960s, due to the exhaustion of alternate options of social and political progress through constitutional means. Successful social democratic revolutions had time and again been undermined by conservative military coups and external forces. The path towards another social democratic revolution had been eradicated by the increased militarization of Latin American politics in the 1950s. Meanwhile the stalwarts of the social democratic movement had moved closer to the United States, through the AFP, and away from their original objectives of legitimate social revolution for the hemisphere. Increasingly, the insurgent path based on the Cuban Revolution became the last option for the disenchanted masses. While insurgency and guerilla warfare are typically associated with rural conflict, Timothy Wickham-Crawley asserts, "guerrilla movements do not begin among the peasants in the countryside but among urban-based intellectuals, especially in the twin milieus of universities and political parties".[878] Meanwhile Radu argues that guerrilla movements were an "elite phenomenon" made by those "unwilling to accept...the prevailing social conventions of his class or group".[879] He continues to identify a "disproportionate amount of upper and middle-class elements among the revolutionaries" and claims "becoming a nationalist is so incompatible with being a Leninist as to be impossible".[880] The insurgent movements were devised amongst urban groups who coopted a regional issue to execute a Castroist insurgency. Left without any other options, the urban revolutionaries committed to the guerilla struggle in many Latin American countries in an attempt to emulate Cuba and to change the balance of power in national politics.

Virtually every guerrilla movement in Latin America emerged within the reformist parties. The Venezuelan Movement of the Revolutionary Left (MIR) evolved out of AD.[881] The MIR opposed Betancourt's moderate platform in the 1958 elections and while Betancourt received 49 per cent of the popular vote, his popularity in Caracas was significantly lower, at 12 per cent.[882] This demonstrated discontent with moderate reform and reflected the radicalism of AD youth who "forged their political thought in the battle against the increasingly bloody Pérez Jiménez regime".[883] In Peru, a similar demographic was drawn away from APRA. The Peruvian MIR charged that Haya had become "pro-yanqui and [was] in collusion with the oligarchy".[884] Luis de la Puente claimed his support for Marxism-Leninism as the only road that "can lead the liberation process" in Peru.[885] In Bolivia, the schism occurred in the months leading to the coup against Estenssoro's MNR. The National Liberation Army (ELN) was founded in 1964.[886] Its leader, Victor Medina, targeted the "political and military domination of the United States" while distancing himself from Marxism and Cuba.[887] The Revolutionary Armed Forces of Colombia (FARC) emerged out of the fallout of *La Violencia* and coalition rule.[888] The FARC leadership was ideologically connected to the Colombian Communist Party (PCC), more so than the other insurgent group in Latin America. The PCC had utilized the demise of Gaitán to gain influence over all actors outside of the oligarchy. The FARC has led the longest insurgency in Latin American history, beginning in 1964. The urban FARC leadership cadre attempted "to secure power through the unorthodox means of military alliance with the peasantry".[889] This followed the example of Castro's Cuba.

The Cubans supported revolution in Latin America by utilizing widespread enthusiasm for the revolutionary ideology. Castro initially provided material support to the pro-Cuba revolutionaries of Nicaragua and the Dominican Republic.[890] Castro's ideology emerged alongside his insurgent tactics. Castro's tactics were enmeshed within the experience of the Sierra Maestra, which was not dependent on the declarations of Socialism and Marxism-Leninism that followed the revolution. Castroism was distinct from doctrinal communism for a number of reasons. Firstly, it did not rely on the USSR or the Cominform for direction. Quite simply, Latin America "had never been one of Moscow's priorities".[891] The experience of Cuba did not overtly change this stance. Secondly, Castroism did not emphasize the appointment of leading communists to head the revolution. As Castro declared in 1962, Cuba made "a socialist revolution without Socialists".[892] Those insurgent groups that had emerged from the social democratic reform parties were sympathetic to Castro's violent struggle. Finally, they saw themselves as the revolutionary vanguard of their nations. According to Aguilar, that "vanguard" did not need to be "a Marxist-Leninist party" and could remain independent of "those parties".[893] Hence Cuba's support of the Latin American revolution was not dependent on its professed communism. Rather, its support was a show of support for other "autochthonous product[s] of the continent".[894] The urban revolutionaries that enacted many of these insurgencies were not therefore committed to enacting a communist state. However, they were committed to reform, especially when it could procure the support of the peasantry. Unlike the social democrats, that would hypothetically open the 'insurgent' movements to outside, potentially Soviet, support if they were to come to power.

Insurgent groups emerged in several Latin American countries. The clearest examples were in Cuba, Venezuela, Colombia and Guatemala. Colombia's insurgency predates its primary organization, the FARC. The eradication of Gaitainism propelled the communists of the PCC to leadership of the leftist community. In 1961, they took a Castroist line, advocating armed struggle.[895] This armed struggle, as elsewhere in Latin America, was small and focused on protecting the peasantry. The communists formed self-defense groups in rural Colombia that the US and the Colombian National Front viewed as 'insurgencies'. The counter-insurgency operations of 1962, discussed below, were the catalyst for the expanded insurgency and the 1964 establishment of the FARC. The continuing militarization of Guatemala led to the creation of the Revolutionary Movement 13th November (MR13) during 1961.[896] The group was composed of Árbenz-era politicians and military officers, and received the political backing of the Cuban government.[897] The MR13 primarily engaged in ambush attacks in rural areas. By 1962 "Guatemala was descending into exactly the kind of violent Third World revolution that the Kennedy administration had feared".[898] Following Guevara's suggestion, the Venezuelan MIR engaged in a Sierra Maestra-type insurgency in mountainous southern Venezuela from 1960.[899] The MIR received greater support in Caracas than in rural areas. Due to its unique social structure, then, the revolutionary model was ill-defined for Venezuela. The long-term MIR struggle was not met with the level of force witnessed in Colombia. Wickham-Crowley's suggestion of the indiscriminate violence appears correct; the Colombian and Guatemalan insurgencies grew due to government action, while the Venezuelan group stagnated.[900]

Counter-Insurgency

The Kennedy administration oversaw the most significant evolution of US military relations towards Latin America in its history. The policies of counterinsurgency and civic action broke down traditional notions of military aid, military training and national sovereignty. Lesley Gill claims "counterinsurgency warfare fascinated President Kennedy".[901] It was evident that Eisenhower's military support for the Batista regime had failed dramatically in 1958 as the regime had been ineffective and received criticism from both sides of the political spectrum. As a result, Kennedy envisaged a new response to the Castroist insurgencies in Latin America. According to Gaillard, "President Kennedy was responsible for organizing US foreign affairs and national security agencies to guide and assist governments he considered threatened…to resist the threat of communist inspired insurgency".[902] As was the case for the AFP, propaganda was key to the success of counter-insurgency operations. It was important that the Latin American militaries win the admiration of their population. To do this, the US had to coordinate all aspects of their mission. These included direct action, training, civic action and allocating resources based on threats. To this end, Kennedy established a "special group" to coordinate counter-insurgency and civic action policies throughout Latin America.[903] This group was composed of Allen Dulles, Robert Kennedy, Admiral Arleigh Burke and General Maxwell Taylor.[904] The special group coordinated between government agencies to ensure that US funds were directed towards the insurgent threat to US interests. Kennedy's counter-insurgency policies were far more advanced than is traditionally recognized. Within three years, national sovereignty was diminished throughout Latin America and the US was coordinating the struggle against Castroist insurgencies in Latin America.

Counter-insurgency training began at Fort Gulick, Panama, on July 31, 1961.[905] The Kennedy administration oversaw the greatest peacetime expansion of the US Special Forces in its history.[906] These Special Forces became instrumental to Kennedy's regional agenda. In the year preceding the inclusion of the counter-insurgency training course, a battalion of the Seventh Special Forces Group visited Panama. Forty Latin American students attended the first counter-insurgency program at the LAGS.[907] They represented twelve Latin American countries and their ranks ranged from Second Lieutenant to Major.[908] The LAGS was rebranded as the School of the Americas (SOA) in 1963, with an increased enrolment of leading military officials representing the greater role of the military in politics.[909] This phenomenon fed itself indefinitely. While military governments expanded their participation within the SOA, its growth expanded military governments. In addition to military tactics, the students at the SOA were also taught about their Soviet, communist and miscellaneous enemies.[910] It was explained that the enemy was directed from Moscow and posed a permanent threat. The SOA intentionally dehumanized insurgents and peasants. For SOA-trained officers, the insurgents were soldiers loyal to Moscow and enemies of the state. The role of the military was to destroy the insurgency by all means necessary. By distorting the definition of communism to include all progressive movements, the US effectively turned the Latin American militaries against their governments, and eventually their own people, to ensure compliant leaders.

This philosophy blurred the definition of national interest and US interest. Insurgents, unionists, peasants and populist governments were seen to represent a 'foreign' interest, while the army were seen to be patriotic. This situation was most evident following the US-backed coup against Salvador Allende in Chile in 1973. According to a member of the democratic Allende administration, Carlos Prats,

> Many of these [soldiers] have responded to the stereotypes and thoughts were inculcated into them during these courses [at the SOA] and, believing they were liberating the country from the internal enemy, have committed a crime which can only be explained by their ingenious, their ignorance and their political short-sightedness.[911]

Given that the students of the SOA were high-ranking military officials, the indoctrination strategies were widely successful. Those men responsible for foiling democracy held close connections to the US through such training programs. However, the infiltration of the military elite meant little without the support of the soldiers involved in counter-insurgency operations. Accordingly, the expansion of the LAGS into the SOA was accompanied by a training surge by the US Special Forces in Latin America. Between 1962 and 1967, more than six hundred Special Forces officers aided in the expansion of counter-insurgency capabilities within Latin America.[912] The Special Forces were divided into Mobile Training Teams consisting of two Special Forces officers and ten military personnel who were sent "to work with conventional armies, intelligence groups, and paramilitary irregulars".[913]

Civic action altered the role of the military within Latin American politics. US military leaders viewed Latin America's militaries as, "… the guardians of the national interest by replacing a government that is confronted by growing strikes, riots, and terrorism or one that seems to be in danger of being taken over by a resurgence of labor leftists".[914] However, the Latin American peasantry viewed that same military as brutally repressive. Given Washington's preference for a militarized Latin America, under the Mann Doctrine of 1964, public image became increasingly important. Civic action, introduced in 1961, sought to utilize military personnel and equipment to build public infrastructure and utilities that benefited the impoverished masses of Latin America.[915] The military took an active role in the construction of ports, roads, wells, schools, hospitals and housing.[916] These projects brought economic and social benefits to many people. While the improvement of the military's image was significant, it was not the intention of civic action. The US increased the size and capabilities of Latin American militaries in order to disperse those personnel to regional areas threatened by potential 'insurgencies'. By utilizing mass amounts of capital from the AFP and AID, the resources of the Latin American militaries significantly increased.[917] Therefore AID, not MAP, was funding the salaries, training, transport and ammunition of many Latin American militaries.

Both AID and the MAP funded counterinsurgency. The MAP's director, Robert Wood, explained that, "The primary purpose of the proposed fiscal year 1965 Military Assistance Program for Latin America is to counter the threat to the entire area by providing equipment and training which will bolster the internal security capabilities of the recipient countries".[918] The official records show a steep decline in MAP funding. There was a 71 per cent decline in MAP funding from the Eisenhower administration averages to the 1965 fiscal year. MAP funding to democratic Venezuela, Costa Rica and Uruguay was essentially eliminated. This was due to the overlapping of MAP and AID resources through the programs of civic action and counter-insurgency. Federico Gil states, "through AID a public safety program was launched under which Latin American internal security and police forces were provided with a variety of arms and special equipment".[919] US AID resources were heavily intertwined with civil military operations. The Latin American military provided the region with stability. However, improperly applied, military involvement could also led to instability by "alienating the populace" or failing to "deliver basic services".[920] Moreover, US AID provisions were spent on coalition building between the Latin American militaries and the civilians., which was intended to alienate the insurgency movements.

Counter-insurgency operations began in Latin America following Kennedy's inauguration in 1961. After the demise of Trujillo, "Kennedy personally ordered aids" to teach the Dominican police force "riot control techniques".[921] The Dominican situation was a priority for the US, as it was concerned that Castroist forces would infiltrate the Bosch government and so sought to bolster Dominican military security. The largest counter-insurgency force emerged in Colombia in 1964. "Plan Laso" was a sophisticated counter-insurgency operation that targeted the communist-controlled areas of rural Colombia.[922] An estimated 7000 US-trained soldiers destroyed the "independent republic of Marquetalia" in 1964.[923] The CIA also worked closely with the counter-insurgency effort, providing anti-communist propaganda via radio and leaflet drops to the affected areas. The Colombian counter-insurgency effort also emphasized civic action. This was ineffective as it is estimated that the Colombian army killed ten peasants for every insurgent. This type of force was detrimental to government control over rural areas in Colombia. In Venezuela, guerrilla zones were regularly bombed. However, civilian casualties were much lower than in Colombia, as the Venezuelan military initiated "voluntary evacuations" of civilian populations.[924] The Betancourt government attempted to maintain the loyalty of the Venezuelan peasantry, eroding the base for the insurgent movement. The early stages of counter-insurgency in Latin America varied in individual countries. However, the rise of small insurgent movements in virtually every nation of Latin America witnessed an increased military presence in Latin America.

Yet another Regression

Washington prioritized the isolation of Cuba between 1959 and 1962. Once that Castro was ostracized, and the Soviet Union had been demonized, the need for American good-will had ended. The AFP rhetorically encouraged democratic regimes to choose American globalism over Castro's version of communism. With that achieved, their preference for security and stability was resumed. While rhetorically committing to a social and democratic revolution, they privately invited a series of military coups in Peru, Bolivia, Honduras, the Dominican Republic, Brazil and Argentina. They also prevented progressive democratic regimes from coming to power in Guatemala and Chile. The politics of anti-communism, had now also extended into greater South America. Even Uruguay, the most democratic nation in all of Latin America, was threatened by their military in the late 1960s. The powerful anti-communist pretext had now been fulfilled in the hemisphere. US diplomats characterized any attempt at social reform as 'communism', and concluded that military regimes were the only defense from Cuban and Soviet advances. The militaries were bound to the US through training, funding and ideology. The US had firmer control over Latin America than at any previous point by 1965.

Military coups were staged against the democracies of Peru and Bolivia during the early years of Kennedy's AFP. In Peru, President Manuel Prado legalized APRA participation in the 1962 presidential elections.[925] However, the APRA schism had, again, brought suspicions of communist infiltration. While the moderate wing remained under the control of Haya de la Torre, MIR was led by ex-*Aprista* Luis De La Puente.[926] The conservatives promoted the candidacy of Fernando Belaúnde.[927] Despite the forthcoming democratic elections, it was clear that the military would not accept an APRA or MIR victory. One key general warned the US ambassador that those "which originally drank at the communist fountains had changed their political programs in a cynical play for power".[928] On July 18, 1962 the military removed Prado, along with the perceived threat of an APRA victory.[929] The US non-response to events in Peru had indicated that Kennedy's rhetorical support for the AFP philosophy had already ended by mid-1962. Meanwhile, the Bolivian Movement of the National Revolution (MNR) faced opposition from both the left and the right during the 1960s. Their party also split between the older MNR and the pro-Cuban ELN of Medina.[930] On November 4, 1964, the Bolivian army staged a coup against the Estenssoro, and began the persecution of both groups.[931] This was a counter-revolutionary coup against a longstanding constitutional revolutionary regime. Soon after the military assumed power a guerrilla struggle began, with the assistance of Cuban forces. It was in Bolivia, in 1967, that the CIA finally killed Guevara.[932]

Democracy was also eradicated in Honduras and the Dominican Republic during this period. The Honduran example highlights the hypocrisy of the AFP period. Ramón Villeda was an exception within the AFP as he naively believed the AFP charter.[933] He followed the recommendations on agrarian reform despite the fact that it discriminated against most Honduran politicians, who were landholders.[934] He enacted a land reform policy that was strikingly similar to Árbenz's 1951 Decree 900. The military and the oligarchy deposed Villeda on October 3, 1963.[935] While the US, under the AFP, promoted 'democracy,' no condemnation eventuated. On December 14, the US recognized the military regime.[936] The Dominican example highlighted US uncertainty over Latin American democracy. Kennedy's Dominican arithmetic left Juan Bosch in a precarious position. Bosch was an idealistic social democrat. He was not a communist. He believed in political freedoms. He asserted, in 1962, that the PRD would allow the communists to participate in the political sphere, despite his negative views on communism and Castroism.[937] Bosch indicated that there was a disconnect between State Department rhetoric and the American military.[938] He argued that the Ambassador sought to strengthen his regime, while the Pentagon colluded with the Dominican military. The Pentagon won. Bosch believed that "the only group in the [Dominican Republic] that had not been corrupted [was] the masses of the people," but he refused to have the people fight the military to return him to power.[939] In his view, the Dominican Republic had missed the opportunity to develop as the military returned power to the Trujillo family.

The anti-communist pretext and its dictatorial regression continued southward towards Brazil and Argentina. The removal of João Goulart was inevitable in the Cold War context. The US had opposed the governments of Quadros and Goulart due to their sympathy for the Cuban Revolution.[940] The State Department foresaw a "foreign policy orientated increasingly toward the Soviet bloc in world affairs....".[941] Ambassador Gordon asserted that the 1964 coup,

> Can indeed be included along with the Marshall Plan proposal, the Berlin Blockade, the defeat of communist aggression in Korea, and the resolution of the missile crisis in Cuba as one of the major turning points in world history in the middle of the twentieth century.[942]

Gordon saw this as a Cold War victory against the USSR despite the limited communist presence in Brazil. This is evidence of an expanding anti-communist pretext. Meanwhile, in Argentina, Arturo Frondizi's four-year showdown with the Argentine military finally ended with his ousting in 1962. The 'deal' made with Perón in 1958 allowed for the eventual transition of Perónists back into Argentine politics.[943] Frondizi confidently asserted that his economic achievements would undermine the populist policies of Perónism, but as Potash demonstrates, "Frondizi failed to break Perón's hold over the working class".[944] The March 1962 municipal elections demonstrated the power of Perón. In line with his 1958 commitment, he allowed Perónists, under the banner of the *Unión Popular*, to participate in municipal elections.[945] Perónists won ten of the fourteen provincial elections, including Buenos Aires.[946] In response, he attempted to overturn seven of the elections, launch a proactive attack on all communists and permanently ban all signs and symbols of Perón, but nevertheless, the armed forces overthrew Frondizi the following month.[947] The US State Department accepted the outcome of the coup as the military condemned Castro's revolution, yet it also requested immediate elections.[948] The results of the 1963 presidential elections were telling. The blank vote, representing the Perónists, received 19 per cent, while the victor only achieved 25.8 per cent. When Perónists re-joined the system in 1965, their success led to the overthrow of another democratic regime the following year.[949] As Szusterman identifies, "democracy in Argentina was liable to produce the 'wrong' result".[950] For the military, that 'wrong result' was Perón's return. The State Department lumped Perónism within the 'communist line' and provided support for the military under this anti-communist pretext.

The ideological battle lines of the Cold War had been drawn. In addition to justifying the prolonged support for these military coups in Peru, Bolivia, the Dominican Republic, Argentina and Brazil, the US also actively prevented the reemergence of democratic movements in the region. Any government that did not conform to the central themes of anti-communism and free trade economics could not exist in Latin America. There could be no 'second' Castro. The US also actively repressed new left-wing governments that emerged. It stifled progressives in elections in both Chile and Guatemala as the US also fought against the election of the Socialist Salvador Allende in the elections of 1960 and 1964.[951] The most blatant support was given to Eduardo Frei in 1964; the CIA donated US$20 million to his electoral campaign.[952] James Petras asserts that: "US government intervention in Chile in 1964 was blatant and almost obscene" and "an unusual influx of US military personnel into Chile" was also evident prior to the election.[953] The US was motivated by two criteria. Firstly, Allende was viewed as a leftist threat. Secondly, Frei was an adherent to US fiscal policy. This led to vast private investments through the AFP infrastructure. Chile was an ideal ally and the US sought to maintain the status quo by utilizing the anti-communist pretext. The US had promoted 'free' elections in Guatemala in 1963; however, when Arévalo ascended as a returning presidential hopeful, the US' position changed. Arévalo's candidacy brought renewed hope to Guatemalans.[954] He promised to reverse the counter-revolution. On March 31, 1963 the head of the armed forces, General Enrique Peralta Azurdia, seized power from Ydígoras Fuentes, claiming that Arévalo was heading a communist conspiracy in Central America.[955] The US would not, under any circumstances, let another ally fall into hostile hands.

In the grip of a psychosis?

The Cold War dominated regional politics throughout the 1960s. The tragedy of the Latin American Cold War is that the insurgent movements were caused by the prolonged anti-democratic position of the US. If democracy had prevailed within the region then the insurgency of the 1960s would not have eventuated. Fidel Castro exemplifies this point. Without Chibás' 1951 death and the 1952 Batista coup, there would not have been a Sierra Maestra movement in Cuban history. And without Castro many other groups to the left of the social democrats would have continued to follow the constitutional road. Despite this fact, a full-scale Cold War was underway by 1965. The Soviet Union supported the Cuban economy and political system, which provided an alternative program for several Latin American revolutionaries. The threat of the Soviets, then, provided a justification for further militarism. President Johnson asserted that "for the first time in the history of the [OAS], it has created and sent… an international peace keeping military force".[956] While some allied OAS troops were involved in the occupation, this was an American led action. The Cold War changed the notion of warfare in Latin America.

The psychosis that dominated Latin America exacerbated social divisions. The anti-communist pretext created enemies within Latin American societies and politics. The key actors within this struggle included: the landed oligarchy, an emerging capitalist class, the military, middle-class workers, the union movement, democratic political movements, radical insurgent groups and, on the periphery, the communists. This is a complicated social structure that varied in individual nations. To understand the interests of each competing class and organization would require a separate study in and of itself. However, the anti-communist pretext provides a framework. The military forces became hegemonic during this period. They were supported, and funded, by the landed oligarchy, the capitalist class and the US. Those who challenged the position of their funders and supporters were characterized as communist and, in turn, enemies. Under this pretext, a war was waged against the

Latin American people. Any dissident activity was closely monitored and eventually persecuted. The expansion of military capabilities was a direct result of US policy during the 1960s. While the US could not foresee, and often condemned, the human rights abuses that followed, it was responsible for the conditions that motivated them.

By 1965, the Cold War had been institutionalized in Latin America. The doctrine of counter-insurgency, under the pretext of anti-communism, established this conflict. This conflict took place in three Cold War theatres during the 1960s: geopolitical, political-economic and militaristic. The primary struggle against Castroism required a submissive response. Castro's alliance with the USSR allowed the Cubans to exist peacefully. Cuba was, hence, isolated from its geopolitical place in the OAS. Second were the domestic theatres that served the political-economic interests of the US. This 'new regression' allowed for a rapid economic integration of Latin America into the world economic system. The extermination of economic nationalism was caused by military coups. These coups were predicated by loans and grants made possible through the AFP. The final form was direct military intervention. In 1933, Cordell Hull forfeited Washington's right to invade sovereign states. Thirty-two years later, the US reclaimed their militaristic imperial presence in Latin America. Hence, the US had come full circle. While their actions responded to individual circumstances, it is difficult to overlook their overall achievements. In that thirty-two years: the US became the dominant trading nation in the Western Hemisphere; it monopolized the finances of Latin America; it monopolized weapons sales and military training; its businesses flourished; and, most significantly, it had demonized all the opponents to US rule who had forced Hull into his 1933 commitment. The Cold War in Latin America provided Washington with the opportunity to reclaim its dominant position in Latin America. It possessed subservient satellite regimes indoctrinated to the psychosis of anti-communism. This accounts for a more pervasive form of Imperialism than it possessed through 'gunboat diplomacy'.

Conclusion

The notion of a 'Cold' War in Latin America had effectively ended by 1965. The anti-communist paranoia of the era had increased and many of the conflicts transitioned into open warfare. Latin American militaries and oligarchies became increasingly indoctrinated by anti-communism. Conveniently, this rebranded many of their long-standing struggles for political and economic control. By the late 1970s, this prolonged struggle against 'communists', 'insurgents', political opponents, academics, journalists, unions had become a total war. The US could no longer control the anti-communist pretext that it had unleashed. Nor could it control the conflicts that their rhetoric had inflamed. The Central American states of Guatemala, Nicaragua, Panama and El Salvador suffered under military rule that led to violent civil wars.[957] Those civil wars cost an estimated 350,000 lives between 1965 and 1990, while also creating millions of internal refugees.[958] The Sandinista victory in 1979 goaded the Reagan administration into launching a covert 'Contra' war against the government of Daniel Ortega during the 1980s, without congressional or public support or approval.[959] The Caribbean region saw the occupation of the Dominican Republic as well as the invasion of Grenada in October 1983, in an attempt to maintain the isolation of the Cuban Revolution.[960] South America also felt the force of this anti-communist crusade. The militarization of South America following their domestic military coups and the infamous US intervention in Chile, 1973, laid the way for the regional 'Operation Condor'.[961] The military regimes of Chile, Argentina and Uruguay waged a war against their populations under the banner of anti-communism.[962] Condor was a transnational 'dirty-war' against intellectuals, progressives, unions, peasants and anyone who could be characterized as a 'communist'.[963] While these events have received more attention due to their immediate devastation, the direct origins of this anti-communist pretext arose in the era between the 1920s and 1965. The effects of this sustained propaganda campaign were these hot wars of Latin America that were waged between 1965 and 1990.

Social Democracy and the Myth of Soviet Communism

The social democratic movement, that emerged in Latin America during the 1930s, was a definable phenomenon with transnational significance. The leaders of this movement have often been relegated within their respective national histories. However, there is a clear ideological correlation between the movements for social democracy in Latin America between 1933 and 1965. Their leaders – Ramón Grau, Eduardo Chibás, and Carlos Prío in Cuba, Rómulo Betancourt in Venezuela, Víctor Raúl Haya de la Torre in Peru, Jorge Eliécer Gaitán in Colombia, Lázaro Cárdenas in Mexico, José Figueres Ferrer in Costa Rica, Juan José Arévalo and Jacobo Árbenz in Guatemala, and Juan Bosch in the Dominican Republic and the movements that they represented – all shared a common ideology. Chibás defined their ideology as "nationalism, socialism and anti-Imperialism".[964] This expressed itself in policies including economic nationalism, education, healthcare, labor reform, land reform and social security. These policies are usually defined within the European political tradition of social democracy, but are also present within the American New Deal. Programs for social democracy are evident throughout the developed world. It is the standing ideology of all parties of the democratic left, including Labor parties. Their emergence in the Latin American struggle for democracy is of historical significance.

Social democrats seek to bring a moderate form of socialism to their societies through the government regulation and income redistribution of high taxation, big government and social services. This was at times evident in Latin America between 1933 and 1965. In forging coalitions with workers and peasants, the Latin Americans were creating a more equitable society and bringing modernity to the hemisphere. Others have suggested that these politicians were mere 'populists'. That is, that their policies were designed to procure maximum support from the urban and rural poor, and that the leaders held no strong ideological convictions. While each of these leaders were somewhat motivated by personal political ambitions, this stance overlooks the participation of sectors of the 'under-classes' within the social democratic program. It also overlooks the fact that these leaders clung to their vision through times of intense hardship, including persecution and exile. Populist leaders routinely alter their ideological stance on the basis of political events. This makes the personal and political sacrifice of the generation of social democratic leaders distinct from populist leaders like Juan Perón and Getulio Vargas. They developed a Latin American variation of a common European ideology designed to deliver incremental social progress without the violence associated with communist or other radical revolutions. Significantly, they kept that vision through their lives and continued their struggles against the military, oligarchy and foreign interests.

A brief biography of the social democratic leaders and their associated movements has demonstrated the correlations, both ideological and chronological, between the social democratic leaders. Several factors bind this group together. The class and educational origins of these leaders were a significant contributor to their adoption of social democratic theory. Most of these leaders were middle-upper class: Betancourt's family owned cattle ranches in Southern Venezuela; Ramón Grau descended from an aristocratic tobacco growing family; Arévalo studied abroad, becoming a professor of philosophy in Buenos Aires prior to his return to Guatemala; while Haya de la Torre, Figueres, Bosch and Gaitán all received family support to go to university. This set them apart from the class of people whose interests they represented. Moreover, the social democrats were middle-class revolutionaries who sought to evolve the political system for both personal and ideological reasons. Their ideologies were developed while studying classical European political ideas in American and European universities. While these ideas would have likely included the remote theory of Marxism, social democracy was also seen as an adaptation of liberalism. Their preference for the notions liberalism and socialism were fostered by the oppressive dictatorships they lived under. Each of these leaders reached physical and political maturity during times of oppression. Their circumstances shaped the central tenet of their movement, the anti-dictatorial struggle. Hence, this freedom from tyranny became the central ideal of their social democracy. This made them hostile the central idea of 'communism', the dictatorship of the proletarian. These leaders were similar in their upbringing, their education and their political situation. This shaped the views of those who created the Latin American social democratic movement.

The policies of economic nationalism were characterized within the 'communist line' by the US. Economic nationalism emphasized serving the interests of the nation over that of foreign empires, both formal and informal. It required the strict regulation of their market economies in order to gradually increase the quality of life of the citizenry. The Latin American version of this philosophy emerged during the 1930s in Mexico. The presidency of Lázaro Cárdenas saw the expropriation of the vast majority of foreign-owned agricultural property and, more significantly, the foreign-owned oil reserves. Mexico also created the platforms for agrarian reform, market reform and labor reform. These actions set the precedent for those emerging social democratic regimes of the 1940s. Expropriation of land and resources was emulated in Venezuela and Guatemala. Market reform was emulated in Peru. Meanwhile, labor reforms were enacted throughout the social democratic regimes. The social democratic governments of the 1940s were engaged in a moderate revolution that swung the balance of power from the ruling oligarchic class towards the urban and rural poor. Unfortunately for those leaders embracing this moderate form of socialism, the global Cold War emerged in the 1940s. This effectively meant that their reforms were viewed within the context of that Cold War. Hence, they were required to abandon the reforms that the US characterized as 'the communist line'. In its dealing with Mexico in 1949, the communist line was defined as "any radical ideas they disapproved of".[965] This demonized their moderate actions of economic nationalists, undermining their potential and relegating their achievements to historical and economic irrelevancy.

Social democracy posed a significant challenge to US global interests in the aftermath of WWII, from which it emerged as the undisputed victor. It had reshaped the international system, including its economy. The European empires had been dismantled and the US stood as the leader of the capitalist world. This reality was pervasive in Latin America. Prior to the Great Depression, the US had not held a dominant economic position in greater Latin America. British and German trade and investment was significant throughout South America, while the US focused on the small Caribbean plantation states. The political effects of WWII brought Latin America into Washington's sphere of influence for the first time. However, the rhetoric of the Atlantic Charter and Four Freedoms masked its political and economic ambitions. With the closure of markets in Eastern Europe in 1945 and China in 1949, the US placed increased emphasis on its economic interaction with Latin America. Unfortunately for the burgeoning social democratic movement, and those populists in Argentina and Brazil, the US philosophy of free trade liberalism was in direct competition to their policies of economic nationalism. The great irony was that the US emerged to economic dominance through economic nationalism. Their neighbors would not experience that luxury. While the Guatemalan case provided the most glaring example of the US interfering in the domestic economy of a sovereign democratic state, it was not unique. During the late 1940s, the US waged economic warfare against the populist government of Argentina.[966] It ensured that Argentina would remain a poor appendage of the capitalist system by blocking finance and markets within Europe and isolating

Argentinean goods within inter-American trade. The US was threatened by economic nationalism as it conflicted with its national interest. While Latin America decreased in global political significance throughout the 1950s and 1960s, due to the decolonization of Asia and Africa, it provided the economic platform for the US to become the global hegemon between the 1920s and 1950.

These social democrats were not communists. This book has provided research into the Latin American communist movement that demonstrates the peripheral nature of Marxism. Communism is a revolutionary philosophy that involves the violent overthrow of a society and establishment of military dictatorship to create class equity. This requires the dismantling of all sectors of government and the capitalist class. The Moscow-orientated parties of Latin America were never able to gain support for this vision. Even those quasi-communist revolutions in Cuba and Nicaragua preached an evolutionary economic program and emerged independently of the formal communist parties. The social democrats advocated an evolutionary response to economic challenges. Similar to their European counterparts, they sought to bring about socialism through slow pragmatic changes that were supported by the majority of the population. These changes improved the lives of the rural and urban poor to a level sufficient enough to gain support and protect their coalitions. The fatal flaw in Latin America, when compared to post-war Western Europe, was the reactionary response to these evolutionary changes by the oligarchic class, the military and the US. Europeans were allowed, by the US, to follow this path under the Marshall Plan; Latin Americans were not. That harsh reality accounts for their failure and their historical obscurity.

The Anti-communist Pretext as the Convenient Enemy

The use of anti-communist propaganda was an intentional mechanism to destabilize governments that confronted US regional interests. This preceded any notion of a Cold War in broader Latin America. America's disdain for progressive politics had created a prolonged paranoia around the term 'communism'. Anti-communist characterizations were levied at: Mexico and Nicaragua in 1927 by Frank Kellogg; APRA in 1931 by Fred Dearing; the PCR-A in 1933-4 by Sumner Welles; Colombian Gaitánistas in 1948 by George C Marshall; Guatemala's democracy in 1954 by John F. Dulles; Peruvian and Venezuelan protesters in 1958 by Richard M. Nixon; and the Dominican Democrats led by Juan Bosch in 1965, leading to Lyndon Johnson's invasion. Moreover, anti-communism was a longstanding philosophy of American diplomats in Latin America. As has been demonstrated, accusations of anti-communism were not only levied at communist parties and associated organizations but also came to include the social democratic movement, and even some right-wing populists. This was an effective pretext as 'communism' was seen as a foreign ideology that posed a threat to Latin American sovereignty.

The US brought the Cold War to Latin America from April 9, 1948. The period preceding the Colombian Bogotázo witnessed a democratic revolution in Latin America. Ten dictatorial governments fell to democratic advocates between 1941 and 1948. This left only five military regimes administering the twenty Latin American republics that existed in early 1948. While social gains were limited and short-lived in Haiti, El Salvador and Honduras, social democratic governments were established in Guatemala, Cuba, Venezuela, Peru and Costa Rica.[967] Additionally, elections in Brazil and Argentina consolidated the gains of those military populist leaders.[968] Moreover, a democratic revolution swept through Latin America during this period. This democratic revolution posed a unique threat to American interests in the hemisphere, as explained above. Hence, when the Colombian *Bogotázo* erupted in response to Gaitán's assassination on April 9, 1948, the US Secretary of State, George C. Marshall, created a calculated anti-communist pretext in Latin America. While in Bogotá for the first meeting of the OAS during the *Bogotázo*, he posited that the domestic unrest was intertwined with the global Cold War that the US was waging in Eurasia. Despite Marshall's department keeping extensive records on Gaitán's movement, and acknowledging that neither he, nor his followers, were communists, Marshall concluded that events in Colombia must be seen within the context of the global Cold War. This calculated falsification led the OAS delegations to commit to condemn regional communism.

This book has explained how this anti-communist pretext evolved into doctrine between 1948 and 1950. Following the establishment of this pretext in April 1948, the gains made by democrats were reversed. Conservative military coups occurred in Peru, Venezuela, Cuba, Colombia, Haiti, Paraguay and Argentina between 1948 and 1955. Additionally, the US overthrew the Guatemalan government and the Brazilian President, Getúlio Vargas, committed suicide while enduring the threat of a military coup. This regional regression was motivated by an altered stance on democracy within the US State Department. Cold War pragmatists overtook the Latin American Bureau of the US State Department during the McCarthyist crusade of the second Truman administration. This caused an abandonment of the pro-democratic vision of Latin America held by the moderate Spruille Braden. Cold War realpolitik replaced "Bradenism" in the aftermath of Bogota. Following the extensive reports into Latin American democracy and the communist threat authored by George Kennan, Louis Halle and Francis Truslow, the US Undersecretary of State for Inter-American Affairs, George Miller, enacted an anti-communist doctrine, which favored Latin American military regimes as a regional bulwark against an advancing 'communist' threat. While the 'communist' threat included progressive thinkers, such as social democrats, the Latin American militaries quickly seized upon the promise of international recognition granted by Washington's anti-democratic stance. These military governments opened their intelligence files to the CIA on democrats and communists alike. They also actively persecuted individuals posing threats to their longevity and US interests in the region. While the US was only actively involved in Guatemala, it was implicitly involved in all of the military coups as it began the regional regression against democracy through the pretext of anti-communism.

The Cuban Revolution altered the notion of the 'Cold War' in Latin America between 1959 and 1965. The Sierra Maestra movement was the pinnacle of a regional backlash against dictatorial governance in Latin America, rather than a unique outlier. Once again, between 1956 and 1961 ten dictatorial leaders succumbed to more progressive forces. Cuba, however, was unique. It had an armed revolution that allied the interests of middle-class urban revolutionaries with the rural peasantry through guerrilla warfare. Castro's ideas originated within the social democratic tradition, however, he became frustrated by its leaders' inability to enact meaningful reform or assert independence from the US. Hence, he followed Chibás into the breakaway organization of the *Ortodoxos*, which was further radicalized by Chibás' death in 1951 and the Batista coup of 1952. This radicalization process led to the development of a revolutionary cadre which, after their failed assault on the Mocada Barracks in 1953, sought to overthrow the Batista regime. The Castro movement was underestimated by every sector. Social democrats, both in Cuba and in greater Latin America, supported it, believing that Castro would restore democracy and pragmatic reform. The US did not believe that a domestic revolution could challenge its position in Latin America until its victory was assured in late 1958. The Soviet Union thought little of Castro's attempts as it had avoided acting in America's sphere of influence prior to 1960. However, during 1959 and 1960 Castro changed politics in Latin

America. He distanced himself from the social democrats and drew closer to Marxism, despite his loathing of the Cuban Moscow-orientated party. The regional euphoria for Castro's revolution led young discontents in Latin America to attempt to emulate his efforts. Throughout the region, the social democratic movement splintered as radical wings turned to armed struggle, in certain cases against their former leaders. While Castro did not begin as a communist, he did change the approach to socialism in Latin America. The constitutional road was replaced by a group of violent insurgencies that shook Latin America between 1961 and 1965. These insurgencies were still not led by communists, but by urban discontents of the social democratic movement.

This book has advocated for a thorough revision of Cold War historiography. It does not claim to be a holistic revision of the Cold War in Latin America. Instead, it has used selected case studies to demonstrate the emergence of a social democratic movement and a sustained American led campaign against it. It has challenged many assumptions, including that: the Latin American Cold War was a proxy theatre of the global struggle; communists were the primary target of anti-communism; the US believed there was a genuine communist menace in the *Bogotázo*; Guatemala was an isolated Cold War error made by the Eisenhower administration; Latin America, as a region, was ever in danger of turning 'communist'; the Cold War began in 1959, with the Cuban Revolution; the insurgent movements were led by Moscow; and that the US wanted to support change through its Alliance for Progress. This book has brought together many narratives to support its central arguments. Yet it has also left several areas open to reinterpretation. This reinterpretation is necessary to a thorough understanding of the Cold War in Latin America. There is a lack of revisionist history in this area beyond the central case studies of Guatemala, Cuba, Chile and Nicaragua. The Latin American Cold War cost hundreds of thousands of lives and created millions of refugees. A revision of its causes is significant to understanding this generational conflict and to preventing a twenty-first century reoccurrence.

This book has also offered a revision of the events that contributed to the Cold War in Latin America, the most violent period in the region's twentieth century history. It has highlighted rhetoric and propaganda. In many ways, the Latin American Cold War emerged through anti-communist propaganda. The mischaracterization of democratic leaders led to two widespread military regressions in Latin America between 1948 and 1965. Latin American history contains several dictatorial-democratic cycles. It would not, therefore, be wise to say that every coup was directly motivated by the US and its version of anti-communism. However, there is a distinct pattern in the causes and timing of dozens of military coups. The domestic militaries definitely exploited the anti-communism as a pretext for coups that they may have undertaken anyway. Ultimately, this is the point. The US created a climate in which the Latin American conservative militaries could remove progressive democratic governments and, in turn, receive US diplomatic and financial support for doing so. While many of these coups may have occurred under the auspices of a different pretext, or simply due to domestic circumstances, the explicit support granted by the US for anti-communist coups is a definitive pattern. The US swung the pendulum in favor of the conservative militaries against the social democrats under the pretext of anti-communism. This was the principal battleground of the Latin American Cold War. The struggle encompassed far more than the famous Cold War battlegrounds of Guatemala, Cuba, Chile and Nicaragua. It was a continental struggle between distinct visions for the region's participation within the global capitalist economy. The US propagated one vision. In doing so, they condoned and supported several military regimes that oppressed their populations.

Finally, this book has provided a historical lens through which to view the political movements of modern Latin America. It has demonstrated the nature of the struggle between two ideological visions. This struggle re-emerged after the Cold War. Once again, propaganda was used to discredit the reform regimes of Venezuela, Bolivia, Ecuador, Nicaragua, Honduras, Argentina and Paraguay. This propaganda highlighted the use of socialism that 'unfairly' targeted the wealthier elements of Latin American society. The US and conservative media sources characterized these leaders as a violent minority that were harming their societies. This propaganda has seriously damaged each of those reform regimes, with the downfall of leaders in Honduras, Paraguay, and most recently, Bolivia, while also the significant weakening of the others, and the creation of chaos in Venezuela. This demonstrates a historical correlation to the Cold War. Propaganda allowed the US to reshape Latin America in its service during the Cold War. This pattern of foreign policy by way of propaganda has re-emerged in recent years. Hence, this remains relevant, as George Santayana famously uttered, "those who cannot remember the past are condemned to repeat it".[969]

Notes

Introduction

1   This research has chosen to categorize the 20 former Spanish and Portuguese colonies that had achieved independence prior to 1900 as "Latin America". This obviously does not include the decolonized former subjects of Britain, the Netherlands and France that come into existence during the study period.

2   S Padgett and W Paterson, *A history of Social Democracy in Europe,* 1.

3   T Meyer, *The Theory of Social Democracy,* 16.

4   S Padgett and W Paterson, *A history of Social Democracy in Europe.*

5   B Ames, *Political Survival,* 7.

6   M Gonzalez, *The Mexican Revolution,* 222-235.

7   S Stein, *Populism in Peru,* 162-163.

8   C Ameringer, *The Cuban Democratic Experience,* 44.

9   D Hellinger, *Venezuela,* 51.

10   H Braun, *The Assassination of Gaitán,* 60.

11   M Leffler, *The Specter of Communism,* 12.

12   W Williams, *The Tragedy of American Diplomacy,* 48-53.

13   S Niblo, *War Diplomacy and Development,* 231.

14   *Ibid.,* 231.

15   M Leffler, *The Specter of Communism,* 15.

16   P Boyle, *Eisenhower,* 21.

17   C Belfrage, *The American Inquisition.*

18   B Wood, *The making of the Good Neighbor Policy,* 20.

19   S Stein, *Populism in Peru,* 172.

20   C Ameringer, *The Cuban Democratic Experience*, 9.

21   S Randall, *Colombia and the United States*, 189.

22   D Hellinger, *Venezuela*, 57.

23   E Galeano, *Open Veins of Latin America*, 1-6.

24   M Brown, *Rethinking British Informal Empire in Latin America*, 29-35.

25   J Dunkerley, *The long war*, 7.

26   E Woodward, *Three studies in European conservatism*, 1-9.

27   *Ibid.*, 5.

28   J Henderson, *Conservative though in twentieth century Latin America*, 6.

29   T Di Tella, *The history of political parties in twentieth century Latin America*.

30   E Fawcett, *Liberalism*, 1-9.

31   *Ibid.*, 11.

32   L Hobhouse, *Liberalism*; M Weber and J Dreijmanis, *Max Webers's complete writing on academic and political vocations.*   .

33   W Grampp, *Economic liberalism*, 167.

34   J Peeler, *Building democracy in Latin America*, 36.

35   *Ibid.*, 36.

36   C Marichal, *Nation building and banking in Latin America*, 339-355.

37   F Chevalier, 'The roots of Caudilloism', 27-33.

38   W Lafeber, *Inevitable Revolutions*, 22-41.

39   *Ibid.*, 22-41.

40   E Tatum, *The United States and Europe, 1815-1823*, 251.

41   A Knight, "Rethinking British Informal Empire in Latin America", 33.

42   O Martínez, *The Great Land Grab*, 25

43   J Schroeder, *Mr. Polk's War*, 6.

44   *Ibid.*, 147.

45   K Bermann, *Under the big stick*, 53.

46   O'Brian, "Copper Kings of the Americas", 201.

47   *Ibid.*, 170-260.

48   W Williams, *The Tragedy of American Diplomacy*, 48-53.

49   L Davis and R Cull, *International capital markets and American economic growth*, 79.

50   *Ibid.*, 81.

51   L Aguilar, "Cuba: The Platt Amendment", 159-166.

52   R Ginger, *The age of excess*, 250.

53   T Roosevelt, "Corollary to the Monroe Doctrine".

54   *Ibid.*

55   *Ibid.*

56   For the 1903 Dominican intervention see, E Curry, *Hoover's Dominican Diplomacy and the origins of the Good Neighbor Policy*; For the 1903 Venezuelan intervention see, B McBeth, *Gunboats, corruption and claims*; For the 1911 Nicaraguan intervention see, A Crawley, *Somoza and Roosevelt*, 1-21; For the 1911 Honduran intervention see, R MacCameron, *Bananas, labor and politics in Honduras*.

57   R Alexander, *Prophets of the Revolution*, 19-24.

58   *Ibid.*, 19-27.

59   G Pendle, *Uruguay*, 41.

60   M Vanger, *Uruguay's Battle y Ordonez*. It should be noted that Vanger is somewhat critical of this glorified interpretation of Ordonez's contribution to Uruguayan democracy and social reform. Despite that, one can at least see the framework established by Ordonez through his work.

61   T Di Tella, *The History of Latin American Political Parties*, 35.

62   *Ibid.*, 36-37.

63   A López, *José Marti and the future of Cuban Nationalisms*, 24.

64   P Turton, *José Marti*, 63.

65   *Ibid.*, 63.

66   L Aguilar, *Marxism in Latin America*, 6.

Chapter 1

67   P Newell, *Zapata*, 9-26; A Rolls, *Emiliano Zapata*, 27-44.

68   E Zapata in A Gilly, *The Mexican Revolution*, 153.

69   P Garner, *Porfirio Diaz*.

70   *Ibid.,* 168-171.

71   L Davis and R Cull, *International capital markets and American economic growth*, 81.

72   R Anderson, *Mexico*, 517.

73   J Hart, *Revolutionary Mexico*, 240.

74   *Ibid*, 241.

75   F Tannenbaum, *The Mexican agrarian revolution*, 163.

76   A Rolls, *Emiliano Zapata*, 110.

77   A Gilly, *The Mexican Revolution*, 162.

78   *Ibid.,* 161-167

79   A Brenner, *The Wind that swept Mexico*, 55.

80   M Gonzalez, *The Mexican Revolution*, 172.

81   Mexico, *The Constitution of Mexico*.

82   *Ibid.,* 11-29.

83   Although not Zapata himself.

84   Mexico, *The Constitution of Mexico*, 3-35.

85   *Ibid.,* 22-39.

86   *Ibid.,* 134-139.

87   A Brenner, *The Wind that swept Mexico*, 53.

88   Mexico, *The Constitution of Mexico*, 11-39, 134-139.

89   *Ibid.,* 29-35.

90   L Schoultz, *Beneath the United States*, 214.

91   F Tannenbaum, *The Mexican agrarian Revolution*, 165.

92   A Gilly, *The Mexican Revolution*, 223.

93   *Ibid.,* 223.

94   C Hughes in C Blasier, *The hovering giant*, 116.

95   C Blasier, *The hovering giant*, 116-119.

96   *Ibid.*, 117.

97   R Henig, *The League of Nations*, 15-19.

98   W Cohen, *Empire without tears*, 18.

99   A Schales, *Coolidge*, 196.

100 K Bermann, *Under the big stick*, 163.

101 P Chapman, *Jungle capitalists*, 61-71.

102 *Ibid.*, 61-71.

103 S Kinzer, *Overthrow*, 60.

104 M Bucheli and R Aguilar, *Political survival, energy politics and multinational corporations*, 362-370.

105 *Ibid*, 362-370.

106 T O'Brien, *Copper kings of the Americas*, 205.

107 F Fejes, *Imperialism, media and the good neighbor*, 23.

108 G Grandin, *Fordlandia*.

109 W Newton, *The perilous sky*, 141.

110 F Fejes, *Imperialism, media and the good neighbor*, 18.

111 D Steward, *Trade and hemisphere*, 4.

112 M Francis, *The Limits of Hegemony*, 27.

113 M Friedman, *Nazis and the good neighbor*, 84.

114 J Jonker and J Luiten van Zander, *A history of Royal Dutch Shell*, 244-250,

115 W Cohen, *Empire without tears*, 23.

116 C Hull, cited in J Dunkerley, *Warriors and Scribes*, 140.

117 M Bucheli, *Bananas and business, 132.*

118 R Service, *Lenin,* 391-400.

119 For example, Edward Bernays led a campaign to legitimize Lithuanian independence in 1919. L Tye, *The Father of Spin*, 55.

120 K Marx and F Engels, *The Communist Manifesto.*

121 M Cabellero, M Caballero, *Latin America and the Comintern*, 27.

122 R Alexander, *Communism in Latin America*, 93, 136, 154, 177, 319.

123 L Aguilar, *Marxism in Latin America*, 8-11.

124 R Alexander, *Communism in Latin America*.

125 K Marx, *The Communist Manifesto*.

126 L Aguilar, *Marxism in Latin America*, 24-31.

127 R Alexander, *International Labor Organizations and organized labor in Latin America*, 49.

128 L Aguilar, *Marxism in Latin America*, 11.

129 M Caballero, *Latin America and the Comintern*, 27.

130 *Ibid.*, 27.

131 M Leffler, *The Specter of Communism*, 1-25.

132 L Haas, *Argentina*, 19; Alexander, *International Labor Organizations and organized labor in Latin America*; M Leffler, *The Specter of Communism*, 14.

133 *Ibid.*, 15.

134 F Kellogg in B Wood, *The making of the good neighbor policy*, 20.

135 *Ibid.*, 20.

136 *Ibid.*, 20.

137 B Ames, *Survival Coalitions*, 9.

138 F Pike, *The Politics of the Miraculous*, 24.

139 *Ibid.*, 25.

140 F Pike, *The Politics of the Miraculous*, 26.

141 C Graham, Peru's APRA, 27.

142 R Alexander, *Communism in Latin America*, 222.

143 S Stein, *Populism in Peru,*140.

144 F Pike, *The Politics of the Miraculous*, 47.

145 *Ibid.*, 49.

146 C Graham, Peru's APRA, 23.

147 S Stein, *Populism in Peru*, 150.

148 R Alexander, *Rómulo Betancourt and the transformation of Venezuela*, 21.

149 *Ibid.*, 22.

150 *Ibid.*, 22.

151 *Ibid.*, 31.

152 *Ibid.*, 36.

153 *Ibid.*, 37.

154 *Ibid.*, 42-43.

155 S Wright, "Ramón Grau San Martin", 197.

156 *Ibid*, 197.

157 *Ibid*, 197.

158 L Aguilar, "Cuba: The Platt Amendment", 159-166.

159 L Aguilar, *Cuba 1933*, 59.

160 *Ibid.,* 60.

161 *Ibid.,* 66.

162 Cited in L Aguilar, *Cuba,* 67.

163 J Suchlicki, *University students and revolution in Cuba,* 26.

164 *Ibid.,* 26.

165 *Ibid.,* 22-34.

166 *Ibid.,* 30-36.

167 C Ameringer, *The Cuban Democratic Experience,* 44.

168 F Safford and M Palacious, *Colombia,* 250.

169 R Sharpless, Gaitán of Colombia, 30.

170 *Ibid.,* 31.

171 H Braun, *The Assassination of Gaitán,*47.

172 R Sharpless, Gaitán of Colombia, 34.

173 H Braun, *The Assassination of Gaitán,*48.

174 *Ibid.,* 49.

175 *Ibid.,* 56.

176 *Ibid.,* 57.

Chapter 2

177 R Grau in S Adler, *The uncertain giant*, 110.

178 R Gellman, *Good Neighbor Diplomacy*, 7.

179 R Biles, *A new deal for the American people*, 11.

180 F Roosevelt, "Inaugural address".

181 *Ibid.*,

182 C Hull in R Gellman, *Good Neighbor Diplomacy*, 29.

183 B Wood, *The making of the Good Neighbor Policy*, 120.

184 W Lafeber, *The Panama Canal*, 68.

185 D Steward, *Trade and hemisphere*, 1-27.

186 C Hull, *The memoirs of Cordell Hull vol. 1*, 320.

187 D Steward, *Trade and hemisphere*, 4.

188 R Bauer, *American business and public policy*, 26.

189 D Steward, *Trade and hemisphere*, 68.

190 S Randall, *Colombia and the United State*, 111.

191 J Osterling, *Democracy in Colombia*, 80.

192 W Williams, *The Tragedy of American Diplomacy*, 130.

193 K Grieb, *Guatemalan Caudillo*, 48.

194 J Aybar de Soto, *Dependency and Intervention*, 77.

195 K LaCharité, R Kennedy and P Thienal, *Case study in insurgency and revolutionary warfare*, 17.

196 D Steward, *Trade and hemisphere*, 215-240.

197 R Bauer, *American business and public policy*, 26.

198 G Grandin, *Empire's Workshop*, 36.

199 W Townsend, *Lazaro Cardenas*, 10.

200 *Ibid.*, 13.

201 *Ibid.*, 14.

202 *Ibid.*, 19-26.

203 *Ibid.*, 24.

204 *Ibid.*, 26.

205 *Ibid.*, 43.

206 *Ibid.*, 62.

207 M Gonzalez, *The Mexican Revolution*, 223.

208 J Dwyer, "The end of US intervention in Mexico", 495-510.

209 M Gonzalez, *The Mexican Revolution*, 235.

210 *Ibid.*, 235.

211 *Ibid.*, 242.

212 L Cardenas in J Britton, *Redefining Interventionism*, 50.

213 F Pike, *FDR's Good Neighbor Policy*, 193.

214 G Gereffi and D Wyman, *Manufacturing miracles*, 307.

215 L Aguilar, *Cuba*, 122.

216 *Ibid.*, 175.

217 B Welles, *Sumner Welles*, 171.

218 L Aguilar, *Cuba*, 224.

219 S Stein, *Populism in Peru*, 163.

220 *Ibid.*, 163.

221 *Ibid.*, 162.

222 *Ibid.*, 172.

223 *Ibid.*, 188.

224 T Di Tella, *The History of Latin American Political Parties*, 59.

225 W Green, *Gaitánism, Left-Liberalism, and popular mobilization in Colombia*, 72-76.

226 *Ibid.*, 72-76.

227 *Ibid.*, 72-76.

228 *Ibid.*, 75.

229 S Randall, *Colombia and the United States*, 66.

230 D Hellinger, *Venezuela*, 51.

231 S Ellner, "Venezuela", 727

232 D Hellinger, *Venezuela*, 54.

233 *Ibid.*, 57.

234 H Peterson, *Argentina and the United States*, 389.

235 F Fejes, *Imperialism, Media and the Good Neighbor*, 67.

236 S Lamas, cited in B Wood, *The making of the Good Neighbor Policy*, 17.

237 S Welles, cited in R Gellman, *Good Neighbor Diplomacy*, 74.

238 Inter-American States, "Declaration of Lima".

239 C Hull, *The memoirs of Cordell Hull vol. 2*, 1139.

240 J Bratzel, "Introduction", 8.

241 R Gellman, *Good Neighbor Diplomacy*, 134.

242 J Child, *Unequal Alliance*, 28.

243 J Jones, cited in R Gellman, *Good Neighbor Diplomacy*, 162.

244 FEAC, 3-7.

245 R Gellman, *Good Neighbor Diplomacy*, 157.

246 *Ibid.*, 167.

247 *Ibid.*, 157.

248 *Ibid.*, 158.

249 *Ibid.*, 198.

Chapter 3

250 S Kinzer, *Overthrow*, 131.

251 F Roosevelt in R Gellman, *Good Neighbor Diplomacy*, 157.

252 C O'Sullivan, *Sumner Welles, post-war planning and the quest for a new world order*, 51.

253 *Ibid.*, 47.

254 F Roosevelt, "The Four Freedoms Speech".

255 *Ibid.*,

256 *Ibid.,*

257 *Ibid.,*

258 L Shoup and W Minter, *Imperial Brain Trust.*

259 *Ibid.,* 141.

260 R Schulzinger, *The wise men of foreign affairs,* 59-65.

261 L Shoup and W Minter, *Imperial Brain Trust,* 126.

262 *Ibid.,* 122.

263 *Ibid.,* 162.

264 *Ibid.,* 167.

265 C Mee, *The Marshall Plan,* 258.

266 G Smith, *The Last Years of the Monroe Doctrine,* 44.

267 While Batista was elected as constitutional President in 1940, his authoritarian rule between 1934 and 1940, and again between 1952 and 1959 places him within this category.

268 G Black, *The Good Neighbor,* 61; C Ameringer, *The Socialist Impulse,* 9-22.

269 W Lafeber, *Inevitable Revolutions,* 85-100; M Trouillot, *Haiti,* 102-106.

270 R Cruz, *Costa Rica,* 280-295.

271 J Arévalo, *Anti-Kommunism in Latin America,* 35.

272 R Betancourt, cited in C Ameringer, *The Democratic Left in exile,* 52.

273 C Ameringer, *The Caribbean Legion,* 11.

274 S Braden, *Diplomats and demagogues,* 316.

275 G Dorm, *Bradenism and beyond,* 63.

276 M Rapoport, "Argentina", 116.

277 S Braden, *Diplomats and demagogues,* 316.

278 G Dorm, *Bradenism and beyond,* 74; M Rapoport, "Argentina", 123.

279 C Ameringer, *The Cuban Democratic Experience,* 15.

280 *Ibid.,* 17.

281 *Ibid.,* 18.

282 *Ibid.,* 18.

283 *Ibid.,* 21.

284 *Ibid.,* 21.

285 *Ibid.,* 22.

286 F Castro, *My Life,* 83.

287 *Ibid.,* 99.

288 N Haworth, "Peru", 177.

289 *Ibid.,* 176.

290 G Betrum, "Peru 1930-60", 402.

291 *Ibid,* 427; P Klaren, *Peru,* 285.

292 R Alexander, *Rómulo Betancourt and the transformation of Venezuela,* 114.

293 *Ibid.,* 115.

294 *Ibid.,* 125.

295 *Ibid.,* 125.

296 P Parkman, *Non-violent insurrection in El Salvador,* 22.

297 *Ibid.,* 35.

298 R MacCameron, *Bananas, labor and politics in Honduras,* 17.

299 *Ibid.,* 17.

300 K Grieb, *Guatemalan Caudillo, the regime of Jorge Ubico,* 272.

301 *Ibid.,* 272.

302 C Ameringer, *The Democratic Left in exile,* 52.

303 K Grieb, *Guatemalan Caudillo, the regime of Jorge Ubico,* 277.

304 *Ibid.,* 279.

305 S Schlesinger and S Kinzer, *Bitter Fruit,* 35.

306 P Gleijeses, *Shattered Hope,* 32.

307 *Ibid,* 32.

308 *Ibid.,* 34.

309 *Ibid.,* 38.

310 *Ibid.,* 38.

311 S Schlesinger and S Kinzer, *Bitter Fruit*, 35.

312 J Aybar de Soto, *Dependency and Intervention*, 150.

313 *Ibid.*, 150.

314 P Gleijeses, *Shattered Hope*, 51.

315 S Schlesinger and S Kinzer, *Bitter Fruit*, 40.

316 *Ibid.*, 44.

317 *Ibid.*, 95.

318 C Ameringer, *The Caribbean Legion*, 9.

319 P Gleijeses, "Juan José Arévalo and the Caribbean Legion", 135.

320 C Ameringer, *The Caribbean Legion*, 95.

321 P Gleijeses, "Juan José Arévalo and the Caribbean Legion", 134.

322 P Gleijeses, *Shattered Hope*, 111.

323 C Ameringer, *The Caribbean Legion*, 12-25.

324 *Ibid.*, 27-30.

325 P Gleijeses, "Juan José Arévalo and the Caribbean Legion", 135.

326 C Ameringer, *The Caribbean Legion*, 52.

327 *Ibid.*, 45-51.

328 C Ameringer, *Don Pepe*, 5.

329 *Ibid.*, 5.

330 *Ibid.*, 6.

331 *Ibid.*, 7.

332 *Ibid.*, 7.

333 *Ibid.*, 14-21.

334 *Ibid.*, 23.

335 *Ibid.*, 43.

336 *Ibid.*, 66.

337 *Ibid.*, 67.

Chapter 4

338 H Braun, *The Assassination of Gaitán*, 63.

339 *Ibid.*, 134.

340 M Moore, *Know your enemy*, 61.

341 The Soviets condoned the 1948 communist overthrow of Czechoslovakia in 1948: J Gaddis, *The Cold War*, 33; They directly attacked Hungary in 1956 to maintain communist control: M Beschloss, *The Crisis Years*, 128.

342 J Hogan, *A Cross of Iron*, 87.

343 X, "The Sources of Soviet Conduct"; Gaddis, *The Cold War*, 29.

344 W Churchill in W Williams, *The Tragedy of American Diplomacy*, 260.

345 D Schmitz, *Thank God They're on our Side*, 240.

346 H De Santi's, *The Diplomacy of Silence*, 81.

347 *Ibid.*, 199.

348 J Gaddis, *The United States and the Origins of the Cold War*, 204.

349 C Davis, *Waterfront Revolts*, 119.

350 C Mee, *The Marshall Plan*, 258.

351 *Ibid.*, 38-49.

352 G Roberts, *Stalin's Wars*, 317.

353 T Weiner, *Legacy of Ashes*, 28.

354 G Marshall in S Pisani, *The CIA and the Marshall Plan*, 68.

355 J Gaddis, *The Cold War*, 37-39.

356 N White, *Decolonization*, 11-19.

357 M Hopkins, *The Cold War*, 42.

358 J Gaddis, *We Now Know*, 70-82.

359 *Ibid.*, 40-52.

360 *Ibid.*, 37-40.

361 *Ibid.*, 99-101.

362 J Gaddis, *The United States and the Origins of the Cold War*, 47.

363 I Gellman, *Roosevelt and Batista*, 186.

364 R Alexander, *Communism in Latin America.*

365 J Ryan, *Earl Browder,* 232-238

366 *Ibid.,* 2.

367 P Smith, *Talons of the Eagle,* 128.

368 The percentage was calculated based on population statistics in J Brea, "Population statistics in Latin America", 6.

369 The US campaigned for the liberty of Brazilian Communist leader Carlos Luis Prestes and supported their democratic participation as shown in, J Dulles, *Vargas in Brazil,* 262. For party membership see, R Poppino, *International Communism and Latin America,* 135.

370 Cuban Communists worked with the Batista government between 1940 and 1944, I Gellman, *Roosevelt and Batista,* 186. For party membership see R Alexander, *Communism in Latin America,* 285

371 R Alexander, *Communism in Latin America,* 131.

372 B Coleman, *Colombia and the United States,* 52.

373 D Levy and G Szelky, *Mexico,* 39.

374 K LaCharité, R Kennedy and P Thienal, *Case study in insurgency and revolutionary warfare,* 44.

375 C Pach, *Arming the free world,* 215.

376 *Ibid.,* 41.

377 L Gill, *The School of the Americas,* 63.

378 *Ibid.,* 63.

379 C Hull in G Smith, *The Last Years of the Monroe Doctrine,* 41.

380 AWhitaker, "The Latin American Bloc", 170.

381 G Smith, *The Last Years of the Monroe Doctrine,* 54.

382   R Pogue, *George C Marshall,* 384.

383 J Child, *Unequal Alliance,* 71.

384 G Roberts, *Stalin's Wars,* 303-310

385 I Prizel, *Latin America Through Soviet Eyes,* 2.

386 B Coleman, *Colombia and the United States,* 54.

387 *Ibid.,* 55.

388 This conversation between ambassador Baulac and Foreign minister Gómez was made available by Paul Wolf's ICDC website in 2007 and has since been removed from online access. W Baulac, "Memorandum of conversation".

389 W Baulac, "Memorandum of conversation".

390 *Ibid.,*

391 *Ibid.,*

392 H Braun, *The Assassination of Gaitán*, 134.

393 S Randall, *Colombia and the United States*, 193.

394 H Braun, *The Assassination of Gaitán*, 135.

395 *Ibid.,* 135.

396 *Ibid.,* 135.

397 Paul Wolf's ICDC website provided an archive of documents between 2007 and 2012. Since then the archive and his story has been removed.

398 P Wolf.

399 B Coleman, *Colombia and the United States*, 55.

400 H Braun, *The Assassination of Gaitán*, 135.

401 W Green, *Gaitánism, Left-Liberalism, and popular mobilization in Colombia*, 261.

402 M Rolden, *Blood and Fire*, 72.

403 A Tunzelman, *Red Heat*, 40.

404 A Darling, *The Central Intelligence Agency*, 243-256.

405 J Hoover, "Liberal Party of Colombia".

406 *Ibid.,*

407 J Ray, "Gaitán and Communism".

408 A Darling, *The Central Intelligence Agency*, 243-256.

409 R Pogue, George C Marshall, 387.

410 *Ibid.,* 387.

411 S Randall, *Colombia and the United States*, 189.

412 *Ibid.,* 193.

413 New York Times, "Marshall Blames Reds in Colombia".

414 M Rolden, *Blood and Fire*, 75.

415 *Ibid.*, 68.

416 S Randell, *Colombia and the United States*, 196.

417 M Rolden, *Blood and Fire*, 75.

418 Organization of American States in Holden and Zolov, *Latin America and the United States*, 193.

419 For example, the parties of Brazil and the Dominican Republic were outlawed during 1947, while the Chilean Communists were made illegal during 1948 for domestic political reasons. Communism was eradicated between 1948 and 1952, with the sole exceptions of Guatemala, Mexico, Argentina and Uruguay. For more detail, see R Alexander, *Communism in Latin America.*

420 Organization of American States in Holden and Zolov, *Latin America and the United States*, 194.

421 *Ibid.*, 194.

422 *Ibid.*, 194.

423 T Weiner, *Legacy of Ashes*, 3-15.

424 *Ibid.*, 65.

425 H Greenberg, "The Doolittle Commission of 1954", 692.

426 M Rolden, *Blood and Fire.*

427 *Ibid.*, 220.

428 H Braun, *The Assassination of Gaitán*, 63.

Chapter 5

429 R Alexander, *Rómulo Betancourt and the transformation of Venezuela*, 360.

430 M Hopkins, *The Cold War*, 42-51.

431 R Freeland, *The Truman Doctrine and the Origins of McCarthyism*, 78.

432 P Steinberg, *The Great Red Menace*, 59.

433 E Schrecker, *The Age of McCarthyism*, 63.

434 J McCarthy, 'The Enemy Within'.

435 E Schrecker, *The Age of McCarthyism*, 37.

436 R Cohen, *McCarthy*, 220.

437 J Dulles, *Vargas of Brazil*, 286.

438 B Loveman, *Chile*, 220.

439 P Drake, *Socialism and Populism in Chile, 1932-52*, 286-290.

440 C Ameringer, *The Cuban Democratic Experience*, 110-120.

441 T Szulc, *Twilight of the Tyrants*.

442 P Gleijeses, *Shattered Hope*, 133.

443 S Rabe, *Eisenhower and Latin America*, 92.

444 G Kennan, cited in G Smith, *The Last Years of the Monroe Doctrine*, 68.

445 G Kennan, "Memorandum by the Counsellor of the Department to the Secretary of State", 600.

446 *Ibid.*, 604.

447 *Ibid.*, 608.

448 *Ibid.*, 607.

449 P Smith, *Talons of the eagle*, 120.

450 E Miller, cited in W Lafeber, *Inevitable Revolutions*, 94.

451 Y, "On a certain impatience on with Latin America".

452 *Ibid.*, 578.

453 *Ibid.*, 579.

454 F Truslow, cited in D Schmitz, *Thank god they're on our side*, 156.

455 C Pach, *Arming the free world*, 51.

456 A Whitaker, "The Latin American Bloc", 186.

457 P Gleijeses, "Juan José Arévalo and the Caribbean Legion", 141.

458 L Gill, *The School of the Americas*, 72.

459 L Shoup and W Minter, *Imperial Brain Trust*, 167.

460 G Marshall, cited in B Coleman, *Colombia and the United States*, 55.

461 S Niblo, *War Diplomacy and Development*, 231.

462 B Schneider, *Business politics and the state in Twentieth Century Latin America*.

463 K Raffner and H Singer, *The economic North-South divide*, 2.

464 *Ibid.*, 3.

465 H James, *International Monetary Cooperation since Bretton Woods*, 47.

466 S Rabe, *Eisenhower and Latin America*, 95.

467 A Frank, *Capitalism and Underdevelopment in Latin America*, 290-297.

468 National Security Council, "144/1", 21.

469 D Rock, *Argentina*; Dulles; Drake, 275-290.

470 National Security Council, "144/1", 21.

471 P Klaren, *Peru*, 299.

472 *Ibid.*, 299.

473 V Alba, *Peru*, 45.

474 *Ibid.*, 45.

475 T Szulc, *Twilight of the Tyrants*, 161.

476 *Ibid.*, 180.

477 *Ibid.*, 178-186.

478 *Ibid.*, 184.

479 G Betrum, "Peru 1930-60", 437.

480 *Ibid.*, 428.

481 T Szulc, *Twilight of the Tyrants*, 191.

482 E Lieuwen, *Venezuela*, 86.

483 *Ibid.*, 87.

484 *Ibid.*, 87.

485 *Ibid.*, 88.

486 T Szulc, *Twilight of the Tyrants*, 280.

487 R Alexander, *Communism in Latin America*, 253-269.

488 T Szulc, *Twilight of the Tyrants*, 250.

489 *Ibid.*, 252.

490 M Bucheli and R Aguilar, *Political survival, energy politics and multinational corporations*, 366.

491 T Szulc, *Twilight of the Tyrants*, 251.

492 S Rabe, *Eisenhower and Latin America*, 39.

493 T Szulc, *Twilight of the Tyrants*, 222.

494 *Ibid*, 223.

495 M Rolden, *Blood and Fire*, 71.

496 C Ameringer, *The Cuban Democratic Experience*, 19.

497 *Ibid.*, 25.

498 M Harnecker, *Fidel Castro's Political Strategy*, 3

499 C Ameringer, *The Cuban Democratic Experience*, 119.

500 J Arboyleya, *The Cuban Counterrevolution*, 26.

501 J Benjamin, *The United States and the origins of the Cuban Revolution*, 121.

502 S Ambrose, *Eisenhower Vol. 2*, 8-15.

Chapter 6

503 P Boyle, *Eisenhower*, 40.

504 J Árbenz, cited in S Schlesinger and S Kinzer, *Bitter Fruit*, 199.

505 P Boyle, *Eisenhower*, 46.

506 M Hopkins, *The Cold War*, 47.

507 P Boyle, *Eisenhower*, 54.

508 H Greenberg, 'The Doolittle Commission of 1954', 692.

509 K Roosevelt, *Countercoup*.

510 S Rabe, *Eisenhower and Latin America*, 29.

511 R Alexander, *Juan Domingo Perón*, 71.

512 *Ibid.*, 71.

513 *Ibid.*, 71.

514 R Bourne, *Getulio Vargas of Brazil, 1883-1954*, 160.

515 *Ibid.*, 165.

516 *Ibid.*, 171.

517 US State Department, "Probable Developments in Brazil".

518 R Bourne, *Getulio Vargas of Brazil, 1883-1954*, 169.

519 US State Department, "Probable Developments in Brazil".

520 *Ibid.,*

521 J Dulles, *Vargas of Brazil*, 317.

522 R Bourne, *Getulio Vargas of Brazil, 1883-1954*, 185.

523 *Ibid.,* 194.

524 J Dulles, *Vargas of Brazil*, 334.

525 D Rock, *Authoritarian Argentina*, 167.

526 R Alexander, *Juan Domingo Perón*, 101.

527 US State Department, "Probable Developments in Argentina".

528 K LaCharité, R Kennedy and P Thienal, *Case study in insurgency and revolutionary warfare* 44.

529 R Schneider, *Communism in Guatemala*, 318.

530 K LaCharité, R Kennedy and P Thienal, *Case study in insurgency and revolutionary warfare* 46-50.

531 R Alexander, *Communism in Latin America*, 356.

532 K LaCharité, R Kennedy and P Thienal, *Case study in insurgency and revolutionary warfare* 62.

533 S Schlesinger and S Kinzer, *Bitter Fruit*, 56.

534 C Beals, *Latin America*, 265.

535 M Grow, *US Presidents and Latin American Interventions*, 5.

536 J Aybar de Soto, *Dependency and Intervention*, 150.

537 *Ibid.,* 150.

538 S Kinzer, *Overthrow*, 132.

539 R Immerman, *The CIA in Guatemala*, 184.

540 J Arévalo, cited in S Schlesinger and S Kinzer, *Bitter Fruit*, 86.

541 Alexander, *Communism in Latin America*, 353-356.

542 R Immerman, *The CIA in Guatemala*, 62.

543 *Ibid.,* 62.

544 *Ibid.*, 182.

545 C Brocket, *Land Power and Poverty*, 97-104.

546 *Ibid.*, 102.

547 J Aybar de Soto, *Dependency and Intervention*, 176-182.

548 *Ibid.*, 176-182.

549 T McCann, *An American Company*, 49.

550 *Ibid.*, 49.

551 R Immerman, *The CIA in Guatemala*, 159.

552 T McCann, *An American Company*, 58.

553 S Schlesinger and S Kinzer, *Bitter Fruit*, 108.

554 *Ibid.*, 108.

555 *Ibid.*, 108

556 E Black, cited in J Aybar de Soto, *Dependency and Intervention*, 182.

557 P Gleijeses, *Shattered Hope* 166.

558 *Ibid.*, 167.

559 *Ibid.*, 166.

560 *Ibid.*, 168.

561 J Árbenz, cited in S Schlesinger and S Kinzer, *Bitter Fruit*, 144-145.

562 CIA, "Program for PB success".

563 T Weiner, *Legacy of Ashes*.

564 P Chapman, *Jungle capitalists*, 129.

565 J Clements, cited in L Tye, *The Father of Spin*, 176.

566 P Chapman, *Jungle capitalists*, 129.

567 L Tye, *The Father of Spin*, 170.

568 *Ibid.*, 177

569 *Ibid.*, 168.

570 NY Times (anonymous), *Guatemalan exiles in anti-red fight; Group in Mexico unites to undermine Árbenz and land reform*; NY Times (anonymous), *Idea of*

Red held ruling Guatemala; Ideologies wear a nationalistic cloak but observers see a Kremlin program.

571 CIA, "Program for PB success", 7.

572 S Schlesinger and S Kinzer, *Bitter Fruit*, 139-152.

573 J Dulles, cited in S Rabe, *Eisenhower and Latin America,* 50.

574 G Toriello, cited in

575 P Mervo, cited in S Rabe, *Eisenhower and Latin America,* 52.

576 S Rabe, *Eisenhower and Latin America,* 52.

577 Organization of American States, "Declaration of Caracas".

578 W Blum, *Killing Hope*, 73.

579 P Gleijeses, "Juan José Arévalo and the Caribbean Legion", 142.

580 P Chapman, *Jungle capitalists*, 146.

581 *Ibid.*, 146.

582 R Immerman, *The CIA in Guatemala*, 155.

583 CIA, "Program for PB success".

584 *Ibid.,*

585 New York Times, cited in S Schlesinger and S Kinzer, *Bitter Fruit*, 70.

586 R Immerman, *The CIA in Guatemala,* 159.

587 *Ibid.*, 160.

588 *Ibid.*, 162.

589 M Grow, *US Presidents and Latin American interventions*, 1.

590 R Immerman, *The CIA in Guatemala,* 163.

591 *Ibid.*, 165.

592 S Rabe, *Eisenhower and Latin America,* 55.

593 *Ibid.*, 55.

594 S Schlesinger and S Kinzer, *Bitter Fruit*, 199.

595 T Szulc, *Twilight of the Tyrants*.

596 R Potash, *The army and politics in Argentina 1945-1962*, 214.

597 S Rabe, *Eisenhower and Latin America*, 39.

598 M Grow, *US Presidents and Latin American Interventions*, 26.

599 R Immerman, *The CIA in Guatemala*, 177.

600 S Schlesinger and S Kinzer, *Bitter Fruit*, 232.

601 Cited in W Lafeber, *Inevitable Revolutions*, 261.

602 M Eisenhower, cited in B Cook, *The declassified Eisenhower*, 218.

Chapter 7

603 J Figueres, in C Ameringer, *Don Pepe*, 146-147.

604 S Rabe, *Eisenhower and Latin America*, 50.

605 J Dulles, cited in S Rabe, *Eisenhower and Latin America*, 95.

606 National Security Council, "144/1", 10-11.

607 J Cabot, cited in S Rabe, *Eisenhower and Latin America*, 78.

608 S Ambrose, *Eisenhower*, 194.

609 K Raffner and H Singer, *The economic North-South divide*, 17.

610 S Rabe, *Eisenhower and Latin America*, 75.

611 R Prebisch, cited in J Dreier, *The Alliance for Progress*, 26.

612 *Ibid.*, cited in Dreier, 26.

613 K Sikkink, *Ideas and Institutions*, 33.

614 S Rabe, *Eisenhower and Latin America*, 79.

615 *Ibid.*, 79.

616 J Dulles, cited in S Rabe, *Eisenhower and Latin America*, 75.

617 R Rubottom, cited in S Rabe, *Eisenhower and Latin America*, 79.

618 S Rabe, *Eisenhower and Latin America*, 88.

619 J Muniz, cited in S Rabe, *Eisenhower and Latin America*, 89.

620 J Kubitschek, cited in R Alexander, *Juscelino Kubitschek and the development of Brazil*, 109.

621 *Ibid.*, 280.

622 *Ibid.*; K Sikkink, *Ideas and Institutions*.

623 R Alexander, *Juscelino Kubitschek and the development of Brazil*, 288.

624 J Kubitschek, cited *ibid.*, 281.

625 J Kubitschek, cited in K Sikkink, *Ideas and Institutions*, 134.

626 K Sikkink, *Ideas and Institutions*, 132-140.

627 A Frondizi, cited in K Sikkink, *Ideas and Institutions*, 85.

628 National Security Counsel "5613/1", cited in S Rabe, *Eisenhower and Latin America*, 91.

629 J Dulles, cited in S Rabe, *Eisenhower and Latin America*, 107.

630 L Schoultz, *National Security and United States Policy towards Latin America*, 105.

631 S Rabe, *Eisenhower and Latin America*, 107.

632 E Crawley, *Dictators never die*, 116.

633 *Ibid.*, 115.

634 *Ibid.*, 116.

635 L Gill, *The School of the Americas*, 72.

636 E Crawley, *Dictators never die*, 118.

637 T Szulc, *Twilight of the Tyrants*, 184.

638 G Betrum, "Peru 1930-60", 439.

639 *Ibid.*, 439.

640 T Szulc, *Twilight of the Tyrants*, 204.

641 G Betrum, "Peru 1930-60", 449.

642 Ibid., 449.

643 T Wickham-Crowley, *Guerillas and Revolution in Latin America*, 37.

644 R Alexander, *Rómulo Betancourt and the transformation of Venezuela*, 326.

645 V Lombardi, *Venezuela*, 228.

646 R Alexander, *The Venezuelan Democratic Revolution*, 49.

647 T Szulc, *Twilight of the Tyrants*, 301.

648 R Alexander, *The Venezuelan Democratic Revolution*, 49.

649 *Ibid.*, 49.

650 *Ibid.*, 52.

651 R Alexander, *Rómulo Betancourt and the transformation of Venezuela*, 466.

652 S Rabe, *Eisenhower and Latin America*, 105.

653 M Rolden, *Blood and Fire*, 220.

654 G Leech, *The FARC*, 12.

655 J Hartlyn, *The politics of coalition rule in Colombia*, 57.

656 *Ibid.*, 67.

657 T Szulc, *Twilight of the Tyrants*, 239.

658 *Ibid.*, 241.

659 *Ibid.*, 242.

660 J Hartlyn, *The politics of coalition rule in Colombia*, 70.

661 S Randall, *Colombia and the United States*, 219.

662 US collaboration in the assignation of the Dominican President Rafael Trujillo will be explored in chapter 9. For more information, see S Rabe, *The Most Dangerous Area in the World*, 39.

663 M Trouillot, *Haiti*, 148.

664 R MacCameron, *Bananas, labor and politics in Honduras*, 79.

665 W Blum, *Killing Hope*, 82.

666 T Wickham-Crowley, *Guerillas and Revolution in Latin America*, 23.

667 *Ibid.*, 17.

668 *Ibid.*, 41.

669 R Nixon, *The Memoirs of Richard Nixon*, 186.

670 *Ibid.*, 186.

671 R Potash, *The army and politics in Argentina 1945-1962*, 230

672 S Stein, *Populism in Peru*, 129-136.

673 R Nixon, *The Memoirs of Richard Nixon*, 187.

674 *Ibid.*, 188.

675 S Rabe, *Eisenhower and Latin America*, 102.

676 NY Times, "The Peruvian Incident", 31.

677 S Rabe, *Eisenhower and Latin America* 103.

678 *Ibid.,* 103.

679 R Nixon, *The Memoirs of Richard Nixon,* 190.

680 *Ibid.,* 190.

681 *Ibid.,* 191.

682 *Ibid.,* 191.

683 S Rabe, *Eisenhower and Latin America,* 103.

684 C Ameringer, *Don Pepe,* 146.

685 *Ibid.,* 147.

686 *Ibid.,* 146.

687 *Ibid.,* 147.

688 *Ibid.,* 147.

689 *Ibid.,* 147.

Chapter 8

690 C Ameringer, *Don Pepe,* 156.

691 *Ibid.,*154-158.

692 V Skierka, *Fidel Castro,* 24.

693 R Alexander, *Juscelino Kubitschek and the development of Brazil,* 269.

694 *Ibid,* 270.

695 I Ehrlich, *Eduardo Chibás,* 1-36.

696 *Ibid.,* 17.

697 C Ameringer, *The Cuban Democratic Experience,* 44.

698 *Ibid.,* 55-90.

699 J Benjamin, *The United States and the origins of the Cuban Revolution,* 141.

700 C Ameringer, *The Cuban Democratic Experience,* 39.

701 T Wickham-Crowley, *Guerrillas and revolution in Latin America,* 38.

702 I Ehrlich, *Eduardo Chibás,* 11-12.

703 *Ibid.,* 233.

704 J Benjamin, *The United States and the origins of the Cuban Revolution*, 143.

705 *Ibid.*, 143.

706 F Castro, "History will absolve me".

707 C Ameringer, *The Cuban Democratic Experience*, 44.

708 F Castro, cited in L Aguilar, "From Immutable Proclamations to Unintended Consequences", 140.

709 M Harnecker, *Fidel Castro's Political Strategy*, 16.

710 *Ibid.*, 17.

711 L Pérez, *Cuba*, 234.

712 L Aguilar, "From Immutable Proclamations to Unintended Consequences", 140.

713 M Beschloss, *The Crisis Years*, 88.

714 L Pérez, *Cuba*, 226.

715 *Ibid.*, 229.

716 *Ibid.*, 225.

717 *Ibid.*, 225.

718 *Ibid.*, 229.

719 *Ibid.*, 228.

720 E Guevara, cited W Blum, *Killing Hope*, 82.

721 M Harnecker, *Fidel Castro's Political Strategy*, 16.

722 T Wickham-Crowley, *Exploring Revolution*, 41.

723 J Sweig, *Inside the Cuban Revolution*, 13.

724 *Ibid.*, 13.

725 *Ibid.*, 14.

726 *Ibid.*, 14.

727 A DePalma, *The Man Who Invented Fidel*, 33.

728 *Ibid.*, 67.

729 *Ibid.*, 77.

730 F Castro, cited in A DePalma, *The Man Who Invented Fidel*, 86.

731 J Sweig, *Inside the Cuban Revolution*, 4.

732 F Pais, cited in J Sweig, *Inside the Cuban Revolution*, 12.

733 A Tunzelman, *Red Heat*, 71.

734 C Ameringer, *Don Pepe*, 147.

735 J Benjamin, *The United States and the origins of the Cuban Revolution*, 153.

736 L Pérez, *Cuba*, 234.

737 *Ibid.*, 236.

738 W Pawley, cited in L Pérez, *Cuba*, 235.

739 M Pérez-Stable, *The Cuban Revolution*, 67.

740 S Lamrani, *The Economic War against Cuba*, 18

741 M Pérez-Stable, *The Cuban Revolution*, 67.

742 L Schoultz, *That infernal little Cuban Republic*, 84.

743 M Pérez-Stable, *The Cuban Revolution*, 68.

744 M Morley, *Imperial State and Revolution*, 74.

745 *Ibid.*, 74.

746 L Schoultz, *That infernal little Cuban Republic*, 91.

747 M Beschloss, *The Crisis Years*, 98.

748 L Schoultz, *That infernal little Cuban Republic*, 90.

749 L Pérez, *Cuba*, 243.

750 *Ibid.*, 243.

751 M Morley, *Imperial State and Revolution*, 83.

752 L Schoultz, *That infernal little Cuban Republic*, 99.

753 *Ibid.*, 96.

754 J Franklin, *The Cuban Revolution and the United States*, 28.

755 *Ibid.*, 28.

756 M Morley, *Imperial State and Revolution*, 85.

757 J Franklin, *The Cuban Revolution and the United States*, 31.

758 M Morley, *Imperial State and Revolution*, 87.

759 J Franklin, *The Cuban Revolution and the United States*, 31.

760 R Alexander, *The Venezuelan Democratic Revolution*, 146.

761 F Castro, "Declaration of Havana".

762 L Garcia, *The Cuban Revolution Reader*, 39-44.

763 H Jones, *The Bay of Pigs*, 34.

764 *Ibid.*, 43.

765 *Ibid.*, 31.

766 *Ibid.*, 35.

767 *Ibid*, 65.

768 A Fursenko and T Naftali, *Khrushchev's Cold War*, 343.

769 H Jones, *The Bay of Pigs*, 70.

770 M Beschloss, *The Crisis Years*, 118.

771 M Pérez-Stable, *The Cuban Revolution*, 82.

772 F Castro, cited in L Aguilar, "From Immutable Proclamations to Unintended Consequences",147.

773 *Ibid.*, 144.

774 M Harnecker, *Fidel Castro's Political Strategy*, 26.

775 C Ameringer, *The Cuban Democratic Experience*, 44.

776 B Goldenberg, *The Cuban Revolution and Latin America*, 311.

777 *Ibid.*, 311.

778 *Ibid.*, 311.

779 *Ibid.*, 312.

780 *Ibid.*, 312.

781 *Ibid.*, 314.

782 R Dallek, *John F Kennedy*, 521.

783 C Ameringer, *Don Pepe*, 154.

784 *Ibid.*, 154.

785 *Ibid.*, 155.

786 R Alexander, *The Venezuelan Democratic Revolution*, 146.

787 C Ameringer, *Don Pepe*, 158.

788 *Ibid.,* 156.

789 *Ibid.,* 169.

790 *Ibid.,* 169.

791 R Alexander, *The Venezuelan Democratic Revolution,* 146.

792 S Rabe, *The Most Dangerous Area in the World,* 46.

793 B Goldenberg, *The Cuban Revolution and Latin America,* 321.

794 F Stern, *Averting the Final Failure,* 17.

795 L Pérez, *Cuba,* 247.

796 M Morley, *Imperial State and Revolution,* 87.

797 L Pérez, *Cuba,* 247.

798 S Lamrani, *The Economic War against Cuba,* 25.

799 A Fursenko and T Naftali, *Khrushchev's Cold War,* 340-390.

800 M Beschloss, *The Crisis Years,* 122-125.

801 J Franklin, *The Cuban Revolution and the United States,* 55.

802 M Beschloss, *The Crisis Years,* 116.

803 F Stern, *Averting the Final Failure,* 23.

804 J Franklin, *The Cuban Revolution and the United States,* 58.

805 F Stern, *Averting the Final Failure,* 23.

806 C Ameringer, *Don Pepe,* 158.

Chapter 9

807 J Figueres, cited in C Ameringer, *Don Pepe,* 169.

808 H Parmet, *JFK,* 65-72.

809 S Rabe, *The Most Dangerous Area in the World,* 15.

810 J Taffet, *Foreign aid as foreign policy,* 38.

811 H Parmet, *JFK,* 68.

812 S Bailey, *The US and the Development of Latin America,* 85.

813 E Flores, *Land Reform and the Alliance for Progress,* 6.

814 E Roorda, *The Good Neighbor Policy and the Trujillo regime.*

815 T Patterson, *Kennedy's quest for victory,* 9.

816 S Rabe, *The Most Dangerous Area in the World*, 39.

817 *Ibid.*, 41.

818 *Ibid.*, 45.

819 Organization of American States, "Charter of Punta del Este".

820 E Guevara, *Our America and Theirs*, 24.

821 A Stevenson, in State Department, "Report from the Representative to the United Nations to President Kennedy".

822 N Cull, *The Cold War and the United States Information Agency*, 195

823 Organization of American States, "Charter of Punta del Este".

824 V Alba, *Alliance without Allies*, 81.

825 E Flores, *Land Reform and the Alliance for Progress*, 7.

826 A Berle, *Latin America – diplomacy and reality*, 8.

827 *Ibid.*, 8.

828 Organization of American States, "Charter of Punta del Este".

829 C Oliver, cited in E Galeano, *Open Veins of Latin America*, 1.

830 Organization of American States, "Charter of Punta del Este".

831 S Rabe, *The most dangerous area in the world*, 31.

832 J Marti, E Guevara, *Our America and Theirs*, 20.

833 E Guevara, *Our America and Theirs*, 25.

834 *Ibid.*, 31.

835 J Kennedy, "Remarks at the Techo Housing Project in Bogota".

836 A Camargo, cited in G Simons, *Colombia*, 48.

837 J Kennedy, "Joint Statement following Discussions with President López Mateos".

838 B Leaming, *Mrs Kennedy*, 237.

839 C Dillon, "Memorandum from Secretary of the Treasury Dillon to President Kennedy".

840 *Ibid.*,

841 *Ibid.*,

842 S Robock, *Brazil's developing Northeast*, 141.

843 R Dallek, *John F Kennedy*, 694.

844 F Kluckhohn, *Lyndon's Legacy*, 11.

845 J Colman, *The Foreign Policy of Lyndon B Johnson*, 164.

846 *Ibid.*, 164.

847 *Ibid.*, 164.

848 D Kunz, *Butter and Guns*, 145-6.

849 M Latham, *Modernization as ideology*, 81.

850 *Ibid.*, 87.

851 H Singer, *Beyond Terms of Trade*, 913-915; A Frank, *The Development of Underdevelopment*; A Frank, *Latin America*.

852 J Taffet, *Foreign aid as foreign policy*, 9.

853 *Ibid.*, 149.

854 J Roddick, *The Dance of the Millions*, 7.

855 J Taffet, *Foreign aid as foreign policy*, 159.

856 *Ibid.*, 166.

857 M Latham, *Modernization as ideology*, 71.

858 R Prebisch, cited in J Dreier, *The Alliance for Progress*, 33.

859 D Kunz, *Butter and Guns*, 136.

860 *Ibid.*, 136.

861 *Ibid.*, 144.

862 A Camargo, cited in D Kunz, *Butter and Guns*, 144.

863 D Kunz, *Butter and Guns*, 144.

864 A Frank, *The Development of Underdevelopment*, 184.

865 *Ibid.*, 184-189.

866 *Ibid.*, 185.

867 *Ibid.*, 185.

868 *Ibid.*, 185.

869 Roddick, 7.

870 Roddick, 7.

871 Roddick, 7.

872 J Kennedy, "Inaugural address".

Chapter 10

873 J Kennedy, "Inaugural address".

874 A Berle, cited in S Rabe, *The Most Dangerous Area in the World*, 24.

875 J Bosch, cited in R Alexander, *Biographical dictionary of Latin American and Caribbean political leaders*, 230.

876 J Kennedy, cited in W Barber and C Ronning, *Internal security and military power*, 31.

877 A Berle, cited in S Rabe, *The Most Dangerous Area in the World*, 24.

878 T Wickham-Crowley, *Guerrillas and revolution in Latin America*, 30.

879 M Radu, *Violence and the Latin American revolutionaries*, 3.

880 *Ibid.*, 6.

881 J Ewell, *Venezuela A Century of Change*, 128.

882 T Wickham-Crowley, *Guerrillas and revolution in Latin America*, 44.

883 *Ibid.*, 44.

884 B Goldenberg, *The Cuban Revolution and Latin America*, 315.

885 W Ratliff, *Revolutionary Warfare*, 100.

886 *Ibid.*, 123.

887 *Ibid.*, 119.

888 G Leech, *The FARC*, 14.

889 T Wickham-Crowley, *Guerrillas and revolution in Latin America*, 44.

890 W Ratliff, *Revolutionary Warfare*, 40.

891 L Aguilar, "From Immutable Proclamations to Unintended Consequences", 145.

892 F Castro, cited in L Aguilar, "From Immutable Proclamations to Unintended Consequences",144.

893 L Aguilar, "From Immutable Proclamations to Unintended Consequences",147.

894 B Goldenberg, *The Cuban Revolution and Latin America*, 311.

895 G Leech, *The FARC*, 14.

896 T Wickham-Crowley, *Exploring Revolution*, 35.

897 *Ibid.*, 35.

898 S Streeter, *Nation Building in the land of eternal counter-insurgency*, 59.

899 T Wickham-Crowley, *Exploring Revolution*, 41.

900 *Ibid.*, 41.

901 L Gill, *The School of the Americas*, 77.

902 R Gaillard, "Civic Action versus counterinsurgency and low-intensity conflict in Latin America", 63.

903 *Ibid.*, 63.

904 W Barber and C Ronning, *Internal security and military power*, 95.

905 L Gill, *The School of the Americas*, 74.

906 *Ibid.*, 75.

907 *Ibid.*, 75.

908 *Ibid.*, 78.

909 *Ibid.*, 79.

910 *Ibid.*, 79.

911 C Prats, cited in L Gill, *The School of the Americas*, 79-80.

912 L Gill, *The School of the Americas*, 78.

913 *Ibid.*, 86.

914 R Wood, cited in W Barber and C Ronning, *Internal security and military power*, 38.

915 Gaillard, 63.

916 Gaillard, 64.

917 F Gil, "The Kennedy and Johnson Years", 19.

918 R Wood, cited in W Barber and C Ronning, *Internal security and military power*, 35.

919 F Gil, "The Kennedy and Johnson Years", 19.

920 J Fishel and E Cowen, 'Civil-military operations and the war for political legitimacy in Latin America, 50.

921 S Rabe, *The Most Dangerous Area in the World*, 44.

922 G Leech, *The FARC*, 14.

923 *Ibid.*, 14.

924 T Wickham-Crowley, *Exploring Revolution*, 70.

925 P Klaren, *Peru*, 320.

926 B Goldenberg, *The Cuban Revolution and Latin America*, 315.

927 P Klaren, *Peru*, 322.

928 *Ibid.*, 320.

929 *Ibid.*, 320.

930 H Klein, *Bolivia*, 249.

931 J Malloy and E Gamarra, *Revolution and Reaction*, 1.

932 P Salmon, *The defeat of Guevara*, 99-120.

933 R MacCameron, *Bananas, labor and politics in Honduras*, 178.

934 *Ibid.*, 178.

935 J Coatsworth, Central America and the United States, 102.

936   *Ibid.*, 102.

937 R Alexander, *Biographical dictionary of Latin American and Caribbean political leaders*, 224.

938 J Bosch, cited in R Alexander, *Biographical dictionary of Latin American and Caribbean political leaders*, 224.

939 *Ibid.*, 232.

940 R Dallek, *John F Kennedy*, 521.

941 *Ibid.*, 521.

942 T Skidmore, *The politics of military rule in Brazil*, 28.

943 D James, Resistance and Integration, 141.

944 R Potash, *The army and politics in Argentina 1945-1962*, 377.

945 C Szusterman, *Frondizi and the politics of development in Argentina*, 212.

946 D James, Resistance and Integration, 152.

947 Potash, 230.

948 R Potash, *The army and politics in Argentina 1945-1962*, 83.

949 C Szusterman, *Frondizi and the politics of development in Argentina*, 210.

950 *Ibid.*, 219.

951 J Petras, *Politics and social forces in Chilean development,* 19.

952 *Ibid.*, 19.

953 *Ibid.*, 19.

954 J Coatsworth, Central America and the United States, 104.

955 *Ibid.*, 104.

956 L Johnson, cited in W Barber and C Ronning, *Internal security and military power*, 210.

Conclusion

957 W Lafeber, *Inevitable Revolutions,* 240-255.

958 *Ibid.*, 240-255.

959 S Kinzer, *Overthrow,* 65-75.

960 R Crandle, *Gunboat Diplomacy,* 66; M Grow, *US Presidents and Latin American Interventions,* 140-143.

961 J Dinges, *The Condor Years,* 1-21.

962 J Klaiber, *The church, dictatorships and democracy in Latin America,* 71-125.

963 J Dinges, *The Condor Years,* 6.

964 E Chibás, cited in C Ameringer, *The Cuban Democratic Experience,* 34.

965 S Niblo, *War Diplomacy and Development*, 236.

966 W Blum, *Killing Hope,* 73.

967 C Ameringer, *The Socialist Impulse,* 130-170.

968 M Rapoport, "Argentina", 117.

969 G Santayana, *The life of reason,* 46.

Bibliography

Adler, S. *The uncertain giant: 1921-1941, American foreign policy between the wars.* New York: The MacMillan Company, 1965.

Aguilar, L. E. *Marxism in Latin America.* New York: Alfred A Knopf, 1968.

--- *Cuba 1933: Prologue to revolution.* Ithaca: Cornell University Press, 1972.

--- "From immutable proclamations to unintended consequences: Marxism-Leninism and the Cuban Government, 1959-1986" in *Cuban Communism.* Edited by I. L. Horowitz. New Brunswick: Transaction Books, 1988.

Alba, V. *Alliance without allies: The mythology of progress in Latin America.* New York: Praeger, 1965.

Alexander, R. J. *Communism in Latin America.* New Jersey: Rutgers University Press, 1963.

--- *The Venezuelan Democratic Revolution: A profile of the regime of Rómulo Betancourt.* New Brunswick: Rutgers University Press, 1964.

--- *Prophets of the revolution,* London: MacMillan, 1969.

--- *Rómulo Betancourt and the transformation of Venezuela.* London: Transaction books, 1982.

--- Biographical dictionary of Latin American and Caribbean political leaders. New York: Greenwood Press, 1988.

--- *Juscelino Kubitschek and the development of Brazil.* Athens: Ohio University Press, 1991.

--- *International labor organizations and organized labor in Latin America and the Caribbean.* Denver: Praeger, 2009.

Ambrose, S. *Eisenhower.* 2 vols. Vol. 2. London: Allen and Unwin, 1984.

Ameringer, C. *The democratic left in exile: The anti-dictatorial struggle in the Caribbean, 1945-1959.* Coral Gables: University of Miami Press, 1974.

--- *Don Pepe: A political biography of José Figueres of Costa Rica.* Albuquerque: University of New Mexico Press, 1978.

--- *The Caribbean Legion: Patriots, Politicians, Soldiers of Fortune 1946-1950.* University Park, Pa: The Pennsylvania State University Press, 1996.

--- *The Cuban democratic experience: The Autentico years, 1944-1952.* Gainesville, University of Florida Press, 2000.

--- The socialist impulse: Latin America in the twentieth century. Gainesville: University of Florida Press, 2009.

Ames, B. *Political survival: Politicians and public policy in Latin America.* Berkeley: University of California Press, 1987.

Anderson, R. "Mexico". In *Latin American labor organizations.* Edited by G Greenfield and S Maram. New York: Greenwood Press, 1987.

Arévalo, J. *Anti-Kommunism in Latin America: An x-ray of the process leading to a new colonialism.* New York: Lyle Stuart Inc, 1963.

Aybar de Soto, J. M. *Dependency and intervention: the case of Guatemala 1954.* Boulder: Westview Press, 1978.

Baily, S. *The United States and the development of South America, 1945-1975,* New York: New Viewpoints, 1976.

Barber, W. F. and Ronning, C. N. *Internal security and military power: Counterinsurgency and civic action in Latin America.* Colombus: Ohio State University Press, 1966.

Bauer, R. *American business and public policy: The politics of foreign trade.* New York: Atherton Press, 1963.

Baulac, W. *Memorandum of conversation. ICDC Bogotazo Archive.* Accessed June 1, 2011. www.icdc.com/Tpaulwolf/Gaitán/baulac8april1948.htm

Beals, C. *Latin America: World in revolution.* New York: Abelard-Schuman, 1963.

Belfrage, C. *The American inquisition, 1945-1960: A profile of the McCarthy era.* New York: Thunder Mouth Press, 1989.

Benjamin, J. *The United States and the origins of the Cuban Revolution: An empire of liberty in an age of national liberation.* Princeton, NJ: Princeton University Press, 1990.

Berle, A. *Latin America - diplomacy and reality.* New York: Harper and Row, 1962.

Bermann, K. *Under the big stick: Nicaragua and the United States since 1848.* Boston: South End Press, 1986.

Beschloss, M. *The crisis years: Kennedy and Khrushchev 1960-1963.* New York: Edward Burlingame Books, 1991.

Betrum, G. "Peru 1930-60". In *the Cambridge history of Latin America: Bibliographical essays.* Edited by Leslie Bethell New York: Cambridge University Press, 1995.

Biles, R. *A new deal for the American people.* Dekalb: Northern Illinois University Press, 1991.

Black, G. *The good neighbor: How the United States wrote the history of Central America and the Caribbean.* New York: Pantheon Books, 1988.

Blasier, C. *The hovering giant: US responses to revolutionary change in Latin America.* Pittsburgh: University Press, 1976.

Blum, W. *Killing hope: US military and CIA interventions since World War II.* Monroe, Maine: Common Courage Press, 2004.

Bourne, R. *Getúlio Vargas of Brazil, 1883-1954: Sphinx of the pampas.* London: Charles Knight and Company, 1974.

Boyle, P. *Eisenhower.* London: Pearson Longman, 2005.

Braden, S. *Diplomats and demagogues: The memoirs of Spruille Braden.* New York: Arlington House, 1971.

Braun, H. *The assassination of Gaitán: Public life and violence in Colombia.* Madison: University of Wisconsin Press, 1985.

Brea, J. "Population statistics in Latin America". *Population bulletin 58* (1). 1-36, 2003.

Bratzel, J. "Introduction". In *Latin America during World War II.* Edited by T Leonard and J Bratzel. New York: Rowman and Littlefield, 2007.

Brenner, A. *The wind that swept Mexico: A history of the Mexican Revolution.* Austin: University of Texas Press, 1971.

Brewer, P. (October 13, 1958). "Figueres chides US on dictators: Ex-President of Costa Rica calls for intervention to overthrow tyrants". *New York Times,* October 13, 1958, New York Times Archives.

Britton, J. A. "Redefining interventionism: Mexico's contribution to Anti-Americanism". In *anti-Americanism in Latin America and the Caribbean.* Edited by A. McPherson. New York: Bergham Books, 2006.

Brocket, C. D. *Land power and poverty: Agrarian transformation and political conflict in Central America.* Boston: Unwin Hyman, 1988.

Brown, M. *Rethinking British informal empire in Latin America: Culture, Commerce and Capital.* Chichester, UK: John Wiley and Sons, 2008.

Bucheli, M. *Bananas and business: The United Fruit Company in Colombia, 1899-2000.* New York: University Press, 2005.

Bucheli, M. and Aguilar, R. V. "Political survival, energy politics and multinational corporations: A historical study for the standard oil of New Jersey in Colombia, Mexico and Venezuela in the twentieth century". In *Management International Review* 50, no. 3 (2010). 347-378.

Cabellero, M. *Latin America and the Comintern, 1919-1943.* New York: Cambridge University Press, 1986.

Castro, F. *My life.* London: Allen Lane, 2007.

--- *History will absolve me.* Castro Internet Archive. Accessed June 1, 2015. https://www.marxists.org/history/cuba/archive/castro/1953/10/16.htm

--- *The Declaration of Havana.* London: Verso, 2008.

Castro, F. and Fernández, J. *Playa Giron: Bay of Pigs, Washington's first military defeat in the Americas.* New York: Pathfinder, 2001.

CIA. *Program for PB success.* CIA Guatemala collection. Accessed September 1, 2011. https://www.cia.gov/library/readingroom/docs/DOC_0000924011.pdf

Chapman, P. *Jungle capitalists: A story of globalization, greed and revolution.* New York: Canongate, 2007.

Chevalier, F. "The roots of caudilloism". *In Caudillos: Dictators in Spanish America.* Norman: University of Oklahoma Press, 1992.

Child, J. *Unequal alliance: The Inter-American military system, 1938-1978.* Boulder: Westview Press, 1980.

Coatsworth, J. *Central American and the United States: The clients and the colossus.* New York: Twayne Publishers, 1994.

Cohen, R. *McCarthy.* New York: New American Library, 1968.

Cohen, W. I. *Empire without tears: America's foreign relations, 1921-1933.* Philadelphia: Templeton University Press, 1987.

Colman, J. *The foreign policy of Lyndon B. Johnson: The United States and the world. 1963-69.* Edinburgh: Edinburgh University Press, 1988.

Coleman, B. *Colombia and the United States: The making of an inter-American alliance, 1939-1960.* Kent: State University Press, 2008.

Cook, B. *The declassified Eisenhower: A divided legacy.* 1 Ed. New York: Double Day, 1981.

Crandle, R. *Gunboat democracy: US intervention in the Dominican Republic, Grenada and Panama.* New York: Rowman and Littlefield, 2006.

Crawley, A. *Somoza and Roosevelt: Good neighbor diplomacy in Nicaragua, 1933-1945.* New York: Oxford University Press, 2007.

Crawley, E. *Dictators never die: A portrait of Nicaragua and the Somoza dynasty.* London: C. Hurst and Company, 1979.

Cruz, R. C. "Costa Rica". In *Latin America between the Second World War and the Cold War, 1944-1948.* Edited by L. Bethell and I Roxborough. New York: Cambridge University Press, 1992.

Cull, N. *The Cold War and the United States Information Agency: American propaganda and public diplomacy, 1945-1989.* Cambridge: Cambridge University Press, 2008.

Curry, E. *Hoover's Dominican diplomacy and the origins of the Good Neighbor Policy.* New York: Garland Publishing Inc, 1979.

Dallek, R. *John F Kennedy: An unfinished life, 1917-1963*. London: Penguin, 2003.

Darling, A. *The Central Intelligence Agency: An instrument of government to 1950*. Philadelphia: The Pennsylvania State University Press, 1990.

Davis, C. *Waterfront Revolts: New York and London dockworkers, 1946-1961*. Chicago: University of Illinois Press.

Davis, L. and R. Cull. *International capital markets and American economic growth, 1820-1914*. New York: Cambridge University Press, 1994.

DePalma, A. *The man who invented Fidel: Cuba, Castro and Herbert L. Matthews of the New York Times*. New York: Public Affairs, 2006.

De Santis, H. *The Diplomacy of Silence: the American foreign service, the Soviet Union, and the Cold War, 1933-1947*. Chicago: University of Chicago Press, 1980.

Dillon, C. 'Memorandum from Secretary of the Treasury Dillon to President Kennedy'. *US State Department office of the historian*. Accessed September 1, 2015. https://history.state.gov/historicaldocuments/frus1961-63v09/d8

Dinges, J. *The Condor years: How Pinochet and his allies brought terrorism to three continents*. New York: New Press, 2004.

Di Tella, T. *The history of political parties in Twentieth Century Latin America*. New Brunswick, NJ: Transaction Publishers, 2004.

Dorm, G. Bradenism and beyond: Argentine anti-Americanism, 1945-1953. In *Anti-Americanism in Latin America and the Caribbean*. Edited by A. McPherson. New York: Bergham Books, 2006.

Drake, P. *Socialism and populism in Chile, 1932-52*. Chicago: University of Illinois Press, 1978.

Dreier, J. *The Alliance for Progress: Problems and perspectives*: Baltimore: John Hopkins Press, 1962.

Dulles, J. *Vargas of Brazil: A political biography*. Austin: University of Texas Press, 1967.

Dunkerley, J. *The long war: Dictatorship and revolution in El Salvador*. London: Junction Books, 1992.

--- *Warriors and scribes: Essays on the history and politics of Latin America.* London: Verso, 2000.

Dwyer, J. "The end of US intervention in Mexico: Franklin Roosevelt and the expropriation of American owned agricultural property". *Presidential Studies Quarterly.* 28, no.3 (1998): 495-509.

Ellner, S. "Venezuela". In *International labor organizations.* Edited by G Greenfield and S Maram. New York: Greenwood Press, 1987.

--- "Venezuela". In *Latin America between the Second World War and the Cold War, 1944-1948.* Edited by L. Bethell and I Roxborough. New York: Cambridge University Press, 1992.

Ewell, J. *Venezuela, a century of change.* Stanford, Calif: Stanford University Press, 1984.

Fawcett, E. *Liberalism: The life of an idea.* Princeton: University Press, 2014.

Financial and Economic Advisory Committee. *Inter-American Financial and Economic Advisory Committee: Handbook of its organization and activities, 1939-1943.* Washington: Government Source, 2004.

Fejes, F. *Imperialism, media and the good neighbor: New deal foreign policy and the United States shortwave broadcasting to Latin America.* Norwood, NJ: ABLEX Publishing Corporation, 1986.

Fishel, J. and E. Cowen. "Civil-military operations and the war for political legitimacy in Latin America". In *Winning the peace: The strategic implications of military civic action.* Edited by J. De Pauw and G. Luz. New York: Praeger, 1992.

Flores, E. *Land reform and the Alliance for Progress.* Princeton: University Press, 1963.

Francis, M. *The limits of hegemony: United States relations with Argentina and Chile during World War II.* London: The University of Notre Dame Press, 1977.

Frank, A. *Capitalism and underdevelopment in Latin America: Historical studies of Chile and Brazil.* New York: Modern Reader Paperbacks, 1967.

--- *Latin America: Underdevelopment or revolution; Essays on the development of underdevelopment and the immediate enemy.* New York: Monthly Review Press, 1970.

Franklin, J. *The Cuban Revolution and the United States: A chronological history* New York: Ocean Press, 1992.

Freeland, R. M. *The Truman Doctrine and the origins of McCarthyism: Foreign policy, domestic politics and internal security, 1946-1948*. New York: University Press, 1985.

Friedman, M. *Nazis and the good neighbor: The United States campaign against the Germans of Latin America in World War II*. Cambridge: Cambridge University Press, 2005.

Fursenko, A. and Naftali, T. *Khrushchev's Cold War: The inside story of an American adversary*. New York: WW Norton and Company, 2006.

Gaillard, R. "Civic action versus counterinsurgency and low-intensity conflict in Latin America: The case for delinkage". In *Winning the peace: The strategic implications of military civic action*. Edited by J. De Pauw and G. Luz. New York: Praeger, 1992.

Galliano, E. *Open veins of Latin America: Five centuries of the pillage of a continent*. New York: Monthly Review Press, 1973.

Gaddis, J. L. *The United States and the origins of the Cold War, 1941-1947*. New York: Columbia University Press, 1972.

--- *We Now Know: Rethinking Cold War history*. Oxford: Clarendon Press, 1997.

--- *The Cold War*. London: Allen Lane, 2005.

García L. *The Cuban Revolution reader: A documentary history of 40 key moments of the Cuban Revolution*. New York: Ocean Press, 2001.

Garner, P. *Porfirio Diaz*. London: Longman, 2001.

Gellman, I. *Good neighbor diplomacy: United States policies in Latin America, 1933-1945*. Baltimore: The John Hopkins University Press, 1979.

--- *Roosevelt and Batista: Good neighbour diplomacy in Cuba, 1933-1945*. Albuquerque: University of New Mexico Press, 1973.

Gereffi, G and Wyman, D. *Manufacturing miracles: Paths of industrialization in Latin American and East Asia*. Princeton: Princeton University Press, 1990.

Gil, F. The Kennedy and Johnson Years. In *United States policy in Latin America: A quarter century of crisis and challenge, 1961-1986*. Edited by J Martz. Lincoln: University of Nebraska Press, 1988.

Gill, L. *The School of the Americas: Military training and political violence in the Americas*. Durham: Duke University Press, 2004.

Gilly, A. *The Mexican Revolution*. London: The United Press, 1983.

Ginger, R. *The age of excess: The United States from 1877 to 1914*. Prospect Heights, Ill: Waveland Press, 1989.

Gleijeses, P. "Juan José Arévalo and the Caribbean legion". *Journal of Latin American Studies*. 21 no. 1 (1989): 133-145, 1989.

--- *Shattered hope: The Guatemalan Revolution and the United States, 1944-1954*. Princeton: University Press, 1991.

Goldenberg, B. *The Cuban Revolution and Latin America*. London: Allen and Unwin, 1965.

González, M. *The Mexican Revolution, 1910-1940*. Albuquerque: University of New Mexico Press, 2002.

Graham, C. *Peru's APRA: Parties, politics, and the elusive quest for democracy*. Boulder: Lynne Rienner Publishers, 1992.

Grampp, W. *Economic liberalism: The beginnings*. New York: Random House, 1965.

Grandin, G. *The last colonial massacre: Latin America in the Cold War*. Chicago: University Press, 2004.

--- *Fordlandia: the rise and fall of Henry Ford's forgotten jungle city*. London: Icon, 2010.

--- *Empire's workshop: Latin America, the United States and the rise of the new imperialism*. New York: Henry Holt Books, 2010.

Green, D. *The containment of Latin America: A history of the myths and realities of the Good Neighbor Policy*. Chicago: Quadrangle Books, 1971.

Green, W. *Gaitánism, Left-Liberalism, and popular mobilization in Colombia*. Gainesville: University of Florida Press, 2003.

Greenberg, H. "The Doolittle Commission of 1954". *Intelligence and National Security.* 22 no. 1, (2007): 687- 694.

Grieb, K. *Guatemalan Caudillo, the regime of George Ubico: Guatemala 1931-1944.* Athens: Ohio University Press, 1979.

Grow, M. *US Presidents and Latin American interventions: Pursuing regime change in the Cold War.* Lawrence: University Press of Kansas, 2008.

Grusen, S. "Ideologies wear a nationalist cloak but observers see a Kremlin program". *New York Times,* May 21, 1952, New York Times Archives.

--- "Guatemala exiles in anti-red fight: Group in Mexico unites with front there to undermine Árbenz and land reform". *New York Times,* June 22, 1952, New York Times Archives.

Guevara, E. *The motorcycle diaries: Notes on a Latin American journey.* New York: Ocean Books, 2004.

--- *Our America and theirs: Kennedy and the Alliance for Progress: The Debate at Punta del Este.* New York: Ocean Press, 2006.

Haas, L. "Argentina". In *International labor organizations.* Edited by G Greenfield and S Maram. New York: Greenwood Press, 1987.

Harnecker, M. *Fidel Castro's political strategy: From Moncada to Victory.* London: Pathfinder Press, 1985.

Hart, J. *Revolutionary Mexico: The coming and process of the Mexican Revolution.* Berkeley: University of California Press, 1987.

Hartlyn, J. *The politics of coalition rule in Colombia.* New York: Cambridge University Press, 1988.

Haworth, N. "Peru". In *Latin America between the Second World War and the Cold War, 1944-1948.* Edited by L. Bethell and I Roxborough. New York: Cambridge University Press, 1992.

Hellinger, D. *Venezuela: Tarnished democracy.* Boulder: Westview Press, 1991.

Henderson, J. *Conservative thought in twentieth century Latin America: the ideas of Laureano Gómez*. Athens, Oh: Ohio University Press, 1988.

Henig, R. *The League of Nations: The Peace conference of 1919-23 and their aftermath*. London: Haus Historians, 2010.

Hobhouse, L. *Liberalism*. New York: Oxford University Press, 1964.

Hogan J. *A cross of iron: Harry S Truman and the origins of the National Security State, 1945-1954*. Cambridge: University Press, 1998.

Holden, R. and Zolov, E. *Latin America and the United States: A documentary history*. New York: Oxford University Press, 2002.

- Hoover, J. "Liberal Party of Colombia". *ICDC Bogotazo Archive*. Accessed June 1, 2011. www.icdc.com/paulwolf/Gaitán/hoover19dec1945.htm

- Hopkins, M. *The Cold War,* London: Thomas and Hudson, 2011.

Hull, C. *The memoirs of Cordell Hull*. Vol 1 and 2. New York: Macmillan Co, 1948.

Immerman, R. *The CIA in Guatemala: The foreign policy of intervention*. Austin: University of Texas Press, 1982.

Inter-American States. "Declaration of Lima". *Avalon Project*. Accessed September 1, 2015. http://avalon.law/yale/edu/subject_menus/interame.asp

James, D. *Resistance and integration: Perónism and the Argentine working class, 1946-1976*. Cambridge: University Press, 1988.

James, H. *International monetary cooperation since Bretton Woods*. New York: Oxford University Press, 1996.

Jones, H. *The Bay of Pigs*. Oxford: Oxford University Press, 2008.

Jonker, J and Luiten van Zanden, J. *A history of Royal Dutch Shell: From Challenger to Joint Industry Leader, 1890-1939*. Amsterdam, Oxford University Press, 2007.

Josephs, R. "Gaitán and Communism". *ICDC Bogotazo Archive*. Accessed June 1, 2011. www.icdc.com/paulwolf/Gaitán/Joséphs8augusts1947.htm

Kennan, G. "Memorandum by the Counsellor of the Department to the Secretary of State". *US State Department office of the historian*. Accessed

September 1, 2015. https://history.state.gov/historicaldocuments/frus1950v02/d330

Kennedy, J. "Remarks at the Techo Housing Project in Bogota". *JFK Library.* Accessed April 1, 2016. https://www.jfklibrary.org/Asset-Viewer/Archives/JFKPOF-036-038.aspx

--- "Joint Statement following Discussions with President López Mateos". *The American President Project.* Accessed April 1, 2016. http://www.presidency.ucsb.edu/ws/index.php?pid=11661

--- "Inaugural address". *JFK Library.* Accessed April 1, 2016. https://www.jfklibrary.org/Research/Research-Aids/Ready-Reference/JFK-Quotations/Inaugural-Address.aspx

Kennedy, P. "Árbenz blames U.S. for his fall; will continue Guatemalan fight: Imperialism subjugating Latin America, deposed leader charges in Mexico". *New York Times,* November 8, 1948, New York Times Archives.

Kinzer, S. *Overthrow: America's century of regime change from Hawaii to Iraq.* New York: Times Books, 2007.

Klaiber, J. *The church, dictatorships, and democracy in Latin America.* Maryknoll, NY: Orbis Books, 1998.

Klaren, P. *Peru: Society and nationhood in the Andes.* New York: Oxford University Press, 2000.

Klein, H. *Bolivia: The evolution of a multi-ethnic society.* New York: Oxford University Press, 1992.

Kluckhohn, F. *Lyndon's Legacy.* New York: Monarch Books, 1964.

Knight, M. "Rethinking British informal Empire in Latin America". In *Informal Empire in Latin America: Culture, Commerce and Capital.* Edited by M Brown. Oxford, Blackwell publishing, 2008.

Kunz, D. *Butter and guns: America's Cold War economic diplomacy.* New York: Free Press, 1997.

LaCharité, N., Kennedy R. and Thienal P. *Case study in insurgency and revolutionary warfare: Guatemala 1944-1954.* Washington, D.C: Special Operations Research Office, the American University, 1964.

Lafeber, W. *Inevitable revolutions: The United States in Central America.* New York: WW Norton and Company, 1984.

---*The Panama Canal: The crisis in historical perspective.* New York: Oxford University Press, 1989.

---"The business community's push for war". In *Imperial surge: The United States abroad, the 1890s to the early 1900s.* Edited by T Patterson and S Rabe. Toronto: DC Health and Company, 1992.

Lamrani, S. *The economic war against Cuba: A historic and legal perspective on the US blockade.* New York: Monthly Review, 2013.

Latham, M. *Modernization as ideology: American social and nation building in the Kennedy era.* Chapel Hill: The University of North Carolina Press, 2000.

Leaming, B. *Mrs Kennedy: The missing history of the Kennedy years.* London: Orion, 2001.

Leech, G. *The FARC: The longest insurgency.* New York: Palgrave MacMillan, 2011.

Leffler, M. *The specter of communism: The United States and the origins of the Cold War, 1917-1953.* New York: Hill and Wang, 1994.

Levy, D. and Szekely, G. *Mexico: Paradoxes of stability and change.* Boulder: Westview Press, 1987.

Lieuwen, E. *Venezuela.* New York: Praeger, 1986.

Lombardi, J. *Venezuela: The search for order the dream of progress.* New York: Oxford University Press, 1982.

López, A. *José Marti and the future of Cuban Nationalisms.* Coral Gables: University of Florida Press, 2006.

Loveman, B. *Chile: The Legacy of Hispanic capitalism.* New York: Oxford University Press, 2001.

Malloy, J and Gamarra, E. *Revolution and reaction: Bolivia, 1964-1985.* New Brunswick: Transaction Books, 1988.

Marichal, C. "Nation building and the origins of banking in Latin America, 1850-1930. In *Banking trade and industry: Europe, America and Asia from the thirteenth to twentieth century.* Edited by A Teichova, G

Kurgan-Van Hentenry and D Ziegler. London: Cambridge University Press, 1997.

Martínez, O. *The great land grab: The Mexican American War 1846-1848.* London: Quartet Books, 1975.

MacCameron, R. *Bananas, labor and politics in Honduras: 1954-1963.* New York: University of Syracuse Press, 1983.

Marx, K and Engels, F. *The Communist Manifesto.* Pontylpool: Merlin Press, 2012.

McBeth, B. *Gunboats, corruption, and claims: Foreign intervention in Venezuela, 1899-1908.* New York: Greenwood Press, 2001.

McCann, T. *An American company: The tragedy of United Fruit.* New York: Crown Publishers, 1976.

Mee, C. *The Marshall Plan: the launching of Pax Americana.* New York: Simon and Schuster, 1984.

Mexico, "The Constitution of Mexico". *The Constitution Project.* Accessed April 1, 2015. https://www.constituteproject.org/constitution/Mexico_2015.pdf?lang=en

Meyer, T. *The theory of social democracy.* Malden, MA: Polity Press, 2007.

M Moore. *Know your enemy: The American debate on Nazism, 1933-1945.* New York: Cambridge University Press, 2010.

National Security Council. "144/1". *State Department Office of the Historian.* Accessed May 1, 2016. https://history.state.gov/historicaldocuments/frus1952-54v04/d3

Newell, P *Zapata of Mexico.* Chicago: Black Rose Books, 1979.

Newton, W. *The perilous sky: US aviation diplomacy and Latin America, 1919-1931.* Coral Gables: The University of Miami Press, 1978.

Niblo, S. *War diplomacy and development: The United States and Mexico, 1938-1954.* New York: Routledge, 2006.

Nixon, R. *The memoirs of Richard Nixon.* New York: Arrow Books, 1978.

No Author. "Marshall blames reds in Colombia; Parley to continue; Secretary tells conferees that world communism set off revolt in country". *New York Times,* April 13, 1948, New York Times Archives.

--- "Guatemala without Árbenz". *New York Times,* September 11, 1954, New York Times Archives.

--- "The Peruvian incident". *New York Times,* May 10, 1958, New York Times Archives.

O'Brien, T. "Copper kings of the Americas: The Guggenheim Brothers". In *Mining tycoons in the age of empire: Entrepreneurship, high finance, politics and territorial expansion.* Edited by R. Dumett. London: Ashgate, 2009.

O'Sullivan, C. *Sumner Welles, postwar planning, and the quest for a new world order, 1937-1943.* New York: Columbia University Press, 2008.

Organization of American States, "Declaration of Caracas". *Avalon Project.* Accessed April 1, 2015. http://avalon.law.yale.edu/20th_century/ intam11.asp

--- "Charter of Punta del Este". *Avalon Project.* Accessed April 1, 2015. http://avalon.law.yale.edu/20th_century/intam16.asp

Osterling, J. *Democracy in Colombia: Clientist politics and guerrilla warfare.* New Brunswick: Transaction Publishers, 1989.

Padgett, S and Paterson, W. *A history of social democracy in post-war Europe.* London: Longman, 1991.

Pach, C. *Arming the free world: The origins of the United States Military Assistance Program, 1945-1950.* Chapel Hill: The University of North Carolina Press, 1991.

Parkman, P. *Nonviolent insurrection in El Salvador: The fall of Maximiliano Hernández Martínez.* Tucson: The University of Arizona Press, 1988.

Parmet, H. *JFK: The Presidency of John F Kennedy.* Detroit: Doubleday, 1983.

Patterson, T. *Kennedy's quest for victory: American foreign policy, 1961-1963.* New York: Oxford University Press, 1989.

Peeler, J. *Building democracy in Latin America.* Boulder: Lynne Rienner Publishers, 1998.

Pendle, G. *Uruguay.* London: Oxford University Press, 1963.

Pérez, L. Cuba: The Platt Amendment. In *Imperial surge: The United States abroad, the 1890s to the early 1900s*. Edited by T Patterson and S Rabe. Toronto: DC Health and Company, 1992.

--- *Cuba: Between reform and revolution*. New York: Oxford University Press, 2011.

Pérez-Stable, M. *The Cuban Revolution: Origins, Cause and Legacy*. London: Oxford University Press, 2012.

Peterson, H. *Argentina and the United States, 1810-1960*. New York: State University Press, 1964.

Petras, J. *Politics and social forces in Chilean development*. Berkeley: University of California Press, 1969.

--- *Politics and social structure in Latin America*. New York: Monthly Review, 1970.

Pike, F. *FDR's Good Neighbor Policy: Sixty years of generally gentle chaos*. Austin: University of Texas Press, 1995.

--- *The Politics of the Miraculous: Haya de la Torre and the spiritualist tradition*. Omaha: University of Nebraska Press, 1986.

Pisani, S. *The CIA and the Marshall Plan*. Lawrence: University Press of Kansas, 1991.

Poppino, R. *International communism in Latin America: A history of the movement, 1917-1963*. New York: Free Press of Glencoe, 1964.

Potash, R. *The army and politics in Argentina 1945-1962: Perón to Frondizi*. London: Athlone, 1980.

Salmon, P. *The defeat of Che Guevara: Military response to guerrilla challenge in Bolivia*. New York: Praeger, 1987.

Prizel, I. *Latin America through Soviet Eyes: The evolution of Soviet perceptions during the Brezhnev era, 1964-1982*. Cambridge: University Press, 1990.

Rabe, S. *Eisenhower and Latin America: The foreign policy of anti-communism*. Chapel Hill: The University of North Carolina Press, 1988.

--- *The most dangerous area in the world: John F. Kennedy confronts communist revolution in Latin America.* Chapel Hill: University of North Carolina Press, 1999.

Radu, M. "Introduction: Revolution and revolutionaries". In *Violence and the Latin American revolutionaries.* Edited by M. Radu. New Brunswick: Transaction   Books, 1988.

Randall, S. *Colombia and the United States: Hegemony and interdependence.* Athens: The University of Georgia Press, 1992.

Raffner, K. and Singer, H. *The economic north-south divide: Six decades of unequal development.* Northampton: Edward Elgar, 2001.

Rapoport, M. "Argentina". In *Latin America between the Second World War and the Cold War, 1944-1948.* Edited by L. Bethell and I Roxborough. New York: Cambridge University Press, 1992.

Rattliff, W. *Castroism and communism in Latin America, 1959-1976: The varieties of the Marxist-Leninist experience.* Washington: American Enterprise Institute, 1976.

--- "Revolutionary warfare". In *Violence and the Latin American revolutionaries.* Edited by M. Radu. New Brunswick: Transaction Books, 1988.

Roberts, G. *Stalin's Wars: From World War to Cold War, 1939-1953.* New Haven: Yale University Press, 2006.

Robock, S. *Brazil's developing north-east: A study of regional planning and foreign aid.* Washington: Brooking's Institute, 1963.

Rock, D. *Argentine: 1516-1982, from Spanish colonization to the Falkland War.* London: IB Taurus and Co Ltd, 1986.

--- *Authoritarian Argentina: The nationalist movement, its history and its impact.* Berkley: University of California Press, 1993.

Roddick, J. *The dance of the millions: Latin America and the debt crisis.* London: Monthly Review, 1988.

Rolden, M. *Blood and fire: La Violencia in Antioquia, Colombia, 1946-1953.* London: Duke University, 2002.

Rolls, A. *Emiliano Zapata: A biography.* Denver: Greenwood Press, 2011.

Roorda, E. *The Good Neighbor Policy and the Trujillo Regime in the Dominican Republic, 1930-1945*. Durham: Duke University Press, 1998.

Roosevelt, F. "Inaugural address". *The American Presidency Project*. Accessed April 1, 2015. http://www.presidency.ucsb.edu/ws/index.php?pid=14473

--- "The Four Freedoms Speech". *FDR Library*. Accessed April 1, 2015. https://fdrlibrary.org/four-freedoms

Roosevelt, K. *Countercoup, the struggle for the control of Iran*. New York McGraw Hill, 1979.

Roosevelt, T. "Corollary to the Monroe Doctrine". State Department Office of the Historian. Accessed April 1, 2015. https://history.state.gov/milestones/1899-1913/roosevelt-and-monroe-doctrine

Rostow, W. *The stage of economic growth: A non-communist manifesto*. Cambridge: University Press, 1971.

Ryan, J. *Earl Browder: The failure of American Communism*. Tuscaloosa: University of Alabama Press, 1997.

Safford, F. and Palacious, M. *Colombia: Fragmented land, divided society*. New York: Oxford University Press, 2002.

Santayana, G. *The life of reason*. Amherst, NY: Prometheus Books, 1998.

Schales, A. *Coolidge*. New York: Harper Collins, 2013.

Schlesinger, S. and Kinzer, S. *Bitter fruit: The untold story of the American coup in Guatemala*. Garden City, N.Y.: Doubleday, 1982.

Schmitz, D. *Thank God they're on our side: The United States and right-wing dictatorships 1921-1965*. Chapel Hill: The University of North Carolina Press, 1999.

Schneider, R. *Communism in Guatemala*. New York: Frederick A Praeger, Publishers, 1958.

Schneider, B. *Business politics and the state in twentieth century Latin America*. New York: Cambridge University Press, 2004.

Schoultz, L. *National security and United States policy towards Latin America*. Princeton, NJ: University Press, 1987.

--- *Beneath the United States: A history of US policy towards Latin America.* Cambridge: Harvard University Press, 1998.

--- *That infernal little Cuban republic: The United States and the Cuban Revolution.* Chapel Hill: The University of North Carolina Press, 2009.

Schrecker, E. *Many are the crimes: McCarthyism in America.* Princeton, NJ: University Press, 1998.

Schroeder, J. *Mr. Polk's War: American opposition and dissent,1846-1848.* Madison: The University of Wisconsin Press, 1973.

Schulzinger, R. *The wise men of foreign affairs: The history of the Council on Foreign Relations.* New York: Columbia University Press, 1984.

Singer, H. "Beyond terms of trade: Convergence and divergence". *Journal of International Development,*11 no. 1, (1999): 911-916.

Sharpless, R. *Gaitán of Colombia: A Political Biography.* Pittsburgh: University of Pittsburgh Press, 1978.

Shoup, L. H. and Minter, W. *Imperial brain trust: The Council on Foreign Relations and United States Foreign Policy.* New York: Monthly Review, 1977.

Sikkink, K. *Ideas and institutions: Developmentalism in Brazil and Argentina.* Ithaca: Cornell University Press, 1991.

Skidmore, T. *The politics of military rule in Brazil, 1964-1985.* New York: Oxford University Press, 1988.

Skierka, V. *Fidel Castro: A biography.* Cambridge: Polity Press, 2004.

Smith, G. *The last years of the Monroe Doctrine, 1945-1993.* New York: Hill and Wang, 1994.

Smith, P. *Talons of the eagle: Dynamics of US-Latin relations.* New York: Oxford University Press, 2000.

Service, R. *Lenin: A Biography.* Kent: Pan Books, 2000.

State Department, "Probable Developments in Brazil". *US State Department office of the historian.* Accessed September 1, 2015. https://history. state.gov/historicaldocuments/frus1952-54v04/d206

--- "Probable Developments in Argentina". *US State Department office of the historian.* Accessed September 1, 2015. https://history.state.gov/historicaldocuments/frus1952-54v04/d125

Stein, S. *Populism in Peru: The emergence of the masses and the politics of social control.* Madison: University of Wisconsin Press, 1980.

Steinberg, P. *The great red menace: United States prosecution of American Communists, 1947-1952.* London: Greenwood Press, 1984.

Stern, F. *Averting the Final Failure: John F Kennedy and the Secret Cuban Missile Crisis Meetings.* Stanford: Stanford University Press, 2003.

Stevenson, A. "Report from the Representative to the United Nations to President Kennedy". *US State Department office of the historian.* Accessed September 1, 2015. http://history.state.gov/historicaldocuments/frus1961-63v12/d14

Steward, D. *Trade and hemisphere: The Good Neighbor Policy and reciprocal trade.* Columbia: University of Missouri Press, 1975.

Streeter, S. "Nation-building in the land of eternal counter-insurgency: Guatemala and the contradictions of the Alliance for Progress". *Third World Quarterly* 27, no 1 (2006): 57-68.

Suchlicki, J. *University students and revolution in Cuba: 1920-1968.* Miami: University of Miami Press, 1972.

Sweig, J. *Inside the Cuban Revolution: Fidel Castro and the Urban Underground.* Cambridge, Ma.: Harvard University Press, 2002.

Szulc, T. "US fly's troops to Caribbean as mobs attack Nixon in Caracas; Eisenhower demands his safety: Vice President unhurt as furious crowds halt reception". *New York Times,* May14, 1958, New York Times Archives.

--- *Twilight of the tyrants.* New York: Henry Holt and Company, 1959.

Szusterman, C. *Frondizi and the politics of developmentalism in Argentina, 1955-1962.* London: Macmillan, 1993.

Taffet, J. *Foreign aid as foreign policy: The Alliance for Progress in Latin America.* New York: Routledge, 2007.

Tannenbaum, F. *The Mexican agrarian revolution.* New York: Archon Books, 1968.

Tatum, E. *The United States and Europe, 1815-1823: A study in the background of the Monroe Doctrine.* New York: Russell and Russell, 1967.

Townsend, W. *Lazaro Cardenas: Mexican Democrat.* Charlotte: International Friendship, 1979.

Trouillot, M. *Haiti: State against nation, the origins and legacy of Duvalierism.* New York: Monthly Review Press, 1990.

Tunzelman, A. *Red Heat: Conspiracy, murder, and the Cold War in the Caribbean.* New York: Henry Holt, 2011.

Turton, P. *José Marti: Architect of Cuba's freedom.* London: Zed Books, 1986.

Tye, L. *The father of spin: Edward L. Bernays & the birth of public relations.* 1st Ed. New York: Crown Publishers, 1998.

M Vanger. *Uruguay's Jose Battle y Ordonez: The determined visionary, 1915-1917.* Bouler: Lienne Rienner, 2010.

Wallerstein, I. *The capitalist world economy: Essays.* New York: Cambridge University Press, 1979.

---*The modern world system III: The second era of great expansion of the capitalist world-economy, 1930-1840s.* New York: Academic Press, 1989.

Weber, M. and Dreijmanis, J. *Max Webers's complete writing on academic and political vocations.* New York: Algora Publishing, 2008.

Weiner, T. *Legacy of ashes: The history of the CIA.* New York: Doubleday, 2007.

Welles, B *Sumner Welles: FDR's global strategist: A Biography.* Basingstoke: Macmillan, 1997.

Whitaker, A. "The Latin American Bloc". In *the United States and the United Nations.* Edited by B. Gross. Norman: University of Oklahoma Press, 1964.

White, N. *Decolonization: The British Experience since 1945.* London: Routeledge, 2014.

Wickham-Crowley, T. *Exploring revolution: Essays on Latin American insurgency and revolutionary theory.* Armond, NY: ME Sharp Inc, 1991.

--- *Guerrillas and revolution in Latin America: A comparative study of insurgents and regimes since 1956.* Princeton: Princeton University Press, 1992.

Williams, W. *The tragedy of American diplomacy.* New York: WW Norton and Company, 1972.

Wood, B. *The making of the Good Neighbor Policy.* New York: WW Norton and Company, 1961.

Woodward, E. *Three studies in European conservatism: Metternich, Guizot and the Catholic Church in the nineteenth century.* London: Frank Cass and Co, 1963.

Woodward, E. *Three studies in European conservatism; Metternich; Guizot; the Catholic Church in the nineteenth century.* London: Frank Cass, 1963.

Wright, S "Ramón Grau San Martin". In *Dictionary of Caribbean and Afro-Latin American biography.* Edited by F Wright and H Gates. Oxford: Oxford University Press, 2016.

Wolf, P. "Wold vs. CIA and FBI: The Legal Battle to release records about Jorge Eleicer Gaitán". *ICDC Bogotazo Archive.* Accessed June 1, 2011. www.icdc/-paulwolf/Gaitán_wolfvcciaandfbi.htm

X (Kennan, G). "The sources of Soviet conduct". *Foreign Affairs,* 25, no 4 (1947): 90-110.

Y (Halle, L). "On a certain impatience with Latin America". *Foreign Affairs* 28 no 4 (1950): 565-570.

Index

T

U

V

www.ingramcontent.com/pod-product-compliance
Lightning Source LLC
LaVergne TN
LVHW040010200726
843493LV00005B/1201